To

EVERY DAY

Every Day

Daily readings for the Christian of today, planned to combine a systematic coverage of Biblical teaching with suitability for devotional use.

SCRIPTURE UNION
47 MARYLEBONE LANE
LONDON W1M 6AX

Silver Jubilee Edition 1977

Printed and Bound in England by
Hazell Watson & Viney Ltd,
Aylesbury, Bucks
ISBN 0 85421 291 4

INTRODUCTION

The first aim of *Every Day* is that the words of Scripture, without comment or explanation, will themselves bring strength and help to the reader, lead to progress in the Christian life, and whet the appetite for further Bible study.

Every Day has also been compiled so that the reader who uses the book daily will work through a systematic scheme of Bible teaching in the course of a year. A syllabus was first prepared, including doctrinal, ethical, devotional and biographical topics; this was fitted into the calendar in order to achieve a balance and also to use the seasons of the Christian year. Finally, verses were collected from all parts of the Revised Standard Version and arranged so as to present a consecutive and logical exposition of each subject.

The result is that the reader has, in addition, a topical concordance and, by making use of the index at the back, he can find many of the most important verses in the Bible on a large number of topics and characters.

*How . . . can man understand his way?**

I know, O Lord, that the way of man is not in himself, that it is not in man who walks to direct his steps.[1] A man's mind plans his way, but the Lord directs his steps.[2] The steps of a man are from the Lord.[3]

I am the Lord your God, who teaches you to profit, who leads you in the way you should go.[4] I will instruct you and teach you the way you should go; I will counsel you with My eye upon you.[5] Be not like a horse or a mule, without understanding, which must be curbed with bit and bridle.[5] Trust in the Lord with all your heart, and do not rely on your own insight. In all your ways acknowledge Him, and He will make straight your paths.[6] Commit your way to the Lord; trust in Him, and He will act.[7]

The God who . . . made my way safe.[8] He will be our guide for ever.[9] The Lord will keep your going out and your coming in from this time forth and for evermore.[10] Lead me, O Lord, in Thy righteousness . . . make Thy way straight before me.[11]

**Prov. 20:24.* [1]*Jer. 10:23.* [2]*Prov. 16:9.* [3]*Ps. 37:23.* [4]*Is. 48:17.* [5]*Ps. 32:8, 9.* [6]*Prov. 3:5, 6.* [7]*Ps. 37:5.* [8]*Ps. 18:32.* [9]*Ps. 48:14.* [10]*Ps. 121:8.* [11]*Ps. 5:8.*

JANUARY 2

*The living and abiding word of God**

All scripture is inspired by God and profitable for teaching, for reproof, for correction, and for training in righteousness.[1] No prophecy ever came by the impulse of man, but men moved by the Holy Spirit spoke from God.[2] The word of God is living and active, sharper than any two-edged sword . . . discerning the thoughts and intentions of the heart.[3]

Think not that I have come to abolish the law and the prophets; I have come not to abolish them but to fulfil them.[4] Heaven and earth will pass away, but My words will not pass away.[5] The Holy Spirit, whom the Father will send in My name, He will teach you all things, and bring to your remembrance all that I have said to you.[6] He will guide you into all the truth . . . and He will declare to you the things that are to come.[7]

The law of Thy mouth is better to me than thousands of gold and silver pieces.[8] Thy testimonies are my delight, they are my counselors.[9] All Thy commandments are sure.[10] He has granted to us His precious and very great promises.[11] Therefore I direct my steps by all Thy precepts.[12]

** 1 Pet. 1:23. [1] 2 Tim. 3:16. [2] 2 Pet. 1:21. [3] Heb. 4:12. [4] Mt. 5:17. [5] Mt. 24:35. [6] Jn. 14:26. [7] Jn. 16:13. [8] Ps. 119:72. [9] Ps. 119:24. [10] Ps. 119:86. [11] 2 Pet. 1:4. [12] Ps. 119:128.*

*Be strong, and let your heart take courage**

When the servant of the man of God rose early in the morning and went out, behold, an army with horses and chariots was round about the city. And the servant said, 'Alas, my master! What shall we do?' He said, 'Fear not, for those who are with us are more than those who are with them.'[1] The angel of the Lord encamps around those who fear Him, and delivers them.[2]

The following night the Lord stood by Paul and said, 'Take courage, for as you have testified about Me at Jerusalem, so you must bear witness also at Rome.'[3] At my first defense no one took my part ... But the Lord stood by me and gave me strength to proclaim the word fully.[4]

Take your share of suffering as a good soldier of Christ Jesus.[5] Be watchful, stand firm in your faith, be courageous, be strong.[6] God did not give us a spirit of timidity but a spirit of power and love and self-control.[7]

Have I not commanded you? Be strong and of good courage; be not frightened, neither be dismayed; for the Lord your God is with you wherever you go.[8]

**Ps. 27:14.* [1] *2 Kings 6:15, 16.* [2] *Ps. 34:7.* [3] *Acts 23:11.* [4] *2 Tim. 4:16, 17.* [5] *2 Tim. 2:3.* [6] *1 Cor. 16:13.* [7] *2 Tim. 1:7.* [8] *Josh. 1:9.*

JANUARY 4

*As I was with Moses, so I will be with you**

By faith Moses, when he was grown up, refused to be called the son of Pharaoh's daughter, choosing rather to share ill-treatment with the people of God than to enjoy the fleeting pleasures of sin. He considered abuse suffered for the Christ greater wealth than the treasures of Egypt.[1]

And Moses said, 'I will turn aside and see this great sight, why the bush is not burnt.' When the Lord saw that he turned aside to see, God called to him out of the bush, 'Moses, Moses!' And he said, 'Here am I.'[2] Then the Lord said, 'I have seen the affliction of My people who are in Egypt.'[3] 'Come, I will send you to Pharaoh that you may bring forth My people . . . out of Egypt.' But Moses said to God, 'Who am I that I should go to Pharaoh?' . . . He said, 'But I will be with you.'[4]

The man Moses was very great in the land of Egypt . . . and in the sight of the people.[5] Now the man Moses was very meek, more than all men that were on the face of the earth.[6] The Lord used to speak to Moses face to face, as a man speaks to his friend.[7] Moses did not know that . . . his face shone because he had been talking with God.[8]

* *Josh. 1:5.* [1] *Heb. 11:24–26.* [2] *Ex. 3:3, 4.* [3] *Ex. 3:7.* [4] *Ex. 3:10, 11, 12.* [5] *Ex. 11:3.* [6] *Num. 12:3.* [7] *Ex. 33:11.* [8] *Ex. 34:29.*

*You were straying like sheep**

'Simon, son of John, do you love Me?'[1] Your love is like a morning cloud, like the dew that goes early away.[2] I have this against you, that you have abandoned the love you had at first.[3]

My little children, I am writing this to you so that you may not sin.[4] He died for all, that those who live might live no longer for themselves but for Him who for their sake died and was raised.[5]

If we confess our sins, He is faithful and just, and will forgive our sins and cleanse us from all unrighteousness.[6] 'Come now, let us reason together,' says the Lord: 'though your sins are like scarlet, they shall be as white as snow.'[7]

Take with you words and return to the Lord; say to Him, 'Take away all iniquity.'[8] Create in me a clean heart, O God, and put a new and right spirit within me.[9]

'Simon, son of John, do you love Me?' He said to Him, 'Yes, Lord; You know that I love You.'[10] You were straying like sheep, but have now returned to the Shepherd and Guardian of your souls.[11]

* *1 Pet. 2:25.* [1] *Jn. 21:16.* [2] *Hos. 6:4.* [3] *Rev. 2:4.* [4] *1 Jn. 2:1.* [5] *2 Cor. 5:15.* [6] *1 Jn. 1:9.* [7] *Is. 1:18.* [8] *Hos. 14:2.* [9] *Ps. 51:10.* [10] *Jn. 21:16.* [11] *1 Pet. 2:25.*

JANUARY 6

*The Almighty—we cannot find Him**

Oh, that I knew where I might find Him![1] Many prophets and righteous men longed to see what you see, and did not see it.[2] Now when Jesus was born in Bethlehem of Judea in the days of Herod the king, behold, wise men from the East came to Jerusalem, saying, 'Where is He who has been born King of the Jews?'[3] Going into the house they saw the child with Mary His mother, and they fell down and worshipped Him.[4]

When the time had fully come, God sent forth His Son, born of woman.[5] And the Word became flesh and dwelt among us, full of grace and truth.[6] That which was from the beginning, which we have heard, which we have seen with our eyes, which we have looked upon and touched with our hands.[7]

Great indeed, we confess, is the mystery of our religion: God was manifested in the flesh.[8] Christ Jesus . . . in the form of God . . . born in the likeness of men.[9] His name shall bc called Emmanuel (which means, God with us).[10] He who has seen Me has seen the Father; how can you say, 'Show us the Father'?[11]

**Job 37:23. [1]Job 23:3. [2]Mt. 13:17. [3]Mt. 2:1, 2. [4]Mt. 2:11. [5]Gal. 4:4. [6]Jn. 1:14. [7]1 Jn. 1:1. [8]1 Tim. 3:16. [9]Phil. 2:5–7. [10]Mt. 1:23. [11]Jn. 14:9.*

JANUARY 7

*When he calls to Me, I will answer him**

Your Father knows what you need before you ask Him.[1] Before they call I will answer, while they are yet speaking I will hear.[2] Jesus said, 'Abba, Father, all things are possible to Thee; remove this cup from Me; yet not what I will, but what Thou wilt.'[3] 'Father, I thank Thee that Thou hast heard Me . . . Thou hearest Me always.'[4]

Ask, and it will be given you; seek, and you will find; knock, and it will be opened to you.[5] Whatever you ask in My name, I will do it, that the Father may be glorified in the Son.[6] If two of you agree on earth about anything they ask, it will be done for them by My Father in heaven.[7] Whatever you ask in prayer, believe that you receive it, and you will.[8]

Have no anxiety about anything, but in everything by prayer and supplication with thanksgiving let your requests be made known to God.[9] This is the confidence which we have in Him, that if we ask anything according to His will He hears us. And if we know that He hears us in whatever we ask, we know that we have obtained the requests made of Him.[10]

**Ps. 91:15.* [1]*Mt. 6:8.* [2]*Is. 65:24.* [3]*Mk. 14:36.* [4]*Jn. 11:41, 42.* [5]*Mt. 7:7.* [6]*Jn. 14:13.* [7]*Mt. 18:19.* [8]*Mk. 11:24.* [9]*Phil. 4:6.* [10]*1 Jn. 5:14, 15.*

JANUARY 8

*Let Us make man in Our image**

So God created man in His own image, in the image of God He created him; male and female He created them. And God blessed them, and God said to them, 'Be fruitful and multiply, and fill the earth and subdue it.'[1] The Lord God formed man of dust from the ground, and breathed into his nostrils the breath of life; and man became a living being.[2] The dust returns to the earth as it was, and the spirit returns to God who gave it.[3]

When I look at Thy heavens, the work of Thy fingers . . . what is man that Thou art mindful of him, and the son of man that Thou dost care for him? Yet Thou hast made him little less than God, and dost crown him with glory and honor.[4] What is man, that Thou dost make so much of him, and that Thou dost set Thy mind upon him, dost visit him every morning, and test him every moment?[5] Thus says the Lord, He who created you . . . 'You are Mine.'[6] In Him we live and move and have our being . . . for we are indeed His offspring.[7]

**Gen. 1:26.* [1]*Gen. 1:27, 28.* [2]*Gen. 2:7.* [3]*Eccles. 12:7.* [4]*Ps. 8:3–5.* [5]*Job 7:17, 18.* [6]*Is. 43:1.* [7]*Acts 17:28.*

*Was it not necessary that the Christ should suffer?**

Like a sheep that before its shearers is dumb, so He opened not His mouth.[1] Jesus gave Pilate no answer, not even to a single charge.[2]

A company of evildoers encircle Me; they have pierced My hands and feet.[3] He . . . was numbered with the transgressors.[4] They crucified Him . . . and with Him . . . two robbers, one on His right and one on His left.[5]

They divide My garments among them, and for My raiment they cast lots.[6] The soldiers . . . took His garments and made four parts, one for each soldier. But His tunic was without seam, woven from top to bottom; so they said to one another, 'Let us not tear it, but cast lots for it to see whose it shall be.'[7]

He . . . made intercession for the transgressors.[8] 'Father, forgive them; for they know not what they do.'[9]

You (Satan) shall bruise His heel.[10] He was wounded for our transgressions, He was bruised for our iniquities.[11] He Himself bore our sins in His body on the tree.[12]

I lay down My life . . . No one takes it from Me.[13] Then I said, 'Lo, I have come to do Thy will, O God,' as it is written of Me in the roll of the book.[14]

**Lk. 24:26.* [1]*Is. 53:7.* [2]*Mt. 27:14.* [3]*Ps. 22:16.* [4]*Is. 53:12.* [5]*Mk. 15:25, 27.* [6]*Ps. 22:18.* [7]*Jn. 19:23, 24.* [8]*Is. 53:12.* [9]*Lk. 23:34.* [10]*Gen. 3:15.* [11]*Is. 53:5.* [12]*1 Pet. 2:24.* [13]*Jn. 10:17, 18.* [14]*Heb. 10:7.*

JANUARY 10

*Keep your conscience clear**

The spirit of man is the lamp of the Lord, searching all his innermost parts.[1] Your ears shall hear a word behind you, saying, 'This is the way, walk in it,' when you turn to the right or when you turn to the left.[2] By rejecting conscience, certain persons have made shipwreck of their faith.[3]

The aim of our charge is love that issues from a pure heart and a good conscience and sincere faith.[4] Owe no one anything, except to love one another . . . Love is the fulfilling of the law.[5] Happy is he who has no reason to judge himself for what he approves. But he who has doubts is condemned . . . because he does not act from faith; for whatever does not proceed from faith is sin.[6]

Paul . . . said, 'Brethren, I have lived before God in all good conscience up to this day.'[7] God whom I serve with a clear conscience.[8] Beloved, if our hearts do not condemn us, we have confidence before God.[9]

Let us draw near with a true heart in full assurance of faith, with our hearts sprinkled clean from an evil conscience.[10] The blood of Jesus His Son cleanses us from all sin.[11]

**1 Pet. 3:16. [1] Prov. 20:27. [2] Is. 30:21. [3] 1 Tim. 1:19. [4] 1 Tim. 1:5. [5] Rom. 13:8, 10. [6] Rom. 14:22, 23. [7] Acts 23:1. [8] 2 Tim. 1:3. [9] 1 Jn. 3:21. [10] Heb. 10:22. [11] 1 Jn. 1:7.*

*Anxiety in a man's heart weighs him down**

Why are you cast down, O my soul, and why are you disquieted within me?[1] Cast all your anxieties on Him, for He cares about you.[2] Therefore . . . do not be anxious about your life . . . Look at the birds of the air: they neither sow nor reap nor gather into barns, and yet your heavenly Father feeds them. Are you not of more value than they?[3] Therefore do not be anxious about tomorrow, for tomorrow will be anxious for itself.[4] When you lie down, your sleep will be sweet.[5]

Have no anxiety about anything, but in everything by prayer . . . let your requests be made known to God. And the peace of God, which passes all understanding, will keep your hearts and your minds in Christ Jesus.[6] Cast your burden on the Lord, and He will sustain you; He will never permit the righteous to be moved.[7]

Blessed is the man who trusts in the Lord . . . He is like a tree planted by water . . . and is not anxious in the year of drought.[8] Return, O my soul, to your rest; for the Lord has dealt bountifully with you.[9]

**Prov. 12:25.* [1]*Ps. 42:5.* [2]*1 Pet. 5:7.* [3]*Mt. 6:25, 26.* [4]*Mt. 6:34.* [5]*Prov. 3:24.* [6]*Phil. 4:6, 7.* [7]*Ps. 55:22.* [8]*Jer. 17:7, 8.* [9]*Ps. 116:7.*

JANUARY 12

*I have called you friends**

The friendship of the Lord is for those who fear Him.[1] You are My friends if you do what I command you.[2] If a man loves Me, he will keep My word, and My Father will love him, and We will come to him and make Our home with him.[3] Behold, I stand at the door and knock; if any one hears My voice and opens the door, I will come in to him and eat with him, and he with Me.[4]

I will not leave you desolate; I will come to you.[5] Even though I walk through the valley of the shadow of death, I fear no evil; for Thou art with me.[6] He has said, 'I will never fail you nor forsake you.' Hence we can confidently say, 'The Lord is my helper, I will not be afraid; what can man do to me?'[7] Lo, I am with you always, to the close of the age.[8]

Love is strong as death.[9] Greater love has no man than this, that a man lay down his life for his friends.[10] God shows His love for us in that while we were yet sinners Christ died for us.[11]

* *Jn. 15:15.* [1] *Ps. 25:14.* [2] *Jn. 15:14.* [3] *Jn. 14:23.* [4] *Rev. 3:20.* [5] *Jn. 14:18.* [6] *Ps. 23:4.* [7] *Heb. 13:5, 6.* [8] *Mt. 28. 20.* [9] *Song of Sol. 8:6.* [10] *Jn. 15:13.* [11] *Rom. 5:8.*

*We aim at what is honorable**

Hear this, you who trample upon the needy . . . saying, 'When will the new moon be over . . . and the Sabbath, that we may . . . deal deceitfully with false balances?' The Lord has sworn . . . 'Surely I will never forget any of their deeds'.[1] Diverse weights and diverse measures are . . . an abomination to the Lord . . . and false scales are not good.[2] A trader, in whose hands are false balances, he loves to oppress. Ephraim has said, 'Ah, but I am rich, I have gained wealth for myself'; but all his riches can never offset the guilt he has incurred.[3] He who is greedy for unjust gain makes trouble for his household.[4]

These are the things that you shall do: Speak the truth to one another, render in your gates judgments that are true and make for peace, do not devise evil in your hearts against one another, and love no false oath, for all these things I hate, says the Lord.[5] Put away from you crooked speech, and put devious talk far from you.[6]

I love Thy commandments above gold, above fine gold. Therefore I direct my steps by all Thy precepts; I hate every false way.[7]

** 2 Cor. 8:21. [1] Amos 8:4, 5, 7. [2] Prov. 20:10, 23. [3] Hos. 12:7, 8. [4] Prov. 15:27. [5] Zech. 8:16, 17. [6] Prov. 4:24. [7] Ps. 119:127, 128.*

JANUARY 14

*Blessed is the man who . . .**

Blessed is he whose transgression is forgiven, whose sin is covered.[1] He who conceals his transgressions will not prosper, but he who confesses and forsakes them will obtain mercy.[2]

Happy is the man who listens to me, watching daily at my gates, waiting beside my doors.[3] He is like a tree planted by streams of water, that yields its fruit in its season, and its leaf does not wither. In all that he does, he prospers.[4]

Blessed is the man who trusts in the Lord, whose trust is the Lord.[5] Happy is he whose help is the God of Jacob, whose hope is in the Lord his God.[6]

Happy is the man whom God reproves; therefore despise not the chastening of the Almighty.[7] If you are reproached for the name of Christ, you are blessed, because the spirit of glory and of God rests upon you.[8]

It is more blessed to give than to receive.[9] Blessed is he who considers the poor.[10]

If you know these things, blessed are you if you do them.[11]

**Ps. 1:1. [1]Ps. 32:1. [2]Prov. 28:13. [3]Prov. 8:34. [4]Ps. 1:3. [5]Jer. 17:7. [6]Ps. 146:5. [7]Job 5:17. [8]1 Pet. 4:14. [9]Acts 20:35. [10]Ps. 41:1. [11]Jn. 13:17.*

*The fool says in his heart, 'There is no God'**

Men say to me continually, 'Where is your God?'[1] The Almighty—we cannot find Him.[2] Oh, that I knew where I might find Him, that I might come even to His seat![3]

The heavens are telling the glory of God; and the firmament proclaims His handiwork.[4] Ever since the creation of the world His invisible nature, namely, His eternal power and deity, has been clearly perceived in the things that have been made. So they are without excuse.[5] By faith we understand that the world was created by the word of God.[6]

No one has ever seen God; the only Son, who is in the bosom of the Father, He has made Him known.[7] For in Him the whole fulness of deity dwells bodily.[8] He reflects the glory of God and bears the very stamp of His nature.[9]

They said to Him therefore, 'Where is Your Father?' Jesus answered, 'You know neither Me nor My Father; if you knew Me, you would know My Father also.'[10] He who has seen Me has seen the Father.[11]

**Ps. 14:1.* [1]*Ps. 42:3.* [2]*Job 37:23.* [3]*Job 23:3.* [4]*Ps. 19:1.* [5]*Rom. 1:20.* [6]*Heb. 11:3.* [7]*Jn. 1:18.* [8]*Col. 2:9.* [9]*Heb. 1:3.* [10]*Jn. 8:19.* [11]*Jn. 14:9.*

JANUARY 16

*Your adversary the devil**

The Lord said to Satan, 'Whence have you come?' Satan answered the Lord, 'From going to and fro on the earth, and from walking up and down on it.'[1] Your adversary the devil prowls around like a roaring lion, seeking some one to devour.[2]

Let no one say when he is tempted, 'I am tempted by God'; for God . . . Himself tempts no one; but each person is tempted when he is lured and enticed by his own desire.[3] For from within, out of the heart of man, come evil thoughts . . .[4]

No temptation has overtaken you that is not common to man. God is faithful, and He will not let you be tempted beyond your strength, but with the temptation will also provide the way of escape, that you may be able to endure it.[5] Blessed is the man who endures trial, for when he has stood the test he will receive the crown of life.[6]

Then Jesus was led up by the Spirit into the wilderness to be tempted by the devil.[7] For we have not a high priest who is unable to sympathize with our weaknesses, but one who in every respect has been tempted as we are, yet without sinning.[8]

**1 Pet. 5:8. [1]Job 1:7. [2]1 Pet. 5:8. [3]Jas. 1:13, 14. [4]Mk. 7:21. [5]1 Cor. 10:13. [6]Jas. 1:12. [7]Mt. 4:1. [8]Heb. 4:15.*

*When words are many, transgression is not lacking**

I am a man of unclean lips, and I dwell in the midst of a people of unclean lips.[1] No human being can tame the tongue—a restless evil, full of deadly poison. With it we bless the Lord and Father, and with it we curse men, who are made in the likeness of God.[2] Out of the abundance of the heart the mouth speaks.[3]

Speak evil of no one . . . avoid quareling.[4] Do not grumble, brethren, against one another.[5] Put them all away: anger, wrath, malice, slander, and foul talk from your mouth. Do not lie to one another.[6]

A word fitly spoken is like apples of gold in a setting of silver.[7] A gentle tongue is a tree of life.[8] Speaking the truth in love.[9]

If any one thinks he is religious, and does not bridle his tongue but deceives his heart, this man's religion is vain.[10] On the day of judgment men will render account for every careless word they utter; for by your words you will be justified, and by your words you will be condemned.[11]

Set a guard over my mouth, O Lord, keep watch over the door of my lips![12]

**Prov. 10:19. [1]Is. 6:5. [2]Jas. 3:8, 9. [3]Mt. 12:34. [4]Tit. 3:2. [5]Jas. 5:9. [6]Col. 3:8, 9. [7]Prov. 25:11. [8]Prov. 15:4. [9]Eph. 4:15. [10]Jas. 1:26. [11]Mt. 12:36, 37. [12]Ps. 141:3.*

JANUARY 18

*Serve the Lord with gladness!**

Preach the word, be urgent in season and out of season, convince, rebuke, and exhort, be unfailing in patience and in teaching.[1] For what we preach is not ourselves, but Jesus Christ as Lord, with ourselves as your servants for Jesus' sake.[2] We were ready to share with you not only the gospel of God but also our own selves.[3]

I have been . . . in danger . . . in toil and hardship, through many a sleepless night, in hunger and thirst, often without food, in cold and exposure. And, apart from other things, there is the daily pressure upon me of my anxiety for all the churches.[4] I will most gladly spend and be spent for your souls.[5] For the Son of Man also came not to be served but to serve.[6]

When you have done all that is commanded you, say, 'We are unworthy servants; we have only done what was our duty.'[7] His master said to him, 'Well done, good and faithful servant; you have been faithful over a little, I will set you over much; enter into the joy of your Master.'[8] A servant who deals wisely has the king's favor.[9]

**Ps. 100:2.* [1]*2 Tim. 4:2.* [2]*2 Cor. 4:5.* [3]*1 Thess. 2:8.* [4]*2 Cor. 11:25–28.* [5]*2 Cor. 12:15.* [6]*Mk. 10:45.* [7]*Lk. 17:10.* [8]*Mt. 25:21.* [9]*Prov. 14:35.*

*Jesus said . . . 'Before Abraham was, I am'**

I am the way, and the truth, and the life; no one comes to the Father, but by Me.[1] There is salvation in no one else, for there is no other name . . . by which we must be saved.[2]

I am the bread of life; he who comes to Me shall not hunger, and he who believes in Me shall never thirst.[3] Why do you spend your money for that which is not bread, and your labor for that which does not satisfy? . . . Incline your ear, and come to Me.[4]

I am the light of the world; he who follows Me will not walk in darkness, but will have the light of life.[5] Men loved darkness rather than light, because their deeds were evil.[6]

I am the resurrection and the life; he who believes in Me, though he die, yet shall he live.[7] Yet you refuse to come to Me that you may have life.[8]

I am the good shepherd. The good shepherd lays down his life for the sheep.[9] All we like sheep have gone astray; we have turned every one to his own way.[10] I am the door; if any one enters by Me, he will be saved.[11]

**Jn. 8:58. [1]Jn. 14:6. [2]Acts 4:12. [3]Jn. 6:35. [4]Is. 55:2, 3. [5]Jn. 8:12. [6]Jn. 3:19. [7]Jn. 11:25. [8]Jn. 5:40. [9]Jn. 10:11. [10]Is 53:6. [11]Jn. 10:9.*

JANUARY 20

*I long for Thy salvation, O Lord**

By grace you have been saved through faith.[1] He has delivered us from the dominion of darkness and transferred us to the kingdom of His beloved Son, in whom we have redemption, the forgiveness of sins.[2] He who hears My word and believes Him who sent Me, has eternal life; he does not come into judgment, but has passed from death to life.[3]

Work out your own salvation with fear and trembling; for God is at work in you, both to will and to work for His good pleasure.[4] He who began a good work in you will bring it to completion at the day of Jesus Christ.[5] He is able to keep you from falling.[6]

An inheritance which is . . . kept in heaven for you, who by God's power are guarded through faith for a salvation ready to be revealed in the last time.[7] Salvation is nearer to us now than when we first believed.[8] Let us be sober, and put on the breastplate of faith and love, and for a helmet the hope of salvation.[9]

He is able for all time to save those who draw near to God through Him.[10]

**Ps. 119:174.* [1]*Eph. 2:8.* [2]*Col. 1:13, 14.* [3]*Jn. 5:24.* [4]*Phil. 2:12. 13,* [5]*Phil. 1:6.* [6]*Jude 24.* [7]*1 Pet. 1:4, 5.* [8]*Rom. 13:11.* [9]*1 Thess. 5:8.* [10]*Heb. 7:25.*

JANUARY 21

*For to me to live is Christ**

Has the Lord as great delight in burnt offerings and sacrifices, as in obeying the voice of the Lord? Behold, to obey is better than sacrifice.[1] You shall love the Lord your God with all your heart, and with all your soul, and with all your might.[2] For this is the love of God, that we keep His commandments. And His commandments are not burdensome.[3]

Whoever of you does not renounce all that he has cannot be My disciple.[4] When they had brought their boats to land, they left everything and followed Him.[5] Indeed I count everything as loss because of the surpassing worth of knowing Christ Jesus my Lord. For His sake I have suffered the loss of all things, and count them as refuse, in order that I may gain Christ.[6] I wholly followed the Lord my God.[7] That in everything He might be preëminent.[8]

Lead a life worthy of the Lord, fully pleasing to Him.[9] Whether you eat or drink, or whatever you do, do all to the glory of God.[10] Never flag in zeal, be aglow with the Spirit, serve the Lord.[11] Be steadfast, immovable, always abounding in the work of the Lord.[12]

**Phil. 1:21.* [1]*1 Sam. 15:22.* [2]*Deut. 6:5.* [3]*1 Jn. 5:3.* [4]*Lk. 14:33.* [5]*Lk. 5:11.* [6]*Phil. 3:8.* [7]*Josh. 14:8.* [8]*Col. 1:18.* [9]*Col. 1:10.* [10]*1 Cor. 10:31.* [11]*Rom. 12:11.* [12]*1 Cor. 15:58.*

JANUARY 22

*None is righteous, no, not one**

The Lord saw that the wickedness of man was great in the earth, and that every imagination of the thoughts of his heart was only evil continually.[1] The Lord looks down from heaven . . . to see if there are any . . . that seek after God. They have all gone astray . . . there is none that does good, no, not one.[2]

Behold, I was brought forth in iniquity.[3] I know that nothing good dwells within me, that is, in my flesh.[4] The heart is deceitful above all things, and desperately corrupt.[5] For from within, out of the heart of man, come evil thoughts, fornication, theft, murder, adultery . . . All these evil things come from within, and they defile a man.[6] What causes wars, and what causes fightings among you? Is it not your passions that are at war in your members?[7]

Wretched man that I am! Who will deliver me from this body of death? Thanks be to God through Jesus Christ our Lord![8] For the law of the Spirit of life in Christ Jesus has set me free from the law of sin and death.[9]

**Rom. 3:10. [1]Gen. 6:5. [2]Ps. 14:2, 3. [3]Ps. 51:5. [4]Rom. 7:18. [5]Jer. 17:9. [6]Mk. 7:21, 23. [7]Jas. 4:1. [8]Rom. 7:24, 25. [9]Rom. 8:2.*

JANUARY 23

*The Savior of all men**

I bring you good news of a great joy . . . for to you is born this day in the city of David a Savior, who is Christ the Lord.[1] And we have seen and testify that the Father has sent His Son as the Savior of the world.[9] Our Savior Christ Jesus, who abolished death and brought life and immortality to light through the gospel.[3] There is salvation in no one else, for there is no other name under heaven given among men by which we must be saved.[4] Christ Jesus came into the world to save sinners.[5]

As Moses lifted up the serpent in the wilderness, so must the Son of man be lifted up, that whoever believes in Him may have eternal life. For God so loved the world that He gave His only Son, that whoever believes in Him should not perish but have eternal life.[6] He who has the Son has life; he who has not the Son has not life.[7]

The Lord is my light and my salvation.[8] When I was brought low, He saved me.[9] Come to Me, all who labor and are heavy-laden, and I will give you rest.[10] Him who comes to Me I will not cast out.[11] Thou hast delivered my soul from death, my eyes from tears, my feet from stumbling; I walk before the Lord in the land of the living.[12]

**1 Tim. 4:10.* [1]*Lk. 2:10, 11.* [2]*1 Jn. 4:14.* [3]*2 Tim. 1:10.* [4]*Acts 4:12.* [5]*1 Tim. 1:15.* [6]*Jn. 3:14–16.* [7]*1 Jn. 5:12.* [8]*Ps. 27:1.* [9]*Ps. 116:6.* [10]*Mt. 11:28.* [11]*Jn. 6:37.* [12]*Ps. 116:8, 9.*

JANUARY 24

*God . . . commands all men everywhere to repent**

David said . . . 'I have sinned against the Lord.'[1] Against Thee, Thee only, have I sinned, and done that which is evil in Thy sight.[2] I despise myself, and repent in dust and ashes.[3]

He came to himself . . . He arose and came to his father.[4] The tax collector, standing far off, would not even lift up his eyes to heaven, but beat his breast, saying, 'God, be merciful to me a sinner!'[5]

The Lord . . . is forbearing toward you, not wishing that any should perish, but that all should reach repentance.[6] Do you not know that God's kindness is meant to lead you to repentance?[7]

I have not come to call the righteous, but sinners to repentance.[8] Repent, for the kingdom of heaven is at hand.[9] Let every one who names the name of the Lord depart from iniquity.[10] Seek the Lord while He may be found, call upon Him while He is near; let the wicked forsake his way, and the unrighteous man his thoughts; let him return to the Lord, that He may have mercy on him, and to our God, for He will abundantly pardon.[11]

**Acts 17:30.* [1]*2 Sam. 12:13.* [2]*Ps. 51:4.* [3]*Job 42:6.* [4]*Lk. 15:17, 20.* [5]*Lk. 18:13.* [6]*2 Pet. 3:9.* [7]*Rom. 2:4.* [8]*Lk. 5:32.* [9]*Mt. 4:17.* [10]*2 Tim. 2:19.* [11]*Is. 55:6, 7.*

*Paul, an apostle of Christ Jesus**

'Saul, Saul, why do you persecute Me? It hurts you to kick against the goads.' And I said, 'Who are You, Lord?' And the Lord said, 'I am Jesus whom you are persecuting. But . . . I have appeared to you for this purpose, to appoint you to serve and bear witness to the things in which you have seen Me and to those in which I will appear to you.'[1]

He who had set me apart before I was born . . . was pleased to reveal His Son to me.[2] The Son of God, who loved me and gave Himself for me.[3] Wherefore . . . I was not disobedient to the heavenly vision.[4]

I do not account my life of any value nor as precious to myself, if only I may accomplish my course and the ministry which I received from the Lord Jesus.[5] For His sake I have suffered the loss of all things, and count them as refuse, in order that I may gain Christ.[6]

I have fought the good fight, I have finished the race, I have kept the faith. Henceforth there is laid up for me the crown of righteousness.[7]

**Col. 1:1.* [1]*Acts 26:14–16.* [2]*Gal. 1:15, 16.* [3]*Gal. 2:20.* [4]*Acts 26:19.* [5]*Acts 20:24.* [6]*Phil. 3:8.* [7]*2 Tim. 4:7, 8.*

JANUARY 26

*Full assurance of faith**

To give knowledge of salvation to His people in the forgiveness of their sins.[1] Jesus said, 'It is finished'; and He bowed His head and gave up His spirit.[2] And behold, the curtain of the temple was torn in two, from top to bottom.[3] We have ... a sure and steadfast anchor of the soul, a hope that enters into the inner shrine behind the curtain, where Jesus has gone ... on our behalf.[4]

To all who received Him, who believed in His name, He gave power to become children of God; who were born, not of blood nor of the will of the flesh nor of the will of man, but of God.[5] Because you are sons, God has sent the Spirit of His Son into our hearts, crying, 'Abba! Father!'[6] By this we know that He abides in us, by the Spirit which He has given us.[7] God ... has shone in our hearts to give the light of the knowledge of the glory of God in the face of Christ.[8]

Truly, truly, I say to you, he who hears My word and believes Him who sent Me, has eternal life; he does not come into judgment, but has passed from death to life.[9] I know whom I have believed.[10]

**Heb.* 10:22. [1]*Lk.* 1:77. [2]*Jn.* 19:30. [3]*Mt.* 27:51. [4]*Heb.* 6:19, 20. [5]*Jn.* 1:12, 13. [6]*Gal.* 4:6. [7]*1 Jn.* 3:24. [8]*2 Cor.* 4:6. [9]*Jn.* 5:24. [10]*2 Tim.* 1:12.

*Jesus . . . said to him, 'Follow Me'**

You shall have no other gods before Me.[1] No one who puts his hand to the plow and looks back is fit for the kingdom of God.[2]

He said to all, 'If any man would come after Me, let him deny himself and take up his cross daily and follow Me.'[3] A man said to Him, 'I will follow You wherever You go.' And Jesus said to him, 'Foxes have holes, and birds of the air have nests; but the Son of man has nowhere to lay His head.'[4]

I have given you an example, that you also should do as I have done to you.[5] This is My commandment, that you love one another as I have loved you.[6] As He is so are we in this world.[7]

Father, I desire that they also, whom Thou hast given Me, may be with Me where I am, to behold My glory.[8] That where I am you may be also.[9]

Caleb . . . wholly followed the Lord.[10] One thing I do, forgetting what lies behind and straining forward to what lies ahead, I press on toward the goal for the prize of the upward call of God in Christ Jesus.[11]

**Jn. 1:43. [1]Exod. 20:3. [2]Lk. 9:62. [3]Lk. 9:23. [4]Lk. 9:57, 58. [5]Jn. 13:15. [6]Jn. 15:12. [7]1 Jn. 4:17. [8]Jn. 17:24. [9]Jn. 14:3. [10]Josh. 14:14. [11]Phil. 3:13, 14.*

JANUARY 28

*Six days you shall labor**

You yourselves know that these hands ministered to my necessities, and to those who were with me.[1] For by trade they were tent-makers.[2] We labor, working with our own hands.[3] We did not eat any one's bread without paying, but with toil and labor we worked night and day, that we might not burden any of you.[4] Is not this the carpenter, the son of Mary?[5]

Man goes forth to his work and to his labor until the evening.[6] A good wife who can find? She . . . works with willing hands . . . She looks well to the ways of her household, and does not eat the bread of idleness.[7] In all toil there is profit, but mere talk tends only to want.[8] Sweet is the sleep of a laborer.[9]

Whatever your task, work heartily, as serving the Lord and not men.[10] And whatever you do, in word or deed, do everything in the name of the Lord Jesus, giving thanks to God the Father through Him.[11] Do all to the glory of God.[12]

**Ex. 20:9.* [1]*Acts 20:34.* [2]*Acts 18:3.* [3]*1 Cor. 4:12.* [4]*2 Thess. 3:8.* [5]*Mk. 6:3.* [6]*Ps. 104:23.* [7]*Prov. 31:10. 13, 27.* [8]*Prov. 14:23.* [9]*Eccl. 5:12.* [10]*Col. 3:23.* [11]*Col. 3:17.* [12]*1 Cor. 10:31.*

JANUARY 29

*Thy kingdom come**

My kingship is not of this world; if My kingship were of this world, My servants would fight.[1] The kingdom of God is not coming with signs to be observed; nor will they say, 'Lo, here it is!' or 'There!' for behold, the kingdom of God is in the midst of you.[2] For the kingdom of God does not mean food and drink but righteousness and peace and joy in the Holy Spirit; he who thus serves Christ is acceptable to God and approved by men.[3] For the kingdom of God does not consist in talk but in power.[4]

All Thy saints shall bless Thee! They shall speak of the glory of Thy kingdom, and tell of Thy power, to make known to the sons of men Thy mighty deeds, and the glorious splendor of Thy kingdom. Thy kingdom is an everlasting kingdom, and Thy dominion endures throughout all generations.[5] The eternal kingdom of our Lord and Savior Jesus Christ.[6] The blessed and only Sovereign, the King of kings and Lord of lords, who alone has immortality and dwells in unapproachable light, whom no man has ever seen or can see.[7]

**Lk. 11:2.* [1]*Jn. 18:36.* [2]*Lk. 17:20, 21.* [3]*Rom. 14:17, 18.* [4]*1 Cor. 4:20.* [5]*Ps. 145:10–13.* [6]*2 Pet. 1:11.* [7]*1 Tim. 6:15, 16.*

JANUARY 30

*Satan, the deceiver of the whole world**

Jesus said . . . 'I saw Satan fall like lightning from heaven.'[1] How you are fallen from heaven, O Day Star, son of Dawn! How you are cut down to the ground, you who laid the nations low! You said in your heart, 'I will ascend to heaven; . . . I will set my throne on high; . . . I will make myself like the Most High.' But you are brought down to . . . the depths . . . Those who see you will stare at you, and ponder over you: 'Is this the man who made the earth tremble?'[2]

Now there was a day when the sons of God came to present themselves before the Lord, and Satan also came among them. The Lord said to Satan, 'Whence have you come?' Satan answered the Lord, 'From going to and fro on the earth, and from walking up and down on it.'[3]

Now the serpent was more subtle than any other wild creature that the Lord God had made.[4] That ancient serpent, who is called the Devil and Satan.[5] Even Satan disguises himself as an angel of light.[6] Your adversary the devil prowls around like a roaring lion, seeking some one to devour.[7]

**Rev. 12:9.* [1]*Lk. 10:18.* [2]*Is. 14:12–16.* [3]*Job 1:6, 7.* [4]*Gen. 3:1.* [5]*Rev. 12:9.* [6]*2 Cor. 11:14.* [7]*1 Pet. 5:8.*

*Be holy, for I am holy**

Who shall ascend the hill of the Lord? And who shall stand in His holy place? He who has clean hands and a pure heart.[1] Blessed are the pure in heart, for they shall see God.[2] Be sure of this, that no immoral or impure man . . . has any inheritance in the kingdom of Christ and of God.[3] Strive for . . . the holiness without which no one will see the Lord.[4]

And I said: 'Woe is me! For I am lost; for I am a man of unclean lips.'[5] Create in me a clean heart, O God, and put a new and right spirit within me.[6] Your guilt is taken away, and your sin forgiven.[7]

Put off your old nature which belongs to your former manner of life and is corrupt through deceitful lusts, and be renewed in the spirit of your minds, and put on the new nature, created after the likeness of God in true righteousness and holiness.[8] That . . . you may escape from the corruption that is in the world . . . and become partakers of the divine nature.[9] That we may share His holiness.[10] He who loves purity of heart . . . will have the king as his friend.[11]

**Lev. 11:44.* [1]*Ps. 24:3, 4.* [2]*Mt. 5:8.* [3]*Eph. 5:5.* [4]*Heb. 12:14.* [5]*Is. 6:5.* [6]*Ps. 51:10.* [7]*Is. 6:7.* [8]*Eph. 4:22–24.* [9]*2 Pet. 1:4.* [10]*Heb. 12:10.* [11]*Prov. 22:11.*

FEBRUARY 1

*Perplexed, but not driven to despair**

O our God . . . we are powerless against this great multitude that is coming against us. We do not know what to do, but our eyes are upon Thee.[1] My eyes are ever toward the Lord, for He will pluck my feet out of the net.[2]

And now, O Lord my God, Thou hast made Thy servant king in place of David my father, although I am but a little child; I do not know how to go out or come in.[3] Lead me, O Lord, in Thy righteousness because of my enemies; make Thy way straight before me.[4]

Now is My soul troubled. And what shall I say, 'Father, save Me from this hour'? No, for this purpose I have come to this hour. 'Father, glorify Thy name.' Then a voice came from heaven, 'I have glorified it, and will glorify it again.'[5]

I said, 'What shall I do, Lord?' And the Lord said to me, 'Rise, and go into Damascus, and there you will be told.'[6] And now, behold, I am going to Jerusalem, bound in the Spirit, not knowing what shall befall me there.[7] We know that in everything God works for good with those who love Him.[8]

* *2 Cor. 4:8.* [1] *2 Chron. 20:12.* [2] *Ps. 25:15.* [3] *1 Kings 3:7.* [4] *Ps. 5:8.* [5] *Jn. 12:27, 28.* [6] *Acts 22:10.* [7] *Acts 20:22.* [8] *Rom. 8:28.*

*Abraham who had faith**

By faith Abraham obeyed when he was called to go out to a place which he was to receive as an inheritance; and he went out, not knowing where he was to go.[1] After these things the word of the Lord came to Abram in a vision, 'Fear not, Abram, I am your shield; your reward shall be very great.'[2]

By faith Abraham, when he was tested, offered up Isaac, and he who had received the promises was ready to offer up his only son.[3] The angel of the Lord called to Abraham a second time from heaven, and said, 'By Myself I have sworn, says the Lord, because you have done this, and have not withheld your son, your only son, I will indeed bless you . . . and by your descendants shall all the nations of the earth bless themselves.'[4]

Abraham believed God, and it was reckoned to him as righteousness.[5] No distrust made him waver concerning the promise of God, but he grew strong in his faith as he gave glory to God, fully convinced that God was able to do what He had promised.[6]

Abraham believed God . . .; and he was called the friend of God.[7]

**Gal. 3:9.* [1]*Heb. 11:8.* [2]*Gen. 15:1.* [3]*Heb. 11:17.* [4]*Gen. 22:15–18.* [5]*Rom. 4:3.* [6]*Rom. 4:20, 21.* [7]*Jas. 2:23.*

FEBRUARY 3

*In the beginning God**

Lord, Thou hast been our dwelling place in all generations. Before the mountains were brought forth, or ever Thou hadst formed the earth and the world, from everlasting to everlasting Thou art God.[1] Ever since the creation of the world His invisible nature, namely, His eternal power and deity, has been clearly perceived in the things that have been made.[2]

Thus says the high and lofty One who inhabits eternity . . . 'I dwell in the high and holy place, and also with him who is of a contrite and humble spirit.'[3] Have you not known? Have you not heard? The Lord is the everlasting God, the Creator of the ends of the earth. He does not faint or grow weary, His understanding is unsearchable.[4] The eternal God is your dwelling place, and underneath are the everlasting arms.[5]

To the King of ages, immortal, invisible, the only God, be honor and glory for ever and ever.[6] I am the Alpha and the Omega, says the Lord God, who is and who was and who is to come, the Almighty.[7]

**Gen. 1:1. [1]Ps. 90:1, 2. [2]Rom. 1:20. [3]Is. 57:15. [4]Is. 40:28. [5]Deut. 33:27. [6]1 Tim. 1:17. [7]Rev. 1:8.*

*The good news**

The day shall dawn upon us from on high to give light to those who sit in darkness and in the shadow of death.[1] The darkness is passing away and the true light is already shining.[2] The light has come into the world.[3] The mystery which was kept secret for long ages but is now disclosed and . . . made known to all nations.[4] The gospel which has come to you, as indeed in the whole world it is bearing fruit and growing.[5]

I am not ashamed of the gospel: it is the power of God for salvation to every one who has faith.[6] God sent the Son into the world, not to condemn the world, but that the world might be saved through Him.[7] That is, God was in Christ reconciling the world to Himself.[8] In Him we have redemption through His blood, the forgiveness of our trespasses, according to the riches of His grace which He lavished upon us.[9]

The kingdom of heaven is like a merchant in search of fine pearls, who, on finding one pearl of great value, went and sold all that he had and bought it.[10] Thanks be to God for His inexpressible gift![11]

**Acts 13:32.* [1]*Lk. 1:78, 79.* [2]*1 Jn. 2:8.* [3]*Jn. 3:19.* [4]*Rom. 16:25, 26.* [5]*Col. 1:5, 6.* [6]*Rom. 1:16.* [7]*Jn. 3:17.* [8]*2 Cor. 5:19.* [9]*Eph. 1:7, 8.* [10]*Mt. 13:45.* [11]*2 Cor. 9:15.*

FEBRUARY 5

*Grow up in every way into Him**

Like newborn babes, long for the pure spiritual milk, that by it you may grow up to salvation; for you have tasted the kindness of the Lord.[1] But I, brethren, could not address you as spiritual men, but as men of the flesh, as babes in Christ. I fed you with milk, not solid food; for you were not ready for it.[2]

Therefore be imitators of God, as beloved children. And walk in love, as Christ loved us and gave Himself up for us.[3] As obedient children, do not be conformed to the passions of your former ignorance, but as He who called you is holy, be holy yourselves in all your conduct; since it is written, 'You shall be holy, for I am holy.'[4]

Brethren, do not be children in your thinking; be babes in evil, but in thinking be mature.[5] Solid food is for the mature, for those who have their faculties trained by practice to distinguish good from evil.[6] I am writing to you, little children, because your sins are forgiven for His sake . . . I am writing to you, young men, because you have overcome the evil one.[7] That the man of God may be complete, equipped for every good work.[8]

**Eph. 4:15.* [1]*1 Pet. 2:2, 3.* [2]*1 Cor. 3:1, 2.* [3]*Eph. 5:1, 2.* [4]*1 Pet. 1:14–16.* [5]*1 Cor. 14:20.* [6]*Heb. 5:14.* [7]*1 Jn. 2:12, 13.* [8]*2 Tim. 3:17.*

*Rich toward God**

Every man also to whom God has given wealth and possessions . . . this is the gift of God.[1] If riches increase, set not your heart on them.[2] Thus says the Lord . . . 'Let not the rich man glory in his riches.'[3] For riches do not last for ever.[4]

As for the rich in this world, charge them not to be haughty, nor to set their hopes on uncertain riches but on God . . . They are to do good, to be rich in good deeds, liberal and generous.[5]

Jesus went on through cities and villages, preaching and bringing the good news of the kingdom of God. And the twelve were with Him, and also some women . . . who provided for them out of their means.[6] Levi made him a great feast in his house; and there was a large company of tax collectors and others sitting at table with them.[7] While Jesus was at Bethany . . . a woman came with an alabaster jar of ointment of pure nard, very costly, and she broke the jar and poured it over His head . . . Jesus said . . . 'She has done a beautiful thing to Me.'[8] When it was evening, there came a rich man . . . named Joseph . . . He went to Pilate and asked for the body of Jesus . . . and laid it in his own new tomb.[9]

**Lk. 12:21.* [1]*Eccl. 5:19.* [2]*Ps. 62:10.* [3]*Jer. 9:23.* [4]*Prov. 27:24.* [5]*1 Tim. 6:17, 18.* [6]*Lk. 8:1–3.* [7]*Lk. 5:29.* [8]*Mk. 14:3, 6.* [9]*Mt. 27:57, 58, 60.*

FEBRUARY 7

*The price of wisdom is above pearls**

But where shall wisdom be found? And where is the place of understanding? Man does not know the way to it, and it is not found in the land of the living. The deep says, 'It is not in me,' and the sea says, 'It is not with me.' It cannot be gotten for gold, and silver cannot be weighed as its price.[1] The wisdom of this world is folly with God.[2] This wisdom is not such as comes down from above, but is earthly, unspiritual, devilish.[3]

God said to man, 'Behold, the fear of the Lord, that is wisdom; and to depart from evil is understanding.'[4] The fear of the Lord is the beginning of wisdom.[5] The knowledge... of Christ, in whom are hid all the treasures of wisdom.[6] Christ Jesus, whom God made our wisdom.[7] The wisdom from above is first pure, then peaceable, gentle, open to reason, full of mercy and good fruits, without uncertainty or insincerity.[8]

Teach me wisdom in my secret heart.[9] If any of you lacks wisdom, let him ask God who gives to all men generously and without reproaching, and it will be given him.[10] Let the word of Christ dwell in you richly . . . in all wisdom.[11]

**Job.* 28:18. [1]*Job* 28:12–15. [2]*1 Cor.* 3:19. [3]*Jas.* 3:15. [4]*Job* 28:28. [5]*Ps.* 111:10. [6]*Col.* 2:2, 3. [7]*1 Cor.* 1:30. [8]*Jas.* 3:17. [9]*Ps.* 51:6. [10]*Jas.* 1:5. [11]*Col.* 3:16.

*Our God . . . is able**

He is able for all time to save those who draw near to God through Him, since He always lives to make intercession for them.[1] Because He Himself has suffered and been tempted, He is able to help those who are tempted.[2] God is able to provide you with every blessing in abundance, so that you may always have enough of everything and may provide in abundance for every good work.[3]

Jesus said to them, 'Do you believe that I am able to do this?' They said to Him, 'Yes, Lord.' Then He touched their eyes, saying, 'According to your faith be it done to you.'[4] Our God whom we serve is able to deliver us from the burning fiery furnace.[5] Able to keep you from falling.[6] He will be upheld, for the Master is able to make him stand.[7]

Now to Him who by the power at work within us is able to do far more abundantly than all that we ask or think, to Him be glory in the Church and in Christ Jesus to all generations, for ever and ever. Amen.[8]

**Dan.* 3:17. [1]*Heb.* 7:25. [2]*Heb.* 2:18. [3]2 *Cor.* 9:8. [4]*Mt.* 9:28, 29. [5]*Dan.* 3:17. [6]*Jude* 24. [7]*Rom.* 14:4. [8]*Eph.* 3:20, 21.

FEBRUARY 9

*The fruit of the Spirit is . . . self-control**

A man without self-control is like a city broken into and left without walls.[1] Urge the younger men to control themselves.[2] The imperishable jewel of a gentle and quiet spirit, which in God's sight is very precious.[3] God did not give us a spirit of timidity but a spirit of power and love and self-control.[4]

He who is slow to anger is better than the mighty, and he who rules his spirit than he who takes a city.[5] If any one strikes you on the right cheek, turn to him the other also.[6] The patient in spirit is better than the proud in spirit.[7] Be angry but do not sin; do not let the sun go down on your anger, and give no opportunity to the devil.[8]

Do not get drunk with wine, for that is debauchery; but be filled with the Spirit.[9] Do not swear at all . . . Let what you say be simply 'Yes' or 'No'; anything more than this comes from evil.[10] The Lord's servant must not be quarrelsome.[11] Those who belong to Christ Jesus have crucified the flesh with its passions and desires.[12]

**Gal. 5:22, 23.* [1]*Prov. 25:28.* [2]*Tit. 2:6.* [3]*1 Pet. 3:4.* [4]*2 Tim. 1:7.* [5]*Prov. 16:32.* [6]*Mt. 5:39.* [7]*Eccl. 7:8.* [8]*Eph. 4:26, 27.* [9]*Eph. 5:18.* [10]*Mt. 5:34, 37.* [11]*2 Tim. 2:24.* [12]*Gal. 5:24.*

*No man ever spoke like this man!**

The crowds were astonished at His teaching, for He taught them as one who had authority, and not as their scribes.[1] They were all amazed and said to one another, 'What is this word? For with authority and power He commands the unclean spirits, and they come out.'[2] Where did this man get this wisdom and these mighty works? Is not this the carpenter's son? . . . Where then did this man get all this?[3]

The word which you hear is not Mine but the Father's who sent Me.[4] My teaching is not Mine, but His who sent Me; if any man's will is to do His will, he shall know whether the teaching is from God or whether I am speaking on My own authority.[5] This is My beloved Son, with whom I am well pleased; listen to Him.[6]

His voice was like the sound of many waters . . . from His mouth issued a sharp two-edged sword.[7] The Lord God has given Me the tongue of those who are taught, that I may know how to sustain with a word him that is weary.[8] The sheep follow him, for they know his voice . . . They do not know the voice of strangers.[9]

**Jn. 7:46.* [1]*Mt. 7:28, 29.* [2]*Lk. 4:36.* [3]*Mt. 13:54–56.* [4]*Jn. 14:24.* [5]*Jn. 7:16, 17.* [6]*Mt. 17:5.* [7]*Rev. 1:15, 16.* [8]*Is. 50:4.* [9]*Jn. 10:4, 5.*

FEBRUARY 11

*The glorious liberty of the children of God**

Jesus answered them, 'Truly, truly, I say to you, every one who commits sin is a slave to sin.'[1] You . . . were once slaves of sin.[2] When you did not know God, you were in bondage.[3] Following the course of this world, following the prince of the power of the air . . . following the desires of body and mind.[4]

The Lord has anointed Me . . . to proclaim liberty to the captives, and the opening of the prison to those who are bound.[5] They came to Jesus, and found the man from whom the demons had gone, sitting at the feet of Jesus, clothed and in his right mind.[6] If the Son makes you free, you will be free indeed.[7] For the law of the Spirit of life in Christ Jesus has set me free from the law of sin and death.[8] Sin will have no dominion over you, since you are not under law but under grace.[9]

Live as free men, yet without using your freedom as a pretext for evil; but live as servants of God.[10] Do not use your freedom as an opportunity for the flesh, but through love be servants of one another.[11]

**Rom. 8:21.* [1]*Jn. 8:34.* [2]*Rom. 6:17.* [3]*Gal. 4:8.* [4]*Eph. 2:2, 3.* [5]*Is. 61:1.* [6]*Lk. 8:35.* [7]*Jn. 8:36.* [8]*Rom. 8:2.* [9]*Rom. 6:14.* [10]*1 Pet. 2:16.* [11]*Gal. 5:13.*

*You said, 'I will not serve'**

After this many of His disciples drew back and no longer went about with Him.[1] My people are bent on turning away from Me.[2]

All that is in the world, the lust of the flesh and the lust of the eyes and the pride of life, is not of the Father but is of the world.[3] Demas, in love with this present world, has deserted me.[4]

When they had fed to the full, they were filled, and their heart was lifted up; therefore they forgot Me.[5] The more they increased, the more they sinned against Me.[6] For the love of money is the root of all evils; it is through this craving that some have wandered away from the faith and pierced their hearts with many pangs.[7]

'Return, faithless Israel,' says the Lord. 'I will not look on you in anger . . . Only acknowledge your guilt, that you rebelled against the Lord your God.'[8] Return . . . to the Lord your God, for you have stumbled because of your iniquity.[9] I will heal their faithlessness; I will love them freely, for My anger has turned from them. I will be as the dew to Israel . . . They shall return and dwell beneath My shadow.[10] For thus said the Lord God . . . 'In returning and rest you shall be saved.'[11]

**Jer. 2:20.* [1]*Jn. 6:66.* [2]*Hos. 11:7.* [3]*1 Jn. 2:16.* [4]*2 Tim. 4:10.* [5]*Hos. 13:6.* [6]*Hos. 4:7.* [7]*1 Tim. 6:10.* [8]*Jer. 3:12, 13.* [9]*Hos. 14:1.* [10]*Hos. 14:4, 5, 7.* [11]*Is. 30:15.*

FEBRUARY 13

*O Lord . . . be not deaf to me**

Behold, the Lord's hand is not shortened, that it cannot save, or His ear dull, that it cannot hear; but your iniquities have made a separation between you and your God . . . so that He does not hear.[1] If I had cherished iniquity in my heart, the Lord would not have listened.[2] You do not have, because you do not ask. You ask and do not receive, because you ask wrongly, to spend it on your passions.[3] Take delight in the Lord, and He will give you the desires of your heart.[4] No good thing does the Lord withhold from those who walk uprightly.[5]

Whatever you ask in My name, I will do it, that the Father may be glorified in the Son; if you ask anything in My name, I will do it.[6] This is the confidence which we have in Him, that if we ask anything according to His will He hears us. And if we know that He hears us in whatever we ask, we know that we have obtained the requests made of Him.[7] But let him ask in faith, with no doubting, for he who doubts is like a wave of the sea that is driven and tossed by the wind.[8]

**Ps. 28:1.* [1]*Is. 59:1, 2.* [2]*Ps. 66:18.* [3]*Jas. 4:2, 3.* [4]*Ps. 37:4.* [5]*Ps. 84:11.* [6]*Jn. 14:13, 14.* [7]*1 Jn. 5:14, 15.* [8]*Jas. 1:6.*

*Ambassadors for Christ**

So we are ambassadors for Christ, God making His appeal through us. We beseech you on behalf of Christ, be reconciled to God.[1] The Lord said to Ananias, 'Go, for he is a chosen instrument of Mine to carry My name before the Gentiles and kings . . . for I will show him how much he must suffer for the sake of My name.[2] Keep alert with all perseverance, making supplication for all the saints, and also for me, that utterance may be given me in opening my mouth boldly to proclaim the mystery of the gospel, for which I am an ambassador in chains.[3]

My chosen people, the people whom I formed for Myself that they might declare My praise.[4] Then Haggai, the messenger of the Lord, spoke to the people with the Lord's message.[5] A bad messenger plunges men into trouble, but a faithful envoy brings healing.[6]

So the woman . . . went away into the city, and said to the people, 'Come, see a man who told me all that I ever did. Can this be the Christ?'[7] Many Samaritans from that city believed in Him because of the woman's testimony.[8]

* *2 Cor. 5:20.* [1] *2 Cor. 5:20.* [2] *Acts 9:15, 16.* [3] *Eph. 6:18–20.* [4] *Is. 43:20, 21.* [5] *Hag. 1:13.* [6] *Prov. 13:17.* [7] *Jn. 4:28, 29.* [8] *Jn. 4:39.*

FEBRUARY 15

*Power belongs to God**

Can you find out the deep things of God? Can you find out the limit of the Almighty?[1] His eternal power.[2]

By the word of the Lord the heavens were made.[3] Upholding the universe by His word of power.[4] O Lord God of hosts, who is mighty as Thou art, O Lord, with Thy faithfulness round about Thee? Thou dost rule the raging of the sea . . . Thou didst scatter Thy enemies with Thy mighty arm.[5] The Lord, strong and mighty, the Lord, mighty in battle.[6]

I am not ashamed of the gospel: it is the power of God for salvation to every one who has faith.[7] That you may know . . . what is the immeasurable greatness of His power in us who believe, according to the working of His great might which He accomplished in Christ when He raised Him from the dead.[8]

The government will be upon His shoulder, and His name will be called 'Wonderful Counselor, Mighty God, Everlasting Father, Prince of Peace'.[9] His dominion is an everlasting dominion, which shall not pass away, and His kingdom one that shall not be destroyed.[10]

**Ps. 62:11.* [1]*Job 11:7.* [2]*Rom. 1:20.* [3]*Ps. 33:6.* [4]*Heb. 1:3.* [5]*Ps. 89:8–10.* [6]*Ps. 24:8.* [7]*Rom. 1:16.* [8]*Eph. 1:18–20.* [9]*Is. 9:6.* [10]*Dan. 7:14.*

*He rewards those who seek Him**

He is not far from each one of us, for in Him we live and move and have our being.[1] Seek the Lord while He may be found, call upon Him while He is near.[2] Call upon Me and come and pray to Me, and I will hear you. You will seek Me and find Me; when you seek Me with all your heart, I will be found by you, says the Lord.[3]

Every one is searching for You.[4] Wise men from the East came to Jerusalem, saying, 'Where is He who has been born king of the Jews?'[5] Zacchaeus . . . climbed up into a sycamore tree to see Jesus.[6] Some Greeks . . . came to Philip . . . and said to him, 'Sir, we wish to see Jesus.'[7] Seek, and you will find.[8]

One thing have I asked of the Lord, that will I seek after; that I may dwell in the house of the Lord all the days of my life, to behold the beauty of the Lord, and to inquire in His temple.[9] O God, Thou art my God, I seek Thee, my soul thirsts for Thee; my flesh faints for Thee, as in a dry and weary land where no water is.[10] Those who seek the Lord lack no good thing.[11]

**Heb. 11:6.* [1]*Acts 17:27, 28.* [2]*Is. 55:6.* [3]*Jer. 29:12–14.* [4]*Mk. 1:37.* [5]*Mt. 2:1, 2.* [6]*Lk. 19:4.* [7]*Jn. 12:20, 21.* [8]*Mt. 7:7.* [9]*Ps. 27:4.* [10]*Ps. 63:1.* [11]*Ps. 34:10.*

FEBRUARY 17

*The Counselor**

The Counselor, the Holy Spirit, whom the Father will send in My name, He will teach you all things, and bring to your remembrance all that I have said to you.[1] He will guide you into all the truth . . . and He will declare to you the things that are to come. He will glorify Me, for He will take what is Mine and declare it to you.[2] He will bear witness to Me.[3]

Do not rely on your own insight.[4] For all who are led by the Spirit of God are sons of God.[5] The Spirit said to Philip, 'Go up and join this chariot.'[6] They attempted to go into Bithynia, but the Spirit of Jesus did not allow them.[7]

I will pour out on the house of David and the inhabitants of Jerusalem a spirit of compassion and supplication.[8] For we do not know how to pray as we ought, but the Spirit Himself intercedes for us with sighs too deep for words.[9]

He who believes in the Son of God has the testimony in himself.[10] By this we know that we abide in Him and He in us, because He has given us of His own Spirit.[11] It is the Spirit Himself bearing witness with our spirit that we are children of God.[12]

**Jn. 15:26.* [1]*Jn. 14:26.* [2]*Jn. 16:13, 14.* [3]*Jn. 15:26.* [4]*Prov. 3:5.* [5]*Rom. 8:14.* [6]*Acts 8:29.* [7]*Acts 16:7.* [8]*Zech. 12:10.* [9]*Rom. 8:26.* [10]*1 Jn. 5:10.* [11]*1 Jn. 4:13.* [12]*Rom. 8:16.*

*Sin . . . deceived me**

There is a way which seems right to a man, but its end is the way to death.[1] The heart is deceitful above all things, and desperately corrupt; who can understand it? I the Lord search the mind and try the heart, to give to every man according to his ways, according to the fruit of his doings.[2] The wages of sin is death.[3]

Do you not know that if you yield yourselves to any one as obedient slaves, you are slaves of the one whom you obey?[4] Every one who commits sin is a slave to sin.[5] Theft, murder, adultery . . . All these evil things come from within, and they defile a man.[6] For he who sows to his own flesh will from the flesh reap corruption.[7]

Your sins have hid His face from you so that He does not hear.[8] If your eye is not sound, your whole body will be full of darkness.[9] I was stupid and ignorant, I was like a beast toward Thee.[10] My iniquities have overtaken me, till I cannot see.[11]

They fell down, with none to help. Then they cried to the Lord in their trouble, and He delivered them from their distress; He brought them out of darkness and gloom, and broke their bonds asunder.[12]

**Rom. 7:11.* [1]*Prov. 16:25.* [2]*Jer. 17:9, 10.* [3]*Rom. 6:23.* [4]*Rom. 6:16.* [5]*Jn. 8:34.* [6]*Mk. 7:21, 23.* [7]*Gal. 6:8.* [8]*Is. 59:2.* [9]*Mt. 6:23.* [10]*Ps. 73:22.* [11]*Ps. 40:12.* [12]*Ps. 107:12–14.*

FEBRUARY 19

*Blessed is he . . . whose sin is covered**

The Lord is merciful and gracious, slow to anger and abounding in steadfast love. He will not always chide, nor will He keep His anger for ever. He does not deal with us according to our sins, nor requite us according to our iniquities. For as the heavens are high above the earth, so great is His steadfast love toward those who fear Him; as far as the east is from the west, so far does He remove our transgressions from us.[1]

He will again have compassion upon us, He will tread our iniquities under foot. Thou wilt cast all our sins into the depths of the sea.[2] I, I am He who blots out your transgressions for My own sake, and I will not remember your sins.[3] For Thou hast cast all my sins behind Thy back.[4]

'Come now, let us reason together,' says the Lord: 'though your sins are like scarlet, they shall be as white as snow; though they are red like crimson, they shall become like wool.'[5]

**Ps. 32:1.* [1]*Ps. 103:8–12.* [2]*Mic. 7:19.* [3]*Is. 43:25.* [4]*Is. 38:17.* [5]*Is. 1:18.*

*The fruit of the Spirit is . . . faithfulness**

Well done, good and faithful servant; you have been faithful over a little, I will set you over much; enter into the joy of your master.[1] He who is faithful in a very little is faithful also in much.[2] I thank God . . . because He judged me faithful by appointing me to His service.[3] Be faithful unto death, and I will give you the crown of life.[4]

Trust in a faithless man in time of trouble is like a bad tooth or a foot that slips.[5] Many a man proclaims his own loyalty, but a faithful man who can find?[6] They all look after their own interests, not those of Jesus Christ.[7] For many, of whom I have often told you and now tell you even with tears, live as enemies of the cross of Christ. Their end is destruction.[8] But we are not of those who shrink back and are destroyed, but of those who have faith and keep their souls.[9]

Know therefore that the Lord your God is God, the faithful God who keeps covenant and steadfast love with those who love Him.[10] He is Lord of lords and King of kings, and those with Him are called and chosen and faithful.[11] The Lord rewards every man for his . . . faithfulness.[12]

**Gal. 5:22.* [1]*Mt. 25:21.* [2]*Lk. 16:10.* [3]*1 Tim. 1:12.* [4]*Rev. 2:10.* [5]*Prov. 25:19.* [6]*Prov. 20:6.* [7]*Phil. 2:21.* [8]*Phil. 3:18, 19.* [9]*Heb. 10:39.* [10]*Deut. 7:9.* [11]*Rev. 17:14.* [12]*1 Sam. 26:23.*

FEBRUARY 21

*His witnesses to the people**

You shall be My witnesses . . . to the end of the earth.[1] I have sent them into the world . . . so that the world may know that Thou hast sent Me.[2] As He is so are we in this world.[3] Thanks be to God, who in Christ always leads us in triumph, and through us spreads the fragrance of the knowledge of Him everywhere. For we are the aroma of Christ.[4] They recognized that they had been with Jesus.[5] You are the salt of the earth; but if salt has lost its taste, how shall its saltness be restored?[6]

Once you were darkness, but now you are light in the Lord; walk as children of light (for the fruit of light is found in all that is good and right and true).[7] You are the light of the world . . . Let your light so shine before men, that they may see your good works and give glory to your Father who is in heaven.[8] Be aglow with the Spirit.[9]

Whatever you do, in word or deed, do everything in the name of the Lord Jesus.[10] Whatever your task, work heartily, as serving the Lord and not men.[11] For it is God's will that by doing right you should put to silence the ignorance of foolish men.[12]

**Acts 13:31.* [1]*Acts 1:8.* [2]*Jn. 17:18, 23.* [3]*1 Jn. 4:17.* [4]*2 Cor. 2:14, 15.* [5]*Acts 4:13.* [6]*Mt. 5:13.* [7]*Eph. 5:8, 9.* [8]*Mt. 5:14, 16.* [9]*Rom. 12:11.* [10]*Col. 3:17.* [11]*Col. 3:23.* [12]*1 Pet. 2:15.*

*The ransom of his life is costly**

What shall a man give in return for his life?[1] No man can ransom himself, or give to God the price of his life, for the ransom of his life is costly, and can never suffice, that he should continue to live on for ever.[2] It is appointed for men to die once, and after that comes judgment.[3] The sting of death is sin.[4]

The Son of man . . . came . . . to give His life as a ransom for many.[5] For there is one God, and there is one mediator between God and men, the man Christ Jesus, who gave Himself as a ransom for all.[6] Jesus, who for a little while was made lower than the angels . . . so that by the grace of God He might taste death for every one.[7]

You were ransomed . . . not with perishable things such as silver or gold, but with the precious blood of Christ.[8] For the wages of sin is death, but the free gift of God is eternal life in Christ Jesus our Lord.[9] Fear not, for I have redeemed you; I have called you by name, you are Mine.[10] Death is swallowed up in victory . . . O death, where is thy sting?[11]

**Ps. 49:8.* [1]*Mt. 16:26.* [2]*Ps. 49:7–9.* [3]*Heb. 9:27.* [4]*1 Cor. 15:56.* [5]*Mk. 10:45.* [6]*1 Tim. 2:5, 6.* [7]*Heb. 2:9.* [8]*1 Pet. 1:18, 19.* [9]*Rom. 6:23.* [10]*Is. 43:1.* [11]*1 Cor. 15:54, 55.*

FEBRUARY 23

*His body, that is, the church**

I am no more in the world, but they are in the world.[1] You shall be My witnesses in Jerusalem and in all Judea and Samaria and to the end of the earth.[2] Go into all the world and preach the gospel to the whole creation.[3] Fear not . . . Behold I will make of you a threshing sledge, new, sharp and having teeth.[4] You will spread abroad to the right and to the left, and your descendants will possess the nations.[5] Your builders outstrip your destroyers.[6]

If two of you agree on earth about anything they ask, it will be done for them by My Father in heaven.[7] Peter was kept in prison; but earnest prayer for him was made to God by the church . . . The Lord . . . brought him out of the prison.[8]

I have tried you in the furnace of affliction.[9] The same experience of suffering is required of your brotherhood throughout the world.[10] For it has been granted to you that for the sake of Christ you should not only believe in Him but also suffer for His sake.[11]

You are a chosen race, a royal priesthood, a holy nation, God's own people, that you may declare the wonderful deeds of Him who called you out of darkness into His marvelous light.[12]

**Col.* 1:24. [1]*Jn.* 17:11. [2]*Acts* 1:8. [3]*Mk.* 16:15. [4]*Is.* 41:14, 15. [5]*Is.* 54:3. [6]*Is.* 49:17. [7]*Mt.* 18:19. [8]*Acts* 12:5, 17. [9]*Is.* 48:10. [10]*1 Pet.* 5:9. [11]*Phil.* 1:29. [12]*1 Pet.* 2:9.

*Faith is . . .**

. . . the assurance of things hoped for, the conviction of things not seen.[1] No one has ever seen God.[2] For we walk by faith, not by sight.[3] So we do not lose heart . . . because we look not to the things that are seen but to the things that are unseen; for the things that are seen are transient, but the things that are unseen are eternal.[4] Blessed are those who have not seen and yet believe.[5]

The world will see Me no more, but you will see Me.[6] In their case the god of this world has blinded the minds of the unbelievers, to keep them from seeing.[7] God . . . has shone in our hearts to give the light of the knowledge of . . . God in the face of Christ.[8] The Lord opened the eyes of the young man, and he saw.[9] He endured as seeing Him who is invisible.[10] Without having seen Him you love Him; though you do not now see Him you believe in Him and rejoice with unutterable and exalted joy.[11]

May the God of hope fill you with all joy and peace in believing.[12] Now we see in a mirror dimly, but then face to face.[13] Therefore do not throw away your confidence, which has a great reward.[14]

**Heb. 11:1.* [1]*Heb. 11:1.* [2]*Jn. 1:18.* [3]*2 Cor. 5:7.* [4]*2 Cor. 4:16, 18.* [5]*Jn. 20:29.* [6]*Jn. 14:19.* [7]*2 Cor. 4:4.* [8]*2 Cor. 4:6.* [9]*2 Kings 6:17* [10]*Heb. 11:27.* [11]*1 Pet. 1:8.* [12]*Rom. 15:13.* [13]*1 Cor. 13:12.* [14]*Heb. 10:35.*

FEBRUARY 25

*Remember the sabbath day, to keep it holy**

It is a sign for ever between Me and the people of Israel that in six days the Lord made heaven and earth, and on the seventh day He rested, and was refreshed.[1] If you turn back your foot from the sabbath, from doing your pleasure on My holy day . . . then you shall take delight in the Lord.[2]

One sabbath . . . Jesus' disciples began to pluck ears of grain. And the Pharisees said to Him, 'Look, why are they doing what is not lawful on the sabbath?' . . . And He said to them, 'The sabbath was made for man, not man for the sabbath; so the Son of man is Lord even of the sabbath.'[3] Again He entered the synagogue, and a man was there who had a withered hand. And they watched Him, to see whether He would heal him on the sabbath . . . And He said to them, 'Is it lawful on the sabbath to do good or to do harm, to save life or to kill?' But they were silent.[4]

Jesus came to Nazareth . . . and He went to the synagogue, as His custom was, on the sabbath day.[5] Let us consider how to stir up one another to love and good works, not neglecting to meet together, as is the habit of some.[6] On the sabbath they rested according to the commandment.[7]

**Ex. 20:8.* [1]*Ex. 31:17.* [2]*Is. 58:13, 14.* [3]*Mk. 2:23, 24, 27.* [4]*Mk. 3:1, 2, 4.* [5]*Lk. 4:16.* [6]*Heb. 10:24, 25.* [7]*Lk. 23:56.*

*You must not be like the hypocrites**

This people draw near with their mouth and honor Me with their lips, while their hearts are far from Me, and their fear of Me is a commandment of men learned by rote.[1] Not every one who says to Me, 'Lord, Lord,' shall enter the kingdom of heaven, but he who does the will of My Father who is in heaven.[2]

And when you pray, you must not be like the hypocrites; for they love to stand and pray in the synagogues and at the street corners, that they may be seen by men.[3] How can you say to your brother, 'Brother, let me take out the speck that is in your eye,' when you yourself do not see the log that is in your own eye? You hypocrite . . .[4] You cleanse the outside of the cup and of the plate, but inside they are full of extortion and rapacity.[5]

What does it profit, my brethren, if a man says he has faith but has not works? Can his faith save him? If a brother or sister is ill-clad and in lack of daily food, and one of you says to them, 'Go in peace, be warmed and filled,' without giving them the things needed for the body, what does it profit? So faith by itself, if it has no works, is dead.[6]

**Mt. 6:5.* [1]*Is. 29:13.* [2]*Mt. 7:21.* [3]*Mt. 6:5.* [4]*Lk. 6:42.* [5]*Mt. 23:25.* [6]*Jas. 2:14–17.*

FEBRUARY 27

*Walk in newness of life**

Blessed is the man who walks not in the counsel of the wicked, nor stands in the way of sinners, nor sits in the seat of scoffers.[1] If sinners entice you . . . hold back your foot from their paths.[2] Walk by the Spirit, and do not gratify the desires of the flesh.[3] There is a way which seems right to a man, but its end is the way to death.[4]

But the path of the righteous is like the light of dawn, which shines brighter and brighter until full day.[5] I will run in the way of Thy commandments when Thou enlargest my understanding.[6] Teach me Thy way, O Lord, that I may walk in Thy truth.[7] He leads me in paths of righteousness for His name's sake.[8]

He has showed you, O man, what is good; and what does the Lord require of you but to do justice, and to love kindness, and to walk humbly with your God?[9] Thou dost show me the path of life; in Thy presence there is fullness of joy, in Thy right hand are pleasures for evermore.[10] Let us go up to the mountain of the Lord . . . that He may teach us His ways and that we may walk in His paths.[11]

**Rom. 6:4.* [1]*Ps. 1:1.* [2]*Prov. 1:10, 15.* [3]*Gal. 5:16.* [4]*Prov. 14:12.* [5]*Prov. 4:18.* [6]*Ps. 119:32.* [7]*Ps. 86:11.* [8]*Ps. 23:3.* [9]*Mic. 6:8.* [10]*Ps. 16:11.* [11]*Is. 2:3.*

*In the shadow of His hand He hid me**

As the mountains are round about Jerusalem, so the Lord is round about His people.[1] The mountains may depart and the hills be removed, but My steadfast love shall not depart from you.[2] The eternal God is your dwelling place, and underneath are the everlasting arms.[3]

Can a woman forget her sucking child, that she should have no compassion on the son of her womb? Even these may forget, yet I will not forget you . . . I have graven you on the palms of My hands.[4] I give them eternal life, and they shall never perish, and no one shall snatch them out of My hand.[5] For I, the Lord your God, hold your right hand; it is I who say to you, 'Fear not, I will help you.'[6] I, the Lord, the first, and with the last.[7]

I will sing of Thy steadfast love, O Lord, for ever; with my mouth I will proclaim Thy faithfulness to all generations. For Thy steadfast love was established for ever, Thy faithfulness is firm as the heavens.[8] Great is Thy faithfulness.[9]

**Is. 49:2.* [1]*Ps. 125:2.* [2]*Is. 54:10.* [3]*Deut. 33:27.* [4]*Is. 49:15, 16.* [5]*Jn. 10:28.* [6]*Is. 41:13.* [7]*Is. 41:4.* [8]*Ps. 89: 1, 2.* [9]*Lam. 3:23.*

FEBRUARY 29

*Why do you not believe?**

He came to His own home, and His own people received Him not.[1] He . . . came to his own country; and his disciples followed Him. And He could do no mighty work there, except that He laid His hands upon a few sick people and healed them. And He marveled because of their unbelief.[2] For even His brothers did not believe in Him.[3]

If I tell the truth, why do you not believe Me?[4] The ones along the path are those who have heard; then the devil comes and takes away the word from their hearts, that they may not believe and be saved.[5] They refused to love the truth and so be saved.[6]

Now Thomas, one of the twelve, called the Twin, was not with them when Jesus came. So the other disciples told him, 'We have seen the Lord.' But he said to them, 'Unless I see in His hands the print of the nails . . . and place my hand in His side, I will not believe.'[7] Then He said to Thomas, 'Put your finger here, and see My hands; and put out your hand, and place it in My side; do not be faithless, but believing.'[8]

**Jn. 8:46.* [1]*Jn. 1:11.* [2]*Mk. 6:15, 6.* [3]*Jn. 7:5.* [4]*Jn. 8:46.* [5]*Lk. 8:12.* [6]*2 Thess. 2:10.* [7]*Jn. 20:24, 25.* [8]*Jn. 20:27.*

*Holy, holy, holy, is the Lord God Almighty**

His head and His hair were white as white wool, white as snow; His eyes were like a flame of fire, His feet were like burnished bronze, refined as in a furnace, and His voice was like the sound of many waters . . . When I saw Him, I fell at His feet as though dead.[1] I the Lord your God am holy.[2] Who is like Thee, majestic in holiness?[3] Who . . . dwells in unapproachable light, whom no man has ever seen or can see.[4] Thou art of purer eyes than to behold evil.[5]

I saw the Lord sitting upon a throne, high and lifted up; and His train filled the temple. Above Him stood the seraphim . . . And one called to another and said: 'Holy, holy, holy is the Lord of hosts; the whole earth is full of His glory . . .' And I said, 'Woe is me! For I am lost; for I am a man of unclean lips, and I dwell in the midst of a people of unclean lips; for my eyes have seen the King, the Lord of hosts!'[6] God is light and in Him is no darkness at all.[7] Our God is a consuming fire.[8] Who among us can dwell with the devouring fire? Who among us can dwell with everlasting burnings?[9] He who has clean hands and a pure heart.[10]

**Rev. 4:8.* [1]*Rev. 1:14, 15, 17.* [2]*Lev. 19:1.* [3]*Ex. 15:11.* [4]*1 Tim. 6:16.* [5]*Hab. 1:13.* [6]*Is. 6:1–3, 5.* [7]*1 Jn. 1:5.* [8]*Heb. 12:29.* [9]*Is. 33:14.* [10]*Ps. 24:4.*

MARCH 2

*Haters of God**

The kings of the earth set themselves . . . against the Lord and His anointed, saying, 'Let us burst their bonds asunder, and cast their cords from us.'[1] We do not want this man to reign over us.[2] He came to His own home, and His own people received Him not.[3] Scorned by men, and despised by the people.[4] They hated Me without a cause.[5]

Men loved darkness rather than light, because their deeds were evil.[6] For although they knew God they did not honor Him as God or give thanks to Him, but they became futile in their thinking and their senseless minds were darkened.[7] For the mind that is set on the flesh is hostile to God; it does not submit to God's law, indeed it cannot; and those who are in the flesh cannot please God.[8] They are darkened in their understanding, alienated from the life of God . . . due to their hardness of heart.[9] Estranged and hostile in mind, doing evil deeds.[10]

But now in Christ Jesus you who once were far off have been brought near in the blood of Christ.[11] For . . . while we were enemies we were reconciled to God by the death of His Son.[12]

**Rom. 1:30.* [1]*Ps. 2:2, 3.* [2]*Lk. 19:14.* [3]*Jn. 1:11.* [4]*Ps. 22:6.* [5]*Jn. 15:25.* [6]*Jn. 3:19.* [7]*Rom. 1:21.* [8]*Rom. 8:7, 8.* [9]*Eph. 4:18.* [10]*Col. 1:21.* [11]*Eph. 2:13.* [12]*Rom. 5:10.*

*Your sins are forgiven for His sake**

David said to the Lord, 'I have sinned greatly in what I have done. But now, O Lord, I pray Thee, take away the iniquity of Thy servant; for I have done very foolishly.'[1] Hide Thy face from my sins, and blot out all my iniquities.[2] Remember not the sins of my youth, or my transgressions; according to Thy steadfast love remember me.[3]

Jesus said, 'Father, forgive them; for they know not what they do.'[4] Behold, the Lamb of God, who takes away the sin of the world![5] He poured out His soul to death, and was numbered with the transgressors; yet He bore the sin of many, and made intercession for the transgressors.[6]

Let it be known to you therefore . . . that through this man forgiveness of sins is proclaimed to you.[7] Every one who believes in Him receives forgiveness of sins.[8] If we confess our sins, He is faithful and just, and will forgive our sins and cleanse us from all unrighteousness.[9]

He, being compassionate, forgave their iniquity.[10] I have swept away your transgressions like a cloud, and your sins like mist.[11] I will forgive their iniquity, and I will remember their sin no more.[12]

***1 *Jn.* 2:12. [1]2 *Sam.* 24:10. [2]*Ps.* 51:9. [3]*Ps.* 25:7. [4]*Lk.* 23:34. [5]*Jn.* 1:29. [6]*Is.* 53:12. [7]*Acts* 13:38. [8]*Acts* 10:43. [9]1 *Jn.* 1:9. [10]*Ps.* 78:38. [11]*Is.* 44:22. [12]*Jer.* 31:34.

MARCH 4

*Repentance to God and . . . faith in our Lord Jesus Christ**

Seek the Lord while He may be found, call upon Him while He is near; let the wicked forsake his way, and the unrighteous man his thoughts; let him return to the Lord, that He may have mercy on him, and to our God, for He will abundantly pardon.[1] That they may turn from darkness to light and from the power of Satan to God.[2] You were straying like sheep, but have now returned to the Shepherd and Guardian of your souls.[3] Truly, I say to you, unless you turn and become like children, you will never enter the kingdom of heaven.[4]

Return to the Lord, your God, for He is gracious and merciful, slow to anger, and abounding in steadfast love.[5] He has delivered us from the dominion of darkness and transferred us to the kingdom of His beloved Son, in whom we have redemption, the forgiveness of sins.[6]

One of the criminals who were hanged railed at Him . . . but the other rebuked him . . . And he said, 'Jesus, remember me when you come in your kingly power.' And He said to him, 'Truly, I say to you, today you will be with me in Paradise.'[7] Your faith has saved you; go in peace.[8]

**Acts 20:21.* [1]*Is. 55:6.* [2]*Acts 26:18.* [3]*1 Pet. 2:25.* [4]*Mt. 18:3.* [5]*Joel 2:13.* [6]*Col. 1:13, 14.* [7]*Lk. 23:39, 40, 42, 43.* [8]*Lk. 7:50.*

*Learn from Me**

Take My yoke upon you, and learn from Me; for I am gentle and lowly in heart, and you will find rest for your souls.[1] His name will be called 'Wonderful Counselor'.[2] Who is a teacher like Him?[3] I bless the Lord who gives me counsel.[4]

The unfolding of Thy words gives light; it imparts understanding to the simple.[5] He . . . teaches the humble His way.[6] Thou hast hidden these things from the wise and understanding and revealed them to babes.[7]

We have received not the spirit of the world but the Spirit which is from God, that we might understand the gifts bestowed on us by God . . . The unspiritual man . . . is not able to understand them because they are spiritually discerned . . But we have the mind of Christ.[8] Privately to His own disciples He explained everything.[9] To you it has been given to know the secrets of the kingdom of God.[10]

Mary . . . sat at the Lord's feet and listened to His teaching. But Martha was distracted with much serving . . . The Lord answered her, 'Martha, Martha, you are anxious and troubled about many things; one thing is needful. Mary has chosen the good portion.'[11]

**Mt. 11:29.* [1]*Mt. 11:29.* [2]*Is. 9:6.* [3]*Job 36:22.* [4]*Ps. 16:7.* [5]*Ps. 119:130.* [6]*Ps. 25:9.* [7]*Mt. 11:25.* [8]*1 Cor. 2:12, 14, 16.* [9]*Mk. 4:34.* [10]*Lk. 8:10.* [11]*Lk. 10:39–42.*

MARCH 6

*Pray at all times**

Have no anxiety about anything, but in everything by prayer and supplication with thanksgiving let your requests be made known to God. And the peace of God, which passes all understanding, will keep your hearts and your minds in Christ Jesus.[1] O Lord, Thou wilt ordain peace for us, Thou hast wrought for us all our works.[2]

They who wait for the Lord shall renew their strength.[3] Jesus withdrew from them about a stone's throw, and knelt down and prayed, 'Father, if Thou art willing, remove this cup from Me; nevertheless not My will, but Thine, be done.' And there appeared to Him an angel from heaven, strengthening Him.[4] On the day I called, Thou didst answer me, my strength of soul Thou didst increase.[5]

And they prayed and said, 'Lord, who knowest the hearts of all men, show which one of these two Thou hast chosen to take the place in this ministry and apostleship from which Judas turned aside.'[6] Teach me Thy way, O Lord; and lead me on a level path.[7] You shall call, and the Lord will answer . . . then shall your light rise in the darkness . . . and the Lord will guide you continually.[8]

**Eph.* 6:18. [1]*Phil.* 4:6, 7. [2]*Is.* 26:12. [3]*Is.* 40:31. [4]*Lk.* 22:41–43. [5]*Ps.* 138:3. [6]*Acts* 1:24, 25. [7]*Ps.* 27:11. [8]*Is.* 58:9–11.

*Clothe yourselves . . . with humility**

What does the Lord require of you but to do justice, and to love kindness, and to walk humbly with your God?[1] For thus says the high and lofty One who inhabits eternity, whose name is Holy: 'I dwell in the high and holy place, and also with him who is of a contrite and humble spirit.'[2] For though the Lord is high, He regards the lowly; but the haughty He knows from afar.[3] Humble yourselves therefore under the mighty hand of God, that in due time He may exalt you.[4]

The meekness and gentleness of Christ.[5] He humbled Himself and became obedient unto death, even death on a cross.[6] I am gentle and lowly in heart.[7] Humble yourselves before the Lord and He will exalt you.[8]

Blessed are the poor in spirit, for theirs is the kingdom of heaven.[9] In humility count others better than yourselves.[10] It is better to be of a lowly spirit with the poor than to divide the spoil with the proud.[11] Let another praise you, and not your own mouth.[12] God opposes the proud, but gives grace to the humble.[13]

**1 Pet. 5:5. [1]Mic. 6:8. [2]Is. 57:15. [3]Ps. 138:6. [4]1 Pet. 5:6. [5]2 Cor. 10:1. [6]Phil. 2:8. [7]Mt. 11:29. [8]Jas. 4:10. [9]Mt. 5:3. [10]Phil. 2:3. [11]Prov. 16:19. [12]Prov. 27:2. [13]Jas. 4:6.*

MARCH 8

*David . . . a man after My heart**

I have exalted one chosen from the people. I have found David, My servant . . . My hand shall ever abide with him, My arm also shall strengthen him.[1] You shall be shepherd of My people Israel, and you shall be prince over Israel.[2]

Then David said to the Philistine, 'You come to me with a sword and with a spear and with a javelin; but I come to you in the name of the Lord of hosts, the God of the armies of Israel, whom you have defied.' . . . So David prevailed over the Philistine with a sling and with a stone.[3] The people who know their God shall stand firm and take action.[4]

Late one afternoon . . . David . . . saw . . . a woman bathing; and the woman was very beautiful . . . So David sent messengers, and took her; and she came to him, and he lay with her.[5] Nathan said to David, 'You are the man . . . Why have you despised the word of the Lord, to do what is evil in His sight?' . . . David said to Nathan, 'I have sinned against the Lord.' And Nathan said to David, 'The Lord also has put away your sin.'[6]

David did what was right in the eyes of the Lord, and did not turn aside from anything that He commanded him all the days of his life, except in the matter of Uriah the Hittite.[7]

**Acts 13:22.* [1]*Ps. 89:19–21.* [2]*2 Sam. 5:2.* [3]*1 Sam. 17:45, 50.* [4]*Dan. 11:32.* [5]*2 Sam. 11:2, 4.* [6]*2 Sam. 12:7, 9, 13.* [7]*1 Kings 15:5.*

MARCH 9

*Be of good cheer**

Let us not grow weary in well-doing, for in due season we shall reap, if we do not lose heart.[1] Jesus told them a parable, to the effect that they ought always to pray and not lose heart.[2] So we do not lose heart. Though our outer nature is wasting away, our inner nature is being renewed every day. Therefore, having this ministry by the mercy of God, we do not lose heart.[3]

The following night the Lord stood by Paul and said, 'Take courage, for as you have testified about Me at Jerusalem, so you must bear witness also at Rome.'[4] In the world you have tribulation; but be of good cheer, I have overcome the world.[5] Jesus spoke to them and said, 'Take heart, it is I; have no fear.' And He got into the boat with them and the wind ceased.[6]

Consider Him who endured from sinners such hostility against Himself, so that you may not grow weary or fainthearted.[7] If you faint in the day of adversity, your strength is small.[8] A cheerful heart is a good medicine, but a downcast spirit dries up the bones.[9]

* *Jn.16:33.* [1]*Gal. 6:9.* [2]*Lk.18: 1.* [3]*2 Cor. 4:16, 1.* [4]*Acts 23:11.* [5]*Jn. 16:33.* [6]*Mk. 6:50, 51.* [7]*Heb. 12:3.* [8]*Prov. 24:10.* [9]*Prov. 17:22.*

MARCH 10

*I am the Lord, your healer**

Now Simon's mother-in-law was ill with a high fever, and they besought Him for her. And He stood over her and rebuked the fever, and it left her . . . Now when the sun was setting, all those who had any that were sick with various diseases brought them to Him; and He laid His hands on every one of them and healed them.[1]

Two demoniacs met Him, coming out of the tombs, so fierce that no one could pass that way . . . Now a herd of many swine was feeding at some distance from them. And the demons begged Him, 'If You cast us out, send us away into the herd of swine.' And He said to them, 'Go.' So they came out and went into the swine; and behold, the whole herd rushed down the steep bank into the sea.[2]

Why will you still be smitten, that you continue to rebel? The whole head is sick, and the whole heart faint.[3] Return, O faithless sons, I will heal your faithlessness.[4] He will revive us . . . that we may live before Him.[5]

Bless the Lord, O my soul . . . who forgives all your iniquity, who heals all your diseases.[6] He took our infirmities and bore our diseases.[7] For you who fear My name the sun of righteousness shall rise, with healing in its wings.[8]

**Ex. 15:26.* [1]*Lk. 4:38–40.* [2]*Mt. 8:28, 30–32.* [3]*Is. 1:5.* [4]*Jer. 3:22.* [5]*Hos. 6:2.* [6]*Ps. 103:2, 3.* [7]*Mt. 8:17.* [8]*Mal. 4:2.*

*You must be born anew**

Can . . . the leopard change his spots?[1] What is man, that he can be clean?[2] Man who drinks iniquity like water.[3] Who can bring a clean thing out of an unclean? There is not one.[4] I know that nothing good dwells within me, that is, in my flesh.[5] And those who are in the flesh cannot please God.[6]

Jesus answered him, 'Truly, truly, I say to you, unless one is born anew, he cannot see the kingdom of God . . . That which is born of the flesh is flesh, and that which is born of the Spirit is spirit. Do not marvel that I said to you, You must be born anew.'[7] And you He made alive, when you were dead through the trespasses and sins in which you once walked.[8] You have been born anew . . . through the living and abiding word of God.[9]

A new heart I will give you, and a new spirit I will put within you; and I will take out of your flesh the heart of stone and give you a heart of flesh. And I will put My Spirit within you, and cause you to walk in My statutes and be careful to observe My ordinances . . . And I will deliver you from all your uncleannesses.[10]

**Jn. 3:7.* [1]*Jer. 13:23.* [2]*Job 15:14.* [3]*Job 15:16.* [4]*Job 14:4.* [5]*Rom. 7:18.* [6]*Rom. 8:8.* [7]*Jn. 3:3, 6, 7.* [8]*Eph. 2:1, 2.* [9]*1 Pet. 1:23.* [10]*Ezek. 36:26, 27, 29.*

MARCH 12

*No one can serve two masters**

Thou art not a God who delights in wickedness.[1] The reason the Son of God appeared was to destroy the works of the devil.[2] He appeared to take away sins, and in Him there is no sin.[3] My little children, I am writing this to you so that you may not sin.[4] Let every one who names the name of the Lord depart from iniquity.[5] God has not called us for uncleanness, but in holiness.[6]

Shun youthful passions and aim at righteousness, faith, love and peace, along with those who call upon the Lord from a pure heart.[7] Choosing rather to share ill-treatment with the people of God than to enjoy the fleeting pleasures of sin.[8]

If any man would come after Me, let him deny himself . . . and follow Me.[9] We . . . ought . . . not to please ourselves . . . for Christ did not please Himself.[10] We are debtors, not to the flesh, to live according to the flesh.[11] Do not yield your members to sin as instruments of wickedness, but yield yourselves to God as men who have been brought from death to life, and your members to God as instruments of righteousness.[12]

**Mt. 6:24.* [1]*Ps. 5:4.* [2]*1 Jn. 3:8.* [3]*1 Jn. 3:5.* [4]*1 Jn. 2:1.* [5]*2 Tim. 2:19.* [6]*1 Thess. 4:7.* [7]*2 Tim. 2:22.* [8]*Heb. 11:25.* [9]*Mt. 16:24.* [10]*Rom. 15:1, 3.* [11]*Rom. 8:12.* [12]*Rom. 6:13.*

*All one in Christ Jesus**

Father, keep them in Thy name which Thou hast given Me, that they may be one, even as We are one . . . I in them and Thou in Me, that they may become perfectly one.[1] Behold, how good and pleasant it is when brothers dwell in unity![2]

The unity of the faith.[3] In Christ Jesus you are all sons of God, through faith.[4] For He is our peace, who has made us both one, and has broken down the dividing wall of hostility.[5] One Lord, one faith, one baptism, one God and Father of us all, who is above all and through all and in all.[6]

The unity of the Spirit.[7] Now there are varieties of gifts, but the same Spirit . . . and there are varieties of working, but it is the same God who inspires them all in every one. To each is given the manifestation of the Spirit for the common good . . . All these are inspired by one and the same Spirit, who apportions to each one individually as He wills.[8] For as in one body we have many members, and all the members do not have the same function, so we, though many, are one body in Christ, and individually members one of another.[9] Live in harmony with one another.[10]

**Gal. 3:28.* [1]*Jn. 17:11, 23.* [2]*Ps. 133:1.* [3]*Eph. 4:13.* [4]*Gal. 3:26.* [5]*Eph. 2:14.* [6]*Eph. 4:5, 6.* [7]*Eph. 4:3.* [8]*1 Cor. 12:4, 6, 7, 11.* [9]*Rom. 12:4, 5.* [10]*Rom. 12:16.*

MARCH 14

*Making the most of the time**

My days are swifter than a weaver's shuttle.[1] The years of our life . . . are soon gone.[2] Look carefully then how you walk, not as unwise men but as wise, making the most of the time, because the days are evil.[3]

Are there not twelve hours in the day?[4] With the Lord one day is as a thousand years.[5] As your days, so shall your strength be.[6] It is in vain that you rise up early, to go late to rest, eating the bread of anxious toil . . . for He gives to His beloved in sleep.[7] A man's mind plans his way, but the Lord directs his steps.[8] Commit your work to the Lord, and your plans will be established.[9]

Whatever your hand finds to do, do it with your might.[10] Jesus . . . went about doing good.[11] I . . . accomplished the work which Thou gavest Me to do.[12] So then, as we have opportunity, let us do good to all men.[13] Good works, which God prepared beforehand, that we should walk in them.[14] Therefore, my beloved brethren, be . . . always abounding in the work of the Lord, knowing that in the Lord your labor is not in vain.[15]

**Eph.* 5:16. [1]*Job* 7:6. [2]*Ps.* 90:10. [3]*Eph.* 5:15, 16. [4]*Jn.* 11:9. [5]*2 Pet.* 3:8. [6]*Deut.* 33:25. [7]*Ps.* 127:2. [8]*Prov.* 16:9. [9]*Prov.* 16:3. [10]*Eccl.* 9:10. [11]*Acts* 10:38. [12]*Jn.* 17:4. [13]*Gal.* 6:10. [14]*Eph.* 2:10. [15]*1 Cor.* 15:58.

*Be angry but do not sin**

Jonah . . . was angry . . . And the Lord said, 'Do you do well to be angry?'[1] Let every man be quick to hear, slow to speak, slow to anger, for the anger of man does not work the righteousness of God.[2] Good sense makes a man slow to anger, and it is his glory to overlook an offense.[3]

Cain was very angry and . . . the Lord said to Cain, 'Why are you angry, and why has your countenance fallen?'[4] A man of wrath stirs up strife, and a man given to anger causes much transgression.[5] Make no friendship with a man given to anger, nor go with a wrathful man, lest you learn his ways, and entangle yourself in a snare.[6] Do not envy a man of violence and do not choose any of his ways.[7]

Put on . . . patience, forbearing one another.[8] Love . . . is not irritable or resentful.[9] He who restrains his words has knowledge, and he who has a cool spirit is a man of understanding.[10] Be angry, but do not sin; do not let the sun go down on your anger, and give no opportunity to the devil.[11]

**Eph. 4:26.* [1]*Jon. 4:1, 4.* [2]*Jas. 1:19, 20.* [3]*Prov. 19:11.* [4]*Gen. 4:5, 6.* [5]*Prov. 29:22.* [6]*Prov. 22:24, 25.* [7]*Prov. 3:31.* [8]*Col. 3:12, 13.* [9]*1 Cor. 13:5.* [10]*Prov. 17:27.* [11]*Eph. 4:26.*

MARCH 16

*I have finished the race**

Do you not know that in a race all the runners compete, but only one receives the prize? So run that you may obtain it. Every athlete exercises self-control in all things. They do it to receive a perishable wreath, but we an imperishable. Well, I do not run aimlessly, I do not box as one beating the air; but I pommel my body and subdue it, lest after preaching to others I myself should be disqualified.[1]

Therefore, since we are surrounded by so great a cloud of witnesses, let us also lay aside every weight, and sin which clings so closely, and let us run with perseverance the race that is set before us, looking to Jesus the pioneer and perfecter of our faith.[2]

As for me, my feet had almost stumbled, my steps had well nigh slipped.[3] But they who wait for the Lord shall renew their strength, they shall mount up with wings like eagles, they shall run and not be weary, they shall walk and not faint.[4] When you walk, your step will not be hampered; and if you run, you will not stumble.[5]

**2 Tim. 4:7. [1] 1 Cor. 9:24–27. [2] Heb. 12:1, 2. [3] Ps. 73:2. [4] Is. 40:31. [5] Prov. 4:12.*

*The man Christ Jesus**

Christ Jesus . . . emptied Himself, taking the form of a servant, being born in the likeness of men.[1] Since therefore the children share in flesh and blood, He Himself likewise partook of the same nature.[2] For we have not a high priest who is unable to sympathize with our weaknesses, but one who in every respect has been tempted as we are, yet without sinning.[3]

God . . . has anointed Thee with the oil of gladness.[4] There was a marriage at Cana in Galilee, and . . . Jesus . . . was invited.[5] The Son of man has come eating and drinking.[6] I have spoken to you, that My joy may be in you, and that your joy may be full.[7]

He was . . . a man of sorrows, and acquainted with grief.[8] Surely He has borne our griefs and carried our sorrows.[9] Then Mary . . . fell at Jesus' feet, saying to Him, 'Lord, if You had been here, my brother would not have died.' When Jesus saw her weeping . . . He was deeply moved . . . and He said, 'Where have you laid him?' They said to Him, 'Lord, come and see.' Jesus wept.[10]

**1 Tim.* 2:5. [1]*Phil.* 2:5, 7. [2]*Heb.* 2:14. [3]*Heb.* 4:15. [4]*Heb.* 1:9. [5]*Jn.* 2:1, 2. [6]*Lk.* 7:34. [7]*Jn.* 15:11. [8]*Is.* 53:3. [9]*Is.* 53:4. [10]*Jn.* 11:32–35.

MARCH 18

*They are seeking a homeland**

For here we have no lasting city, but we seek the city which is to come.[1] The city . . . whose builder and maker is God.[2] Where Jesus has gone as a forerunner on our behalf.[3] The city has no need of sun or moon to shine upon it, for the glory of God is its light, and its lamp is the Lamb . . . But nothing unclean shall enter it . . . but only those who are written in the Lamb's book of life.[4]

In my Father's house are many rooms; if it were not so, would I have told you that I go to prepare a place for you?[5] No eye has seen, nor ear heard, nor the heart of man conceived, what God has prepared for those who love Him.[6] An inheritance which is imperishable, undefiled, and unfading, kept in heaven for you.[7]

Father, I desire that they also, whom Thou hast given Me, may be with Me where I am, to behold My glory.[8] For now we see in a mirror dimly, but then face to face. Now I know in part; then I shall understand fully.[9] Your eyes will see the King in His beauty.[10] His servants . . . shall see His face.[11]

Heb. 11:14. [1]Heb. 13:14. [2]Heb. 11:10. [3]Heb. 6:20. [4]Rev. 21:23, 27. [5]Jn. 14:2. [6]1 Cor. 2:9. [7]1 Pet. 1:4. [8]Jn. 17:24. [9]1 Cor. 13:12. [10]Is. 33:17. [11]Rev. 22:3, 4.

*Called to belong to Jesus Christ**

The kingdom of heaven may be compared to a king who gave a marriage feast for his son, and sent his servants to call those who were invited . . . but they would not come . . . Then he said to his servants . . . 'Go . . . and invite . . . as many as you find.' And those servants went out into the streets and gathered all whom they found, both bad and good; so the wedding hall was filled with guests.[1] Blessed are those who are invited to the marriage supper of the Lamb.[2] The Spirit and the Bride say, 'Come.' And let him who hears say, 'Come.'[3]

I came not to call the righteous, but sinners.[4] Jesus . . . saw a tax collector, named Levi, sitting at the tax office; and He said to him, 'Follow Me.' And he left everything, and rose and followed Him.[5] Today, when you hear His voice, do not harden your hearts.[6] Incline your ear, and come to Me; hear, that your soul may live.[7]

To this He called you through our gospel, so that you may obtain the glory of our Lord Jesus Christ.[8] Called you out of darkness into His marvelous light.[9] Called . . . to His own glory and excellence.[10] Called to belong to Jesus Christ.[11]

**Rom. 1:6.* [1]*Mt. 22:2, 3, 8–10.* [2]*Rev. 19:9.* [3]*Rev. 22:17.* [4]*Mt. 9:13.* [5]*Lk. 5:27, 28.* [6]*Heb. 3:7, 8.* [7]*Is. 55:3.* [8]*2 Thess. 2:14.* [9]*1 Pet. 2:9.* [10]*2 Pet. 1:3.* [11]*Rom. 1:6.*

MARCH 20

*You shall worship the Lord your God**

Worthy art Thou, our Lord and God, to receive glory and honor and power, for Thou didst create all things, and by Thy will they existed and were created.[1] Worthy is the Lamb who was slain, to receive power and wealth and wisdom and might and honor and glory and blessing![2]

Ascribe to the Lord, O families of the peoples, ascribe to the Lord glory and strength! Ascribe to the Lord the glory due His name; bring an offering, and come before Him! Worship the Lord in holy array.[3]

I was glad when they said to me, 'Let us go to the house of the Lord.'[4] I will offer to Thee the sacrifice of thanksgiving and call on the name of the Lord. I will pay my vows to the Lord in the presence of all His people, in the courts of the house of the Lord . . . Praise the Lord![5]

God is spirit, and those who worship Him must worship in spirit and truth.[6] For we are the true circumcision, who worship God in spirit, and glory in Christ Jesus, and put no confidence in the flesh.[7] Let us offer to God acceptable worship, with reverence and awe.[8]

**Mt. 4:10.* [1]*Rev. 4:11.* [2]*Rev. 5:12.* [3]*1 Chron. 16:28, 29.* [4]*Ps. 122:1.* [5]*Ps. 116:17–19.* [6]*Jn. 4:24.* [7]*Phil. 3:3.* [8]*Heb. 12:28.*

*Wait patiently for Him**

We exhort you, brethren, admonish the idle, encourage the fainthearted, help the weak, be patient with them all.[1] Love bears all things . . . hopes all things, endures all things.[2] The fruit of the Spirit is love, joy, peace, patience, kindness, goodness, faithfulness, gentleness, self-control; against such there is no law.[3]

As for that in the good soil, they are those who, hearing the word, hold it fast in an honest and good heart, and bring forth fruit with patience.[4] He who sows to the Spirit will from the Spirit reap eternal life. And let us not grow weary in well-doing, for in due season we shall reap, if we do not lose heart.[5] Be patient, therefore, brethren, until the coming of the Lord. Behold, the farmer waits for the precious fruit of the earth, being patient over it until it receives the early and the late rain. You also be patient. Establish your hearts, for the coming of the Lord is at hand.[6]

If when you do right and suffer for it you take it patiently, you have God's approval. For to this you have been called, because Christ also suffered for you, leaving you an example, that you should follow in His steps.[7] I waited patiently for the Lord; He inclined to me and heard my cry.[8]

**Ps. 37:7.* [1]*1 Thess. 5:14.* [2]*1 Cor. 13:7.* [3]*Gal. 5:22, 23.* [4]*Lk. 8:15.* [5]*Gal. 6:8, 9.* [6]*Jas. 5:7, 8.* [7]*1 Pet. 2:20, 21.* [8]*Ps. 40:1.*

MARCH 22

*The eternal Spirit**

In the beginning God created the heavens and the earth. The earth was without form and void, and darkness was upon the face of the deep; and the Spirit of God was moving over the face of the waters.[1] Yonder is the sea, great and wide, which teems with . . . living things . . . When Thou sendest forth Thy Spirit, they are created; and Thou renewest the face of the ground.[2]

The Spirit of God came upon Balaam, and he took up his discourse, and said . . .[3] The Spirit of the Lord took possession of Gideon; and he sounded the trumpet . . .[4] The Spirit of the Lord came mightily upon Samson, and he tore the lion asunder as one tears a kid; and he had nothing in his hand.[5] The Spirit of the Lord came mightily upon David from that day forward.[6]

No prophecy ever came by the impulse of man, but men moved by the Holy Spirit spoke from God.[7] It was revealed to them that they were serving not themselves but you, in the things which have now been announced to you.[8] The Spirit of the Lord God is upon Me, because the Lord has anointed Me to . . . proclaim the year of the Lord's favor.[9]

**Heb. 9:14.* [1]*Gen. 1:1, 2.* [2]*Ps. 104:25, 30.* [3]*Num. 24:2.* [4]*Judg. 6:34.* [5]*Judg. 14:6.* [6]*1 Sam. 16:13.* [7]*2 Pet. 1:21.* [8]*1 Pet. 1:12.* [9]*Is. 61:1, 2.*

*If a man die, shall he live again?**

He has put eternity into man's mind.[1] Who knows whether the spirit of man goes upward and the spirit of the beast goes down to the earth?[2] The dust returns to the earth as it was, and the spirit returns to God who gave it.[3] My soul thirsts for God, for the living God.[4]

Flesh and blood cannot inherit the kingdom of God . . . This mortal nature must put on immortality.[5] Enoch walked with God; and he was not, for God took him.[6] Enoch was taken up so that he should not see death.[7] Truly, truly, I say to you, if any one keeps My word, he will never see death.[8]

Jesus said to her, 'I am the resurrection and the life; he who believes in Me, though he die, yet shall he live, and whoever lives and believes in Me shall never die.'[9] If for this life only we have hoped in Christ, we are of all men most to be pitied.[10]

What does it profit a man if he gains the whole world and loses . . . himself?[11] You have been born anew, not of perishable seed but of imperishable.[12] They cannot die any more.[13]

**Job 14:14.* [1]*Eccl. 3:11.* [2]*Eccl. 3:21.* [3]*Eccl. 12:7.* [4]*Ps. 42:2.* [5]*1 Cor. 15:50, 53.* [6]*Gen. 5:24.* [7]*Heb. 11:5.* [8]*Jn. 8:51.* [9]*Jn. 11:25, 26.* [10]*1 Cor. 15:19.* [11]*Lk. 9:25.* [12]*1 Pet. 1:23.* [13]*Lk. 20:36.*

MARCH 24

*Teach me to do Thy will, for Thou art my God**

Do not be conformed to this world but be transformed by the renewal of your mind, that you may prove what is the will of God, what is good and acceptable and perfect.[1] If any man's will is to do His will, he shall know whether the teaching is from God.[2] Therefore do not be foolish, but understand what the will of the Lord is.[3] That you may stand mature and fully assured in all the will of God.[4]

While Jesus was still speaking to the people, behold, His mother and His brothers stood outside, asking to speak to Him. But He replied to the man who told Him, 'Who is My mother, and who are My brothers?' And stretching out His hand toward His disciples, He said, 'Here are My mother and My brothers! For whoever does the will of My Father in heaven is My brother, and sister, and mother.'[5]

I delight to do Thy will, O my God; Thy law is within my heart.[6] Teach me, O Lord, the way of Thy statutes; and I will keep it to the end. Give me understanding, that I may keep Thy law and observe it with my whole heart . . . Incline my heart to Thy testimonies.[7] Thy will be done, on earth as it is in heaven.[8]

**Ps. 143:10. [1]Rom. 12:2. [2]Jn. 7:17. [3]Eph. 5:17. [4]Col. 4:12. [5]Mt. 12:46–50. [6]Ps. 40:8. [7]Ps. 119:33, 34, 36. [8]Mt. 6:10.*

*A sword will pierce through your own soul also**

'Son, why have You treated us so? Behold, Your father and I have been looking for You anxiously.' And Jesus said to them, 'How is it that you sought Me? Did you not know that I must be in My Father's house?' And they did not understand the saying which He spoke to them. And He went down with them and came to Nazareth, and was obedient to them; and His mother kept all these things in her heart.[1]

There was a marriage at Cana in Galilee . . . When the wine failed, the mother of Jesus said to Him, 'They have no wine.' And Jesus said to her, 'O woman, what have you to do with Me? My hour has not yet come.' His mother said to the servants, 'Do whatever He tells you.'[2]

When Jesus saw His mother, and the disciple whom He loved standing near, He said to His mother, 'Woman, behold your son!' Then He said to the disciple, 'Behold your mother!' And from that hour the disciple took her to his own home.[3]

Behold, I am the handmaid of the Lord; let it be to me according to your word.[4] Behold, henceforth all generations will call me blessed.[5]

**Lk. 2:35.* [1]*Lk. 2:48–51.* [2]*Jn. 2:1, 3–5.* [3]*Jn. 19:26, 27.* [4]*Lk. 1:38.* [5]*Lk. 1:48.*

MARCH 26

*Let a man examine himself**

Examine yourselves, to see whether you are holding to your faith. Test yourselves.[1] Search me, O God, and know my heart! Try me and know my thoughts! And see if there be any wicked way in me, and lead me in the way everlasting![2] Prove me, O Lord, and try me; test my heart and my mind.[3] For it is not the man who commends himself that is accepted, but the man whom the Lord commends.[4]

Why do you see the speck that is in your brother's eye, but do not notice the log that is in your own eye? . . . You hypocrite, first take the log out of your own eye, and then you will see clearly to take the speck out of your brother's eye.[5] Love is patient and kind; love is not jealous or boastful; it is not arrogant or rude. Love does not insist on its own way; it is not irritable or resentful; it does not rejoice at wrong.[6]

Not that I . . . am already perfect.[7] For I am the least of the apostles, unfit to be called an apostle.[8] I am the very least of all the saints.[9] I am the foremost of sinners.[10]

* *1 Cor. 11:28.* [1] *2 Cor. 13:5.* [2] *Ps. 139:23, 24.* [3] *Ps. 26:2.* [4] *2 Cor. 10:18.* [5] *Mt. 7:3, 5.* [6] *1 Cor. 13:4–6.* [7] *Phil. 3:12.* [8] *1 Cor. 15:9.* [9] *Eph. 3:8.* [10] *1 Tim. 1:15.*

*Two are better than one**

A friend loves at all times, and a brother is born for adversity.[1] The soul of Jonathan was knit to the soul of David, and Jonathan loved him as his own soul.[2] Jonathan knew that his father was determined to put David to death. And Jonathan rose from the table in fierce anger . . . for he was grieved for David.[3] Then Jonathan said to David, 'Go in peace . . . The Lord shall be between me and you . . . for ever.'[4]

Faithful are the wounds of a friend.[5] Samuel rose early to meet Saul in the morning . . . Then Samuel said to Saul, 'Stop! I will tell you what the Lord said to me this night.' And he said to him, 'Say on.'[6] Nathan said to David . . . 'Why have you despised the word of the Lord, to do what is evil in His sight?' . . . David said to Nathan, 'I have sinned against the Lord.'[7] Jesus said to him the third time, 'Simon, son of John, do you love Me?' Peter was grieved because He said to him the third time, 'Do you love Me?' And he said to Him, 'Lord . . . You know that I love You.'[8]

There is a friend who sticks closer than a brother.[9] Standing by the cross of Jesus were His mother, and His mother's sister, Mary the wife of Clopas, and Mary Magdalene.[10] Do your best to come to me soon . . . Luke alone is with me.[11]

**Eccl. 4:9.* [1]*Prov. 17:17.* [2]*1 Sam. 18:1.* [3]*1 Sam. 20:33, 34.* [4]*1 Sam. 20:42.* [5]*Prov. 27:6.* [6]*1 Sam. 15:12, 16.* [7]*2 Sam. 12:7, 9, 13.* [8]*Jn. 21:17.* [9]*Prov. 18:24.* [10]*Jn. 19:25.* [11]*2 Tim. 4:9, 11.*

MARCH 28

*They have not wholly followed Me**

I know your works: you are neither cold nor hot. Would that you were cold or hot! So, because you are lukewarm, and neither cold nor hot, I will spew you out of My mouth.[1] As for what was sown on rocky ground, this is he who hears the word and immediately receives it with joy; yet he has no root in himself, but endures for a while, and when tribulation or persecution arises on account of the word, immediately he falls away. As for what was sown among thorns, this is he who hears the word, but the cares of the world and the delight in riches choke the word, and it proves unfruitful.[2] They all look after their own interests, not those of Jesus Christ.[3]

No one can serve two masters; for either he will hate the one and love the other, or he will be devoted to the one and despise the other. You cannot serve God and mammon.[4] Elijah came near to all the people, and said, 'How long will you go limping with two different opinions? If the Lord is God, follow Him; but if Baal, then follow him.'[5] A double-minded man, unstable in all his ways.[6] Draw near to God and He will draw near to you. Cleanse your hands, you sinners, and purify your hearts, you men of double mind.[7]

**Num. 32:11.* [1]*Rev. 3:15, 16.* [2]*Mt. 13:20–22.* [3]*Phil. 2:21.* [4]*Mt. 6:24.* [5]*1 Kings 18:21.* [6]*Jas. 1:8.* [7]*Jas. 4:8.*

*Open my eyes, that I may behold wondrous things out of Thy law**

Behold, I was brought forth in iniquity, and in sin did my mother conceive me.[1] All have sinned and fall short of the glory of God.[2] The wages of sin is death.[3]

Behold, the Lamb of God, who takes away the sin of the world![4] You know that you were ransomed from the futile ways inherited from your fathers, not with perishable things such as silver or gold, but with the precious blood of Christ, like that of a lamb without blemish or spot.[5] He Himself bore our sins in His body on the tree.[6]

Behold, I stand at the door and knock; if any one hears My voice and opens the door, I will come in to him and eat with him, and he with Me.[7] Jesus appeared to be going further, but they constrained Him, saying, 'Stay with us, for it is toward evening and the day is now far spent.' So He went in to stay with them.[8] That Christ may dwell in your hearts through faith.[9] Christ in you, the hope of glory.[10] A dwelling place of God in the Spirit.[11]

**Ps. 119:18.* [1]*Ps. 51:5.* [2]*Rom. 3:23.* [3]*Rom. 6:23.* [4]*Jn. 1:29.* [5]*1 Pet. 1:18, 19.* [6]*1 Pet. 2:24.* [7]*Rev. 3:20.* [8]*Lk. 24:28, 29.* [9]*Eph. 3:17.* [10]*Col. 1:27.* [11]*Eph. 2:22.*

MARCH 30

*The builder of all things is God**

In the beginning God created the heavens and the earth.[1] He spoke, and it came to be; He commanded, and it stood forth.[2] God calls into existence the things that do not exist.[3] By faith we understand that the world was created by the word of God, so that what is seen was made out of things which do not appear.[4]

O Lord, how manifold are Thy works! In wisdom hast Thou made them all; the earth is full of Thy creatures.[5] Great are the works of the Lord, studied by all who have pleasure in them.[6] He has made everything beautiful in its time.[7] The wondrous works of Him who is perfect in knowledge.[8] Who forms the mountains, and creates the wind.[9] Who has measured the waters in the hollow of His hand?[10]

Before the mountains were brought forth, or ever Thou hadst formed the earth and the world, from everlasting to everlasting Thou art God.[11] Worthy art Thou, our Lord and God, to receive glory and honor and power, for Thou didst create all things, and by Thy will they existed and were created.[12]

**Heb.* 3:4. [1]*Gen.* 1:1. [2]*Ps.* 33:9. [3]*Rom.* 4:17. [4]*Heb.* 11:3. [5]*Ps.* 104:24. [6]*Ps.* 111:2. [7]*Eccl.* 3:11. [8]*Job* 37:16. [9]*Amos* 4:13. [10]*Is.* 40:12. [11]*Ps.* 90:2. [12]*Rev.* 4:11.

MARCH 31

*But some doubted**

When John heard in prison about the deeds of the Christ, he sent word by his disciples and said to Him, 'Are You He who is to come, or shall we look for another?' And Jesus answered them, 'Go and tell John what you hear and see: the blind receive their sight and the lame walk . . .'[1]

And beginning to sink Peter cried out, 'Lord, save me.' Jesus immediately reached out His hand and caught him, saying to him, 'O man of little faith, why did you doubt?'[2]

But Thomas said to them, 'Unless I see . . . I will not believe.' Eight days later . . . Jesus came and stood among them . . . He said to Thomas, 'Put your finger here, and see My hands; and put out your hand, and place it in My side; do not be faithless, but believing.' Thomas answered Him, 'My Lord and my God!' Jesus said to him . . . 'Blessed are those who have not seen and yet believe.'[3]

Now Jesus did many other signs . . . which are not written in this book; but these are written that you may believe that Jesus is the Christ, the Son of God, and that believing you may have life in His name.[4]

**Mt. 28:17.* [1]*Mt. 11:2–5.* [2]*Mt. 14:30, 31.* [3]*Jn. 20:25–29.* [4]*Jn. 20:30, 31.*

APRIL 1

*Daniel prospered**

The king assigned them a daily portion of the rich food which the king ate, and of the wine which he drank . . . But Daniel resolved that he would not defile himself with the king's rich food, or with the wine which he drank . . . At the end of ten days it was seen that they were better in appearance . . . than all the youths who ate the king's rich food.[1] My heart is steadfast, O God, my heart is steadfast![2]

'All the presidents of the kingdom . . . are agreed that the king should . . . enforce an interdict, that whoever makes petition to any god . . . except to you, O king, shall be cast into the den of lions . . .' When Daniel knew that the document had been signed, he went to his house . . . and he got down upon his knees three times a day and prayed and gave thanks before his God, as he had done previously.[3] I call upon God; and the Lord will save me. Evening and morning and at noon . . . He will hear my voice.[4]

Then King Darius wrote . . . 'I make a decree, that in all my royal dominion men tremble and fear before the God of Daniel, for He is the living God . . . He who has saved Daniel from the power of the lions.' So this Daniel prospered during the reign of Darius.[5] For those who honor Me I will honor.[6]

**Dan. 6:28.* [1]*Dan. 1:5, 8, 15.* [2]*Ps. 57:7.* [3]*Dan. 6:7, 10.* [4]*Ps. 55:16, 17.* [5]*Dan. 6:25–28.* [6]*1 Sam. 2:30.*

*His banner over me was love**

That you . . . may have power to comprehend . . . what is the breadth and length and height and depth, and to know the love of Christ which surpasses knowledge, that you may be filled with all the fullness of God.[1]

The love of Christ controls us, because we are convinced that one has died for all; therefore all have died. And He died for all, that those who live might live no longer for themselves but for Him who for their sake died and was raised.[2] I have been crucified with Christ; it is no longer I who live, but Christ who lives in me; and the life I now live in the flesh I live by faith in the Son of God, who loved me and gave Himself for me.[3] You are not your own; you were bought with a price.[4] I am my beloved's, and my beloved is mine.[5]

I have loved you with an everlasting love; therefore I have continued My faithfulness to you.[6] Who shall separate us from the love of Christ? . . . I am sure that neither death, nor life . . . nor anything else in all creation, will be able to separate us from the love of God in Christ Jesus our Lord.[7] Having loved His own who were in the world, He loved them to the end.[8] For love is strong as death.[9]

**Song of Sol. 2:4.* [1]*Eph. 3:17–19.* [2]*2 Cor. 5:14, 15.* [3]*Gal. 2:20.* [4]*1 Cor. 6:19, 20.* [5]*Song of Sol. 6:3.* [6]*Jer. 31:3.* [7]*Rom. 8:35, 38, 39.* [8]*Jn. 13:1.* [9]*Song of Sol. 8:6.*

APRIL 3

*He who endures to the end**

He . . . endures for a while, and when tribulation or persecution arises on account of the word, immediately he falls away.[1]

Now Paul and his company . . . came to Perga in Pamphylia. And John (Mark) left them and returned to Jerusalem.[2] Paul said to Barnabas, 'Come, let us return and visit the brethren in every city where we proclaimed the word of the Lord, and see how they are.' And Barnabas wanted to take with them John called Mark. But Paul thought best not to take with them one who had withdrawn from them in Pamphylia, and had not gone with them to the work.[3] And Peter said to Him, 'Lord, I am ready to go with You to prison and to death.' He said, 'I tell you, Peter, the cock will not crow this day, until you three times deny that you know Me.'[4] The fear of man lays a snare.[5]

Having begun with the Spirit, are you now ending with the flesh?[6] I am sure that He who began a good work in you will bring it to completion at the day of Jesus Christ.[7] They sent Barnabas to Antioch. When he came and saw the grace of God, he was glad; and he exhorted them all to remain faithful to the Lord with steadfast purpose.[8] Perfect love casts out fear.[9]

**Mt. 24:13. [1]Mt. 13:21. [2]Acts 13:13. [3]Acts 15:36–38. [4]Lk. 22:33, 34. [5]Prov. 29:25. [6]Gal. 3:3. [7]Phil. 1:6. [8]Acts 11:22, 23. [9]1 Jn. 4:18.*

*Spend and be spent**

I was hungry and you gave Me food, I was thirsty and you gave Me drink, I was a stranger and you welcomed Me.[1] Learn to do good; seek justice, correct oppression; defend the fatherless, plead for the widow.[2]

One must help the weak, remembering the words of the Lord Jesus, how He said, 'It is more blessed to give than to receive.'[3] If you pour yourself out for the hungry and satisfy the desire of the afflicted, then shall your light rise in the darkness and your gloom be as the noonday.[4] The blessing of him who was about to perish came upon me, and I caused the widow's heart to sing for joy.[5]

As we have opportunity, let us do good to all men.[6] A Samaritan, as he journeyed, came to where he was; and when he saw him, he had compassion, and went to him and bound up his wounds, pouring on oil and wine; then he set him on his own beast and brought him to an inn, and took care of him.[7] As you did it to one of the least of these My brethren, you did it to Me.[8]

**2 Cor. 12:15. [1]Mt. 25:35. [2]Isa. 1:17. [3]Acts 20:35. [4]Isa. 58:10. [5]Job 29:13. [6]Gal. 6:10. [7]Lk. 10:33, 34. [8]Mt. 25:40.*

APRIL 5

*King of kings and Lord of lords**

Sing praises to God, sing praises! Sing praises to our King, sing praises! For God is the King of all the earth . . . God reigns over the nations; God sits on His holy throne.[1] I am a great King, says the Lord of hosts, and my name is feared among the nations.[2] The Lord is the true God; He is the living God and the everlasting King.[3] The King of glory.[4]

Therefore God has highly exalted Him and bestowed on Him the name which is above every name, that at the name of Jesus every knee should bow, in heaven and on earth and under the earth, and every tongue confess that Jesus Christ is Lord, to the glory of God the Father.[5]

Of the increase of His government and of peace there will be no end.[6] And He shall reign for ever and ever.[7] To the King of ages, immortal, invisible, the only God, be honor and glory for ever and ever.[8] The blessed and only Sovereign, the King of kings and Lord of lords, who alone has immortality and dwells in unapproachable light, whom no man has ever seen or can see. To Him be honor and eternal dominion.[9]

**Rev. 19:16.* [1]*Ps. 47:6–8.* [2]*Mal. 1:14.* [3]*Jer. 10:10.* [4]*Ps. 24:9.* [5]*Phil. 2:9–11.* [6]*Is. 9:7.* [7]*Rev. 11:15.* [8]*1 Tim. 1:17.* [9]*1 Tim. 6:15, 16.*

*He knows the secrets of the heart**

The Lord sees not as man sees; man looks on the outward appearance, but the Lord looks on the heart.[1] For the Lord searches all hearts, and understands every plan and thought.[2] Keep your heart with all vigilance; for from it flow the springs of life.[3] My heart has gone after my eyes.[4] Create in me a clean heart, O God, and put a new and right spirit within me.[5]

A broken and contrite heart, O God, Thou wilt not despise.[6] He heals the brokenhearted, and binds up their wounds.[7] I dwell . . . also with him who is of a contrite and humble spirit, to revive the spirit of the humble, and to revive the heart of the contrite.[8] My son, give Me your heart.[9] For where your treasure is, there will your heart be also.[10]

I will give them a heart to know that I am the Lord; and they shall be My people and I will be their God, for they shall return to Me with their whole heart.[11] I will give them one heart, and put a new spirit within them; I will take the stony heart out of their flesh and give them a heart of flesh.[12]

**Ps. 44:21.* [1]*1 Sam. 16:7.* [2]*1 Chron. 28:9.* [3]*Prov. 4:23.* [4]*Job 31:7.* [5]*Ps. 51:10.* [6]*Ps. 51:17.* [7]*Ps. 147:3.* [8]*Is. 57:15.* [9]*Prov. 23:26.* [10]*Mt. 6:21.* [11]*Jer. 24:7.* [12]*Ezek. 11:19.*

APRIL 7

*Stand in awe of Him**

There is none like Thee, O Lord; Thou art great, and Thy name is great in might. Who would not fear Thee, O King of the nations? For this is Thy due; for . . . there is none like Thee.[1] For who in the skies can be compared to the Lord? Who among the heavenly beings is like the Lord, a God feared in the council of the holy ones, great and terrible above all that are round about Him?[2]

The fear of the Lord is hatred of evil.[3] Fear God, and keep His commandments; for this is the whole duty of man.[4] I will make with them an everlasting covenant, that I will not turn away from doing good to them; and I will put the fear of Me in their hearts, that they may not turn from Me.[5]

The fear of the Lord is the beginning of knowledge.[6] My son, if you receive my words . . . then you will understand the fear of the Lord and find the knowledge of God.[7] This is eternal life, that they know Thee the only true God, and Jesus Christ whom Thou hast sent.[8] That I may know Him and the power of His resurrection.[9] The friendship of the Lord is for those who fear Him.[10]

**Ps. 22:23.* [1]*Jer. 10:6, 7.* [2]*Ps. 89:6, 7.* [3]*Prov. 8:13.* [4]*Eccl. 12:13.* [5]*Jer. 32:40.* [6]*Prov. 1:7.* [7]*Prov. 2:1, 5.* [8]*Jn. 17:3.* [9]*Phil. 3:10.* [10]*Ps. 25:14.*

*The armor of light**

We are not contending against flesh and blood, but against the principalities, against the powers, against the world rulers of this present darkness, against the spiritual hosts of wickedness in the heavenly places.[1] For though we live in the world we are not carrying on a worldly war, for the weapons of our warfare are not worldly but have divine power to destroy strongholds.[2]

Put on the whole armor of God, that you may be able to stand against the wiles of the devil.[3] Stand therefore, having girded your loins with truth, and having put on the breastplate of righteousness . . . above all taking the shield of faith . . . and take the helmet of salvation, and the sword of the Spirit, which is the Word of God.[4] The weapons of righteousness for the right hand and for the left.[5]

There is no discharge from war.[6] Wage the good warfare.[7] Fight the good fight of the faith.[8] Not by might, nor by power, but by My Spirit, says the Lord of hosts.[9] More than conquerors through Him who loved us.[10] This is the victory that overcomes the world, our faith.[11]

**Rom. 13:12.* [1]*Eph. 6:12.* [2]*2 Cor. 10:3, 4.* [3]*Eph. 6:11.* [4]*Eph. 6:14, 16, 17.* [5]*2 Cor. 6:7.* [6]*Eccl. 8:8.* [7]*1 Tim. 1:18.* [8]*1 Tim. 6:12.* [9]*Zech. 4:6.* [10]*Rom. 8:37.* [11]*1 Jn. 5:4.*

APRIL 9

*All his riches can never offset the guilt he has incurred**

You say, 'I am rich, I have prospered, and I need nothing'; not knowing that you are wretched, pitiable, poor, blind, and naked.[1] Riches do not profit in the day of wrath, but righteousness delivers from death.[2]

We know that . . . the whole world is in the power of the evil one.[3] The god of this world has blinded the minds of the unbelievers, to keep them from seeing the light of the gospel of the glory of Christ.[4] He who does evil has not seen God.[5] No one who sins has either seen Him or known Him.[6]

Before Him no creature is hidden, but all are open and laid bare to the eyes of Him with whom we have to do.[7] Sheol and Abaddon lie open before the Lord, how much more the hearts of men![8] Who can say, 'I have made my heart clean; I am pure from my sin'?[9]

Therefore I counsel you to buy from me gold refined by fire, that you may be rich, and white garments to clothe you and to keep the shame of your nakedness from being seen, and salve to anoint your eyes, that you may see.[10]

**Hos. 12:8.* [1]*Rev. 3:17.* [2]*Prov. 11:4.* [3]*1 Jn. 5:19.* [4]*2 Cor. 4:4.* [5]*3 Jn. 11.* [6]*1 Jn. 3:6.* [7]*Heb. 4:13.* [8]*Prov. 15:11.* [9]*Prov. 20:9.* [10]*Rev. 3:18.*

*The royal law**

You shall love your neighbor as yourself.[1] Let no one seek his own good, but the good of his neighbor.[2] Owe no one anything, except to love one another; for he who loves his neighbor has fulfilled the law . . . love is the fulfilling of the law.[3] The stranger who sojourns with you shall be to you as the native among you, and you shall love him as yourself.[4] But I say to you that hear, Love your enemies, do good to those who hate you, bless those who curse you, pray for those who abuse you.[5]

Love is patient and kind; love is not jealous or boastful; it is not arrogant or rude. Love does not insist on its own way; it is not irritable or resentful; it does not rejoice at wrong, but rejoices in the right.[6] Make love your aim.[7]

He who does not love does not know God; for God is love.[8] God's love has been poured into our hearts through the Holy Spirit which has been given to us.[9] May the Lord make you increase and abound in love to one another and to all men.[10]

**Jas. 2:8.* [1]*Lev. 19:18.* [2]*1 Cor. 10:24.* [3]*Rom. 13:8, 10.* [4]*Lev. 19:34.* [5]*Lk. 6:27, 28.* [6]*1 Cor. 13:4–6.* [7]*1 Cor. 14:1.* [8]*1 Jn. 4:8.* [9]*Rom. 5:5.* [10]*1 Thess. 3:12.*

APRIL 11

*For this purpose I have come**

Then I said, 'Lo, I have come to do Thy will, O God.'[1] I seek not My own will but the will of Him who sent Me.[2] Think not that I have come to abolish the law and the prophets; I have come not to abolish them but to fulfil them.[3]

The Son of man came to seek and to save the lost.[4] Not . . . to judge the world but to save the world.[5] Not to be served but to serve, and to give His life as a ransom for many.[6] Christ Jesus came into the world to save sinners.[7]

Jesus answered them, 'Those who are well have no need of a physician, but those who are sick; I have not come to call the righteous, but sinners to repentance.'[8] I came that they may have life, and have it abundantly.[9]

Do not think that I have come to bring peace on earth; I have not come to bring peace, but a sword. For I have come to set a man against his father, and a daughter against her mother . . . and a man's foes will be those of his own household.[10] There was a division among the people over Him.[11]

**Jn. 12:27.* [1]*Heb. 10:7.* [2]*Jn. 5:30.* [3]*Mt. 5:17.* [4]*Lk. 19:10.* [5]*Jn. 12:47.* [6]*Mk. 10:45.* [7]*1 Tim. 1:15.* [8]*Lk. 5:31, 32.* [9]*Jn. 10:10.* [10]*Mt. 10:34–36.* [11]*Jn. 7:43.*

*The Lord is my shepherd, I shall not want**

He makes me lie down in green pastures. He leads me beside still waters; He restores my soul.[1] He satisfies him who is thirsty, and the hungry He fills with good things.[2] Those who seek the Lord lack no good thing.[3]

He leads me in paths of righteousness for His name's sake.[4] Lead me, O Lord, in Thy righteousness because of my enemies; make Thy way straight before me.[5]

Even though I walk through the valley of the shadow of death, I fear no evil; for Thou art with me; Thy rod and Thy staff, they comfort me.[6] When I am afraid, I put my trust in Thee . . . in God I trust without a fear.[7]

Thou preparest a table before me in the presence of my enemies; Thou anointest my head with oil, my cup overflows.[8] Be not far from me, for trouble is near and there is none to help. Many bulls encompass me, strong bulls . . . surround me.[9]

Surely goodness and mercy shall follow me all the days of my life; and I shall dwell in the house of the Lord for ever.[10] I am continually with Thee; Thou dost hold my right hand. Thou dost guide me with Thy counsel, and afterward Thou wilt receive me to glory.[11]

**Ps. 23:1.* [1]*Ps. 23:2, 3.* [2]*Ps. 107:9.* [3]*Ps. 34:10.* [4]*Ps. 23:3.* [5]*Ps. 5:8.* [6]*Ps. 23:4.* [7]*Ps. 56:3, 4.* [8]*Ps. 23:5.* [9]*Ps. 22:11, 12.* [10]*Ps. 23:6.* [11]*Ps. 73:23, 24.*

APRIL 13

*No other name**

The Lord has become like an enemy.[1] Oh, that I knew where I might find Him![2] Why dost Thou hide Thy face, and count me as Thy enemy?[3] Behold, Thou wast angry, and we sinned; in our sins we have been a long time, and shall we be saved? . . . For Thou hast hid Thy face from us.[4]

Jesus said to him, 'I am the way, and the truth, and the life; no one comes to the Father, but by Me.'[5] And there is salvation in no one else, for there is no other name under heaven given among men by which we must be saved.[6] For there is one God, and there is one mediator between God and men, the man Christ Jesus, who gave Himself as a ransom for all.[7]

Through Him we have obtained access to this grace in which we stand.[8] By the blood of Jesus, by the new and living way which He opened for us . . . through His flesh.[9] But now in Christ Jesus you who once were far off have been brought near in the blood of Christ.[10] I am the door; if any one enters by Me, he will be saved, and will go in and out and find pasture.[11]

**Acts 4:12.* [1]*Lam. 2:5.* [2]*Job 23:3.* [3]*Job 13:24.* [4]*Is. 64:5, 7.* [5]*Jn. 14:6.* [6]*Acts 4:12.* [7]*1 Tim. 2:5.* [8]*Rom. 5:2.* [9]*Heb. 10:19, 20.* [10]*Eph. 2:13.* [11]*Jn. 10:9.*

*The hand of the Lord was on Elijah**

Elijah was a man of like nature with ourselves.[1] And the word of the Lord came to him . . . 'Hide yourself by the brook Cherith . . . You shall drink from the brook, and I have commanded the ravens to feed you there.'[2] Then the word of the Lord came to him . . . 'Go to Zarephath . . . Behold, I have commanded a widow there to feed you.'[3] Is anything too hard for the Lord?[4] The young lions suffer want and hunger; but those who seek the Lord lack no good thing.[5]

Elijah . . . prayed fervently.[6] 'O Lord my God, let this child's soul come into him again.' And the Lord hearkened to the voice of Elijah; and the soul of the child came into him again, and he revived.[7] Then Elijah said to the people . . . 'You call on the name of your god and I will call on the name of the Lord; and the God who answers by fire, He is God.'[8] And . . . Elijah . . . said . . . 'Answer me, O Lord, answer me, that this people may know that Thou, O Lord, art God' . . . Then the fire of the Lord fell.[9] I know that Thou canst do all things, and that no purpose of Thine can be thwarted.[10] The prayer of a righteous man has great power in its effects.[11]

**1 Kings 18:46.* [1]*Jas. 5:17.* [2]*1 Kings 17:2–4.* [3]*1 Kings 17:8, 9.* [4]*Gen. 18:14.* [5]*Ps. 34:10.* [6]*Jas. 5:17.* [7]*1 Kings 17:21, 22.* [8]*1 Kings 18:22, 24.* [9]*1 Kings 18:36–38.* [10]*Job 42:2.* [11]*Jas. 5:16.*

APRIL 15

*The gift of God**

Having gifts that differ according to the grace given to us, let us use them: if prophecy, in proportion to our faith; if service, in our serving; he who teaches, in his teaching.[1] Do not neglect the gift you have, which was given you.[2] I remind you to rekindle the gift of God that is within you through the laying on of my hands.[3]

Therefore it is said, When He ascended on high He led a host of captives, and He gave gifts to men . . . and His gifts were that some should be apostles, some prophets, some evangelists, some pastors and teachers, for the equipment of the saints, for the work of ministry, for building up the body of Christ.[4]

'I was afraid, and I went and hid your talent in the ground. Here you have what is yours.' But his master answered him, 'You wicked and slothful servant! . . . You ought to have invested my money with the bankers, and at my coming I should have received what was my own with interest.'[5] Do your best to present yourself to God as one approved, a workman who has no need to be ashamed.[6] Every one to whom much is given, of him will much be required.[7]

**2 Tim. 1:6.* [1]*Rom. 12:6, 7.* [2]*1 Tim. 4:14.* [3]*2 Tim. 1:6.* [4]*Eph. 4:8, 11, 12.* [5]*Mt. 25:25–27.* [6]*2 Tim. 2:15.* [7]*Lk. 12:48.*

*Never be conceited**

By the grace given to me I bid every one among you not to think of himself more highly than he ought to think, but to think with sober judgment.[1] Talk no more so very proudly, let not arrogance come from your mouth.[2] Do nothing from selfishness or conceit, but in humility count others better than yourselves.[3] For every one who exalts himself will be humbled, and he who humbles himself will be exalted.[4] And those who walk in pride He is able to abase.[5]

When you are invited by any one to a marriage feast, do not sit down in a place of honor . . . But when you are invited, go and sit in the lowest place, so that when your host comes he may say to you, 'Friend, go up higher.'[6] Do not be haughty, but associate with the lowly.[7]

The Lord makes poor and makes rich; He brings low, He also exalts. He raises up the poor from the dust; He lifts the needy from the ash heap, to make them sit with princes and inherit a seat of honor.[8] He removes kings and sets up kings.[9] Putting down one and lifting up another.[10] By the grace of God I am what I am.[11]

**Rom. 12:16.* [1]*Rom. 12:3.* [2]*1 Sam. 2:3.* [3]*Phil. 2:3.* [4]*Lk. 14:11.* [5]*Dan. 4:37.* [6]*Lk. 14:8, 10.* [7]*Rom. 12:16.* [8]*1 Sam. 2:7, 8.* [9]*Dan. 2:21.* [10]*Ps. 75:7.* [11]*1 Cor. 15:10.*

APRIL 17

*The eternal God is your dwelling place, and underneath are the everlasting arms**

He found him in a desert land, and in the howling waste of the wilderness; He encircled him, He cared for him, He kept him as the apple of His eye. Like an eagle that stirs up its nest, that flutters over its young, spreading out its wings, catching them, bearing them on its pinions, the Lord alone did lead him.[1] Keep me as the apple of the eye; hide me in the shadow of Thy wings.[2] In the shadow of Thy wings I will take refuge, till the storms of destruction pass by.[3]

The name of the Lord is a strong tower; the righteous man runs into it and is safe.[4] The Lord is good, a stronghold in the day of trouble; He knows those who take refuge in Him.[5] The Lord is . . . my fortress . . . my rock, in whom I take refuge, my shield and the horn of my salvation, my stronghold and my refuge.[6]

Behold, a king will reign in righteousness, and princes will rule in justice. Each will be like a hiding place from the wind, a covert from the tempest, like streams of water in a dry place, like the shade of a great rock in a weary land.[7] He who dwells in the shelter of the Most High, who abides in the shadow of the Almighty.[8]

**Deut. 33:27.* [1]*Deut. 32:10–12.* [2]*Ps. 17:8.* [3]*Ps. 57:1.* [4]*Prov. 18:10.* [5]*Nahum 1:7.* [6]*2 Sam. 22:2, 3.* [7]*Is. 32:1, 2.* [8]*Ps. 91:1.*

*In the name of the Father and of the Son and of the Holy Spirit**

The Holy Spirit will come upon you, and the power of the Most High will overshadow you; therefore the child to be born will be called holy, the Son of God.[1] When He came up out of the water, immediately He saw the heavens opened and the Spirit descending upon Him like a dove; and a voice came from heaven, 'Thou art My beloved Son; with Thee I am well pleased.'[2]

And I will pray the Father, and He will give you another Counselor, to be with you for ever.[3] When the Counselor comes, whom I shall send to you from the Father, even the Spirit of truth, who proceeds from the Father, He will bear witness to Me.[4]

Through Him we both have access in one Spirit to the Father.[5] For this reason I bow my knees before the Father . . . that . . . He may grant you to be strengthened with might through His Spirit in the inner man, and that Christ may dwell in your hearts through faith; . . . that you may be filled with all the fullness of God.[6]

The grace of the Lord Jesus Christ and the love of God and the fellowship of the Holy Spirit be with you all.[7]

**Mt. 28:19. [1]Lk. 1:35. [2]Mk. 1:10, 11. [3]Jn. 14:16. [4]Jn. 15:26. [5]Eph. 2:18. [6]Eph. 3:14, 16, 17, 19. [7]2 Cor. 13:14.*

APRIL 19

*Remove far from me falsehood and lying**

Who shall dwell on Thy holy hill? He who walks blamelessly, and does what is right, and speaks truth from his heart.[1] God is spirit, and those who worship Him must worship in spirit and truth.[2] Behold, Thou desirest truth in the inward being; therefore teach me wisdom in my secret heart.[3]

A man named Ananias with his wife Sapphira sold a piece of property, and with his wife's knowledge he kept back some of the proceeds, and brought only a part and laid it at the apostles' feet. But Peter said, '. . . You have not lied to men but to God.'[4] The getting of treasures by a lying tongue is a fleeting vapor and a snare of death.

Do not lie to one another, seeing that you have put off the old nature with its practices.[6] Therefore, putting away falsehood, let every one speak the truth with his neighbor, for we are members one of another.[7] As servants of God we commend ourselves . . . by . . . the Holy Spirit, genuine love, truthful speech, and the power of God.[8] The Holy Spirit will teach you . . . what you ought to say.[9] The Spirit of truth.[10]

**Prov. 30:8.* [1]*Ps. 15:1, 2.* [2]*Jn. 4:24.* [3]*Ps. 51:6.* [4]*Acts 5:1–4.* [5]*Prov. 21:6.* [6]*Col. 3:9.* [7]*Eph. 4:25.* [8]*2 Cor. 6:4, 6, 7.* [9]*Lk. 12:12.* [10]*Jn. 16:13.*

*Lord, teach us to pray**

Hezekiah received the letter . . . and spread it before the Lord. And Hezekiah prayed to the Lord: . . . 'Incline Thy ear, O Lord, and hear; open Thy eyes, O Lord, and see; and hear all the words of Sennacherib, which he has sent to mock the living God . . . O Lord our God, save us from his hand, that all the kingdoms of the earth may know that Thou alone art the Lord.'[1]

Then I (Daniel) turned my face to the Lord God, seeking Him by prayer . . . 'O our God, hearken to the prayer of Thy servant and . . . cause Thy face to shine upon Thy sanctuary, which is desolate. O my God, incline Thy ear and hear . . . for we do not present our supplications before Thee on the ground of our righteousness, but on the ground of Thy great mercy'.[2]

Jabez called on the God of Israel, saying, 'Oh that Thou wouldst bless me . . . and that Thy hand might be with me, and that Thou wouldst keep me from harm so that it might not hurt me!'[3]

They cried to the Lord in their trouble, and He delivered them from their distress.[4] Call upon Me in the day of trouble; I will deliver you, and you shall glorify Me.[5] In everything by prayer . . . let your requests be made known to God.[6]

**Lk. 11:1.* [1]*Is. 37:14, 15, 17, 20.* [2]*Dan. 9:3, 19.*
[3]*1 Chron. 4:10.* [4]*Ps. 107:13.* [5]*Ps. 50:15.* [6]*Phil. 4:6.*

APRIL 21

*Do not be conformed to this world**

Do not love the world or the things in the world. If any one loves the world, love for the Father is not in him. For all that is in the world, the lust of the flesh and the lust of the eyes and the pride of life, is not of the Father but is of the world.[1] The whole world is in the power of the evil one.[2] Do not be conformed to this world but be transformed by the renewal of your mind, that you may prove what is the will of God, what is good and acceptable and perfect.[3]

If the world hates you, know that it has hated Me before it hated you. If you were of the world, the world would love its own; but because you are not of the world, but I chose you out of the world, therefore the world hates you.[4] Of whom the world was not worthy.[5]

I do not pray that Thou shouldst take them out of the world, but that Thou shouldst keep them from the evil one.[6] You are the salt of the earth.[7] You are the light of the world.[8] That you may be blameless and innocent, children of God without blemish in the midst of a crooked and perverse generation, among whom you shine as lights in the world.[9]

**Rom. 12:2. [1]1 Jn. 2:15, 16. [2]1 Jn. 5:19. [3]Rom. 12:2. [4]Jn. 15:18, 19. [5]Heb. 11:38. [6]Jn. 17:15. [7]Mt. 5:13. [8]Mt. 5:14. [9]Phil. 2:15.*

*Persecuted, but not forsaken**

Remember the word that I said to you, 'A servant is not greater than his master.' If they persecuted Me, they will persecute you.[1] Indeed all who desire to live a godly life in Christ Jesus will be persecuted.[2] Indeed, the hour is coming when whoever kills you will think he is offering service to God.[3]

Beloved, do not be surprised at the fiery ordeal which comes upon you to prove you, as though something strange were happening to you. But rejoice in so far as you share Christ's sufferings, that you may also rejoice and be glad when His glory is revealed. If you are reproached for the name of Christ, you are blessed.[4] Blessed are you when men revile you and persecute you and utter all kinds of evil against you falsely on My account. Rejoice and be glad, for your reward is great in heaven.[5]

Do not wonder, brethren, that the world hates you.[6] Do not fear what you are about to suffer . . . Be faithful unto death, and I will give you the crown of life.[7] Hence we can confidently say, 'The Lord is my helper, I will not be afraid; What can man do to me?'[8]

*2 *Cor. 4:9.* [1]*Jn. 15:20.* [2]*2 Tim. 3:12.* [3]*Jn. 16:2.* [4]*1 Pet. 4:12–14.* [5]*Mt. 5:11, 12.* [6]*1 Jn. 3:13.* [7]*Rev. 2:10.* [8]*Heb. 13:6.*

APRIL 23

*You are not your own**

You are Christ's.[1] For the love of Christ controls us, because we are convinced that one has died for all; therefore all have died. And He died for all, that those who live might live no longer for themselves but for Him who for their sake died and was raised.[2] Yield yourselves to God as men who have been brought from death to life.[3]

Do you not know that your body is a temple of the Holy Spirit . . . ? You are not your own; you were bought with a price. So glorify God in your body.[4] I appeal to you therefore, brethren, by the mercies of God, to present your bodies as a living sacrifice, holy and acceptable to God.[5] To me to live is Christ.[6]

Blessed are those who hunger and thirst for righteousness, for they shall be satisfied.[7] Thou hast said, 'Seek ye My face.' My heart says to Thee, 'Thy face, Lord, do I seek'.[8] With my whole heart I seek Thee; let me not wander from Thy commandments![9] I love those who love me, and those who seek me diligently find me.[10] As long as he sought the Lord, God made him prosper.[11]

**1 Cor. 6:19.* [1]*1 Cor. 3:23.* [2]*2 Cor. 5:14, 15.* [3]*Rom. 6:13.* [4]*1 Cor. 6:19, 20.* [5]*Rom. 12:1.* [6]*Phil. 1:21.* [7]*Mt. 5:6.* [8]*Ps. 27:8.* [9]*Ps. 119:10.* [10]*Prov. 8:17.* [11]*2 Chron. 26:5.*

*I died, and behold, I am alive for evermore**

They found the stone rolled away from the tomb, but when they went in they did not find the body.[1] You seek Jesus of Nazareth, who was crucified. He has risen, He is not here; see the place where they laid Him.[2] The Lord has risen indeed. . . . ![3]

But Mary stood weeping outside the tomb . . . Jesus said to her, 'Mary.' She turned and said to Him in Hebrew, 'Rabboni!'[4] After this He appeared in another form to two of them, as they were walking into the country.[5] He was known to them in the breaking of the bread.[6] Then He appeared to more than five hundred brethren at one time, most of whom are still alive . . . Then He appeared to James, then to all the apostles.[7] Witnesses, who ate and drank with Him after He rose from the dead.[8]

If Christ has not been raised, your faith is futile and you are still in your sins . . . But in fact Christ has been raised from the dead.[9] Christ being raised from the dead will never die again; death no longer has dominion over him.[10] Designated Son of God in power . . . by His resurrection from the dead.[11]

**Rev. 1:18.* [1]*Lk. 24:2, 3.* [2]*Mk. 16:6.* [3]*Lk. 24:34.* [4]*Jn. 20:11, 16.* [5]*Mk. 16:12.* [6]*Lk. 24:35.* [7]*1 Cor. 15:6, 7.* [8]*Acts 10:41.* [9]*1 Cor. 15:17, 20.* [10]*Rom. 6:9.* [11]*Rom. 1:4.*

APRIL 25

*But He gives more grace**

Now Paul and his company set sail from Paphos, and came to Perga in Pamphylia. And John (Mark) left them and returned to Jerusalem.[1] If you faint in the day of adversity, your strength is small.[2] If you have raced with men on foot, and they have wearied you, how will you compete with horses? And if in a safe land you fall down, how will you do in the jungle of the Jordan?[3]

Barnabas wanted to take with them John called Mark. But Paul thought best not to take with them one who had withdrawn from them in Pamphylia, and had not gone with them to the work.[4] My righteous one shall live by faith, and if he shrinks back, My soul has no pleasure in him.[5] As for me, I said, 'O Lord, be gracious to me; heal me, for I have sinned against Thee!'[6]

Luke alone is with me. Get Mark and bring him with you; for he is very useful in serving me.[7] Formerly . . . useless . . ., but now . . . indeed useful.[8] He gives power to the faint, and to him who has no might He increases strength.[9] The Master is able to make him stand.[10]

**Jas. 4:6.* [1]*Acts 13:13.* [2]*Prov. 24:10.* [3]*Jer. 12:5.* [4]*Acts 15:37, 38.* [5]*Heb. 10:38.* [6]*Ps. 41:4.* [7]*2 Tim. 4:11.* [8]*Philemon 11.* [9]*Is. 40:29.* [10]*Rom. 14:4.*

*Sons of the living God**

You shall be called by a new name which the mouth of the Lord will give.[1] And I will be a Father to you, and you shall be My sons and my daughters, says the Lord Almighty.[2] To all who received Him . . . He gave power to become children of God; who were born, not of blood nor of the will of the flesh nor of the will of man, but of God.[3] God sent forth His Son . . . so that we might receive adoption as sons.[4] For in Christ Jesus you are all sons of God, through faith.[5] See what love the Father has given us, that we should be called children of God; and so we are.[6]

God is treating you as sons.[7] Know then in your heart that, as a man disciplines his son, the Lord your God disciplines you.[8] For the Lord reproves him whom He loves, as a father the son in whom he delights.[9] For those whom He foreknew He also predestined to be conformed to the image of His Son.[10] That when He appears we shall be like Him . . . And every one who thus hopes in Him purifies himself as He is pure.[11]

**Hos. 1:10.* [1]*Is. 62:2.* [2]*2 Cor. 6:18.* [3]*Jn. 1:12, 13.* [4]*Gal. 4:4, 5.* [5]*Gal. 3:26.* [6]*1 Jn. 3:1.* [7]*Heb. 12:7.* [8]*Deut. 8:5.* [9]*Prov. 3:12.* [10]*Rom. 8:29.* [11]*1 Jn. 3:2, 3.*

APRIL 27

*I need nothing**

The king said, 'Is not this great Babylon, which I have built by my mighty power as a royal residence and for the glory of my majesty?' While the words were still in the king's mouth, there fell a voice from heaven, 'O King Nebuchadnezzar . . . the kingdom has departed from you, and you shall be driven from among men . . . until you have learned that the Most High rules the kingdom of men.'[1]

On an appointed day Herod put on his royal robes, took his seat upon the throne, and made an oration to them. And the people shouted, 'The voice of a god, and not of man!' Immediately an angel of the Lord smote him, because he did not give God the glory; and he was eaten by worms and died.[2] The God in whose hand is your breath, and whose are all your ways, you have not honored.[3]

Take heed lest . . . when . . . your silver and gold is multiplied . . . then your heart be lifted up, and you forget the Lord your God . . . Beware lest you say in your heart, 'My power and the might of my hand have gotten me this wealth.'[4] For the Lord gives wisdom.[5] It is He who gives you power.[6] Who spread forth the earth . . . who gives breath to the people upon it.[7]

**Rev. 3:17.* [1]*Dan. 4:30–32.* [2]*Acts 12:21–23.* [3]*Dan. 5:23.* [4]*Deut. 8:11, 13, 14, 17.* [5]*Prov. 2:6.* [6]*Deut. 8:18.* [7]*Is. 42:5.*

*You have been saved through faith**

But now the righteousness of God has been manifested apart from law, although the law and the prophets bear witness to it, the righteousness of God through faith in Jesus Christ for all who believe.[1] To Him all the prophets bear witness that every one who believes in Him receives forgiveness of sins through His name.[2]

The jailer brought Paul and Silas out of prison and said, 'Men, what must I do to be saved?' And they said, 'Believe in the Lord Jesus, and you will be saved, you and your household.' And they spoke the word of the Lord to him and to all that were in his house. . . . And he was baptized at once, with all his family. . . . and he rejoiced with all his household that he had believed in God.[3]

For by grace you have been saved through faith; and this is not your own doing, it is the gift of God —not because of works, lest any man should boast.[4] For . . . a man is justified by faith apart from works of law.[5] For in Christ Jesus you are all sons of God, through faith.[6] Your faith has saved you; go in peace.[7]

**Eph.* 2:8. [1]*Rom.* 3:21, 22. [2]*Acts* 10:43. [3]*Acts* 16:30–34. [4]*Eph.* 2:8, 9. [5]*Rom.* 3:28. [6]*Gal.* 3:26. [7]*Lk.* 7:50.

APRIL 29

*Peace with God**

Wilt Thou be angry with us for ever? Wilt Thou prolong Thy anger to all generations?[1] Let me hear what God the Lord will speak, for He will speak peace to His people, to His saints, to those who turn to Him in their hearts.[2] Let them lay hold of My protection, let them make peace with Me.[3]

Remember that you were at that time separated from Christ, alienated from the commonwealth of Israel, and strangers to the covenants of promise, having no hope and without God in the world. But now in Christ Jesus you who once were far off have been brought near in the blood of Christ. For He is our peace.[4] For in Him all the fullness of God was pleased to dwell, and through Him to reconcile to Himself all things, whether on earth or in heaven, making peace by the blood of His cross.[5]

Therefore, since we are justified by faith, we have peace with God through our Lord Jesus Christ.[6] For the mountains may depart and the hills be removed, but My steadfast love shall not depart from you, and My covenant of peace shall not be removed, says the Lord, who has compassion on you.[7]

**Rom. 5:1.* [1]*Ps. 85:5.* [2]*Ps. 85:8.* [3]*Is. 27:5.* [4]*Eph. 2:12–14.* [5]*Col. 1:19, 20.* [6]*Rom. 5:1.* [7]*Is. 54:10.*

*Give no opportunity to the devil**

The whole world is in the power of the evil one.[1] Following the prince of the power of the air, the spirit that is now at work in the sons of disobedience.[2]

We are not ignorant of his designs.[3] A sower went out to sow his seed; and as he sowed, some fell along the path, and was trodden under foot, and the birds of the air devoured it. Now the parable is this: The seed is the word of God. The ones along the path are those who have heard; then the devil comes and takes away the word from their hearts, that they may not believe and be saved.[4]

Simon, Simon, behold, Satan demanded to have you, that he might sift you like wheat.[5] Satan stood up . . . and incited David to number Israel.[6] Then Satan entered into Judas called Iscariot, who was of the number of the twelve.[7]

There was a woman who had had a spirit of infirmity . . . whom Satan bound for eighteen years.[8] We wanted to come to you—I, Paul, again and again—but Satan hindered us.[9]

Get behind Me, Satan![10] Begone, Satan![11] Resist him, firm in your faith.[12] Then the God of peace will soon crush Satan under your feet.[13]

**Eph.* 4:27. [1]*1 Jn.* 5:19. [2]*Eph.* 2:2. [3]*2 Cor.* 2:11. [4]*Lk.* 8:5, 11, 12. [5]*Lk.* 22:31. [6]*1 Chron.* 21:1. [7]*Lk.* 22:3. [8]*Lk.* 13:11, 16. [9]*1 Thess.* 2:18. [10]*Mt.* 16:23. [11]*Mt.* 4:10. [12]*1 Pet.* 5:9. [13]*Rom.* 16:20.

MAY 1

*How are the mighty fallen!**

Saul said, 'I have done wrong.'[1] And Samuel said, Has the Lord as great delight in burnt offerings and sacrifices, as in obeying the voice of the Lord? Behold, to obey is better than sacrifice . . . Because you have rejected the word of the Lord, He has also rejected you from being king.[2] Every way of a man is right in his own eyes, but the Lord weighs the heart. To do righteousness and justice is more acceptable to the Lord than sacrifice.[3]

Saul said 'I. . . have played the fool.'[4] Saul was afraid of David, because the Lord was with him but had departed from Saul.[5] So Saul was David's enemy continually.[6] A fool gives full vent to his anger, but a wise man quietly holds it back.[7]

Saul said . . . 'I have . . . erred exceedingly'.[8] Then Saul said to his servants, 'Seek out for me a woman who is a medium, that I may go to her and inquire of her'.[9] Do not turn to mediums or wizards.[10] It is the glory of God to conceal things.[11] Should not a people consult their God? Should they consult the dead on behalf of the living?[12] Who is the man that fears the Lord? Him will He instruct in the way that he should choose.[13]

**2 Sam. 1:19.* [1]*1 Sam. 26:21.* [2]*1 Sam. 15:22, 23.* [3]*Prov. 21:2, 3.* [4]*1 Sam. 26:21.* [5]*1 Sam. 18:12* [6]*1 Sam. 18:29.* [7]*Prov. 29:11.* [8]*1 Sam. 26:21.* [9]*1 Sam. 28:7.* [10]*Lev. 19:31.* [11]*Prov. 25:2.* [12]*Is. 8:19.* [13]*Ps. 25:12.*

*By this it may be seen who are the children of God**

Every one who believes that Jesus is the Christ is a child of God.[1] To all who received Him, who believed in His name, He gave power to become children of God.[2]

Beloved, let us love one another; for love is of God, and he who loves is born of God and knows God.[3] We are bound to give thanks to God always for you, brethren . . . because your faith is growing abundantly, and the love of every one of you for one another is increasing.[4]

Whatever is born of God overcomes the world; and this is the victory that overcomes the world, our faith.[5] In the world you have tribulation; but be of good cheer, I have overcome the world.[6] Little children, you are of God and have overcome them; for He who is in you is greater than he who is in the world.[7]

We know that any one born of God does not sin, but He who was born of God keeps him, and the evil one does not touch him.[8] I do not pray that Thou shouldst take them out of the world, but that Thou shouldst keep them from the evil one.[9] The Lord is faithful; He will strengthen you and guard you from evil.[10]

**1 Jn. 3:10.* [1]*1 Jn. 5:1.* [2]*Jn. 1:12.* [3]*1 Jn. 4:7.* [4]*2 Thess. 1:3.* [5]*1 Jn. 5:4.* [6]*Jn. 16:33.* [7]*1 Jn. 4:4.* [8]*1 Jn. 5:18.* [9]*Jn. 17:15.* [10]*2 Thess. 3:3.*

MAY 3

*And Samuel said, 'Speak, for Thy servant hears!'**

Joshua said to the people of Israel, 'Come hither, and hear the words of the Lord your God.'[1] Ezra opened the book in the sight of all the people . . . and when he opened it all the people stood . . . And they read from the book, from the law of God, clearly; and they gave the sense, so that the people understood the reading.[2] The two disciples said to each other, 'Did not our hearts burn within us while He talked to us on the road, and while He opened to us the scriptures?'[3] He opened their minds to understand the scriptures.[4]

They received the word with all eagerness, examining the scriptures daily to see if these things were so.[5] I will meditate on Thy precepts, and fix my eyes on Thy ways. I will delight in Thy statutes; I will not forget Thy word . . . Open my eyes, that I may behold wondrous things out of Thy law.[6]

Give me understanding, that I may keep Thy law and observe it with my whole heart. Lead me in the path of Thy commandments, for I delight in it.[7] He who looks into the perfect law . . . and perseveres, being no hearer that forgets but a doer that acts, he shall be blessed in his doing.[8]

**1 Sam. 3:10.* [1]*Josh. 3:9.* [2]*Neh. 8:5, 8.* [3]*Lk. 24:32.* [4]*Lk. 24:45.* [5]*Acts 17:11.* [6]*Ps. 119:15, 16, 18.* [7]*Ps. 119:34, 35.* [8]*Jas. 1:25.*

*Take heed lest you forget the Lord your God**

God who made the world and everything in it . . . gives to all men life and breath and everything . . . In Him we live and move and have our being.[1]

God . . . richly furnishes us with everything to enjoy.[2] Therefore do not be anxious, saying, 'What shall we eat?' or 'What shall we drink?' or 'What shall we wear?' For the Gentiles seek all these things; and your heavenly Father knows that you need them all. But seek first His kingdom and His righteousness, and all these things shall be yours as well.[3]

Because you have made the Lord your refuge, the Most High your habitation, no evil shall befall you, no scourge come near your tent. For He will give His angels charge of you to guard you in all your ways.[4] He will not let your foot be moved, He who keeps you will not slumber.[5] The Lord will keep your going out and your coming in from this time forth and for evermore.[6]

Take heed lest you forget the Lord your God . . . lest, when you have eaten and are full . . . and all that you have is multiplied, then your heart be lifted up, and you forget the Lord your God.[7]

**Deut. 8:11.* [1]*Acts 17:24, 25, 28.* [2]*1 Tim. 6:17.* [3]*Mt. 6:31–33.* [4]*Ps. 91:9–11.* [5]*Ps. 121:3.* [6]*Ps. 121:8.* [7]*Deut. 8:11–14.*

MAY 5

*Jacob whom He loves**

But Isaac said, 'Your brother came with guile, and he has taken away your blessing.' Esau said, 'Is he not rightly named Jacob (=Supplanter)? For he has supplanted me these two times. He took away my birthright; and behold, now he has taken away my blessing.'[1]

Then Jacob awoke from his sleep and said, 'Surely the Lord is in this place; and I did not know it.' And he was afraid, and said, 'How awesome is this place! This is none other than the house of God, and this is the gate of heaven' . . . Then Jacob made a vow, saying, 'If God will be with me . . . then the Lord shall be my God.'[2]

And Jacob was left alone; and a man wrestled with him . . . Then he said, 'Let me go, for the day is breaking.' But Jacob said, 'I will not let you go, unless you bless me.' And he said to him, 'What is your name?' And he said, 'Jacob'. Then he said, 'Your name shall no more be called Jacob, but Israel, for you have striven with God and with men, and have prevailed.'[3]

Therefore, if any one is in Christ, he is a new creation; the old has passed away, behold, the new has come.[4]

**Ps. 47:4.* [1]*Gen. 27:35, 36.* [2]*Gen. 28:16, 17, 20, 21.* [3]*Gen. 32:24, 26–28.* [4]*2 Cor. 5:17.*

*The blood of the Lamb**

Jesus took a cup, and when He had given thanks He gave it to them, saying, 'Drink of it, all of you; for this is My blood of the covenant, which is poured out for many for the forgiveness of sins.'[1] For the life of the flesh is in the blood.[2] And without the shedding of blood there is no forgiveness of sins.[3]

John saw Jesus coming toward him, and said, 'Behold, the Lamb of God, who takes away the sin of the world![4] For if the sprinkling of defiled persons with the blood of goats and bulls . . . sanctifies for the purification of the flesh, how much more shall the blood of Christ, who through the eternal Spirit offered Himself without blemish to God, purify your conscience from dead works to serve the living God.[5] The blood of Jesus His Son cleanses us from all sin.[6]

In Him we have redemption through His blood, the forgiveness of our trespasses, according to the riches of His grace which He lavished upon us.[7] Ransomed . . . with the precious blood of Christ.[8] Justified by His blood.[9] To Him who loves us and has freed us from our sins by His blood . . . be glory and dominion for ever and ever. Amen.[10]

**Rev. 7:14.* [1]*Mt. 26:27, 28.* [2]*Lev. 17:11.* [3]*Heb. 9:22.* [4]*Jn. 1:29.* [5]*Heb. 9:13, 14.* [6]*1 Jn. 1:7.* [7]*Eph. 1:7, 8.* [8]*1 Pet. 1:18, 19.* [9]*Rom. 5:9.* [10]*Rev. 1:5, 6.*

MAY 7

*There is no authority except from God**

Be subject for the Lord's sake to every human institution, whether it be to the emperor as supreme, or to governors as sent by him to punish those who do wrong and to praise those who do right.[1] Let every person be subject to the governing authorities. For there is no authority except from God, and those that exist have been instituted by God. Therefore he who resists the authorities resists what God has appointed.[2]

The high priest questioned them, saying, 'We strictly charged you not to teach in this name, yet here you have filled Jerusalem with your teaching and you intend to bring this man's blood upon us.' But Peter and the apostles answered, 'We must obey God rather than men.'[3] The king of Egypt said to the Hebrew midwives . . . 'If it is a son, you shall kill him . . .' But the midwives feared God, and did not do as the king of Egypt commanded them, but let the male children live.[4] Be it known to you, O king, that we will not serve your gods or worship the golden image which you have set up.[5]

Jesus said to them, 'Render therefore to Caesar the things that are Caesar's, and to God the things that are God's.'[6]

**Rom. 13:1.* [1]*1 Pet. 2:13, 14.* [2]*Rom. 13:1, 2.* [3]*Acts 5:27, 28, 29.* [4]*Ex. 1:15–17.* [5]*Dan. 3:18.* [6]*Mt. 22:21.*

*You shall not covet**

Jesus said to them, 'Take heed, and beware of all covetousness; for a man's life does not consist in the abundance of his possessions.'[1] Achan answered Joshua, 'Of a truth I have sinned against the Lord God of Israel, and this is what I did: when I saw among the spoil a beautiful mantle from Shinar, and two hundred shekels of silver, and a bar of gold weighing fifty shekels, then I coveted them, and took them; and behold, they are hidden in the earth inside my tent, with the silver underneath.'[2]

Keep your life free from love of money, and be content with what you have.[3] But those who desire to be rich fall into temptation, into a snare, into many senseless and hurtful desires that plunge men into ruin.[4] So is he who lays up treasure for himself, and is not rich toward God.[5]

Do not lay up for yourselves treasures on earth, . . . but lay up for yourselves treasures in heaven . . . . For where your treasure is, there will your heart be also.[6] If the Almighty is your gold, and your precious silver; then you will delight yourself in the Almighty, and lift up your face to God.[7]

**Ex. 20:17.* [1]*Lk. 12:15.* [2]*Josh. 7:20, 21.* [3]*Heb. 13:5.* [4]*1 Tim. 6:9.* [5]*Lk. 12:21.* [6]*Mt. 6:19–21.* [7]*Job 22:25, 26.*

MAY 9

*Tempted as we are**

Then Jesus was led up by the Spirit into the wilderness to be tempted by the devil.[1] And the tempter came and said to Him, 'If You are the Son of God, command these stones to become loaves of bread. . . . If You are the Son of God, throw Yourself down. . . . All these I will give You, if You will fall down and worship me.'[2] And when the devil had ended every temptation, he departed from Him until an opportune time.[3]

When the people saw the sign which He had done, they said, 'This is indeed the prophet who is to come into the world!' Perceiving then that they were about to come and take Him by force to make Him king, Jesus withdrew again to the hills by Himself.[4] Jesus began to show His disciples that He must go to Jerusalem and suffer. . . . And Peter took Him and began to rebuke Him, saying, 'God forbid, Lord! This shall never happen to You.' But He turned and said to Peter, 'Get behind Me, Satan!'[5]

For because He Himself has suffered and been tempted, He is able to help those who are tempted.[6] For we have not a high priest who is unable to sympathize with our weaknesses, but one who in every respect has been tempted as we are, yet without sinning.[7]

**Heb. 4:15.* [1]*Mt. 4:1.* [2]*Mt. 4:3, 6, 9.* [3]*Lk. 4:13.* [4]*Jn. 6:14, 15.* [5]*Mt. 16:21–23.* [6]*Heb. 2:18.* [7]*Heb. 4:15.*

*Abide in Me, and I in you**

I am the vine, you are the branches. He who abides in Me, and I in him, he it is that bears much fruit, for apart from Me you can do nothing.[1] He is the source of your life in Christ Jesus, whom God made our wisdom, our righteousness and sanctification and redemption.[2] I say to the Lord, 'Thou art my Lord; I have no good apart from Thee.'[3]

If you keep My commandments, you will abide in My love, just as I have kept My Father's commandments and abide in His love.[4] You know that He appeared to take away sins, and in him there is no sin. No one who abides in Him sins; no one who sins has either seen Him or known Him.[5] Keep yourselves in the love of God.[6]

If you abide in Me, and My words abide in you, ask whatever you will, and it shall be done for you.[7] When he calls to Me, I will answer him; I will be with him in trouble, I will rescue him and honor him.[8] Thou dost keep him in perfect peace, whose mind is stayed on Thee, because he trusts in Thee.[9]

**Jn. 15:4.* [1]*Jn. 15:5.* [2]*1 Cor. 1:30.* [3]*Ps. 16:2.* [4]*Jn. 15:9.* [5]*1 Jn. 3:5, 6.* [6]*Jude 21.* [7]*Jn. 15:7.* [8]*Ps. 91:15.* [9]*Is. 26:3.*

MAY 11

*He was marvelously helped**

O Lord, how many are my foes! Many are rising against me; many are saying . . . there is no help for him in God.[1] As for me, I am poor and needy; but the Lord takes thought for me. Thou art my help and my deliverer; do not tarry, O my God![2] Behold, God is my helper; the Lord is the upholder of my life.[3] The Lord upholds all who are falling, and raises up all who are bowed down.[4] The hapless commits himself to Thee; Thou hast been the helper of the fatherless.[5] My father and my mother have forsaken me, but the Lord will take me up.[6]

Hitherto the Lord has helped us.[7] Thus says the Lord: In a time of favor I have answered you, in a day of salvation I have helped you . . . saying to the prisoners, 'Come forth,' to those who are in darkness, 'Appear'.[8] I was pushed hard, so that I was falling, but the Lord helped me.[9] Uzziah was marvelously helped.[10]

Let them thank the Lord for His steadfast love, for His wonderful works to the sons of men! For He satisfies him who is thirsty, and the hungry He fills with good things.[11] God is our refuge and strength, a very present help in trouble.[12]

**2 Chron. 26:15. [1]Ps. 3:1, 2. [2]Ps. 40:17. [3]Ps. 54:4. [4]Ps. 145:14. [5]Ps. 10:14. [6]Ps. 27:10. [7]1 Sam. 7:12. [8]Is. 49:8, 9. [9]Ps. 118:13. [10]2 Chron. 26:15. [11]Ps. 107: 8, 9. [12]Ps. 46:1.*

*Useful to the master**

I went down to the potter's house, and there he was working at his wheel. And the vessel he was making of clay was spoiled in the potter's hand, and he reworked it into another vessel, as it seemed good to the potter to do. Then the word of the Lord came to me: 'O house of Israel, can I not do with you as this potter has done?' says the Lord.[1]

In a great house there are not only vessels of gold and silver but also of wood and earthenware, and some for noble use, some for ignoble. If any one purifies himself from what is ignoble, then he will be a vessel for noble use, consecrated and useful to the master of the house, ready for any good work.[2]

And His gifts were that some should be apostles, some prophets, some evangelists, some pastors and teachers, for the equipment of the saints, for the work of ministry, for building up the body of Christ.[3] Therefore . . . understand what the will of the Lord is. And . . . be filled with the Spirit.[4]

**2 Tim. 2:21.* [1]*Jer. 18:3–6.* [2]*2 Tim. 2:20, 21.* [3]*Eph. 4:11, 12.* [4]*Eph. 5:17, 18.*

MAY 13

*Apart from Me you can do nothing**

But Moses said to God, 'Who am I that I should go to Pharaoh, and bring the sons of Israel out of Egypt?' He said, 'But I will be with you'.[1] Then I said, 'Ah, Lord God! Behold, I do not know how to speak, for I am only a youth.' But the Lord said to me . . . Be not afraid of them, for I am with you to deliver you.'[2] But Ananias answered, 'Lord, I have heard from many about this man, how much evil he has done to Thy saints at Jerusalem . . .' But the Lord said to him, 'Go, for he is a chosen instrument of Mine to carry My name before the Gentiles.'[3]

Help us, O Lord our God, for we rely on Thee, and in Thy name we have come against this multitude. O Lord, Thou art our God; let not man prevail against Thee.[4] When I am weak, then I am strong.[5] Strong in the Lord and in the strength of His might.[6] He gives power to the faint, and to him who has no might He increases strength.[7] I can do all things in Him who strengthens me.[8]

And what more shall I say? For the time would fail me to tell of . . . the prophets who through faith . . . won strength out of weakness.[9]

**Jn. 15:5.* [1]*Ex. 3:11, 12.* [2]*Jer. 1:6–8.* [3]*Acts 9:13, 15.* [4]*2 Chron. 14:11.* [5]*2 Cor. 12:10.* [6]*Eph. 6:10.* [7]*Is. 40:29.* [8]*Phil. 4:13.* [9]*Heb. 11:32–34.*

*Sold under sin**

So when the woman saw that the tree was good for food, and that it was a delight to the eyes, and that the tree was to be desired to make one wise, she took of its fruit and ate; and she also gave some to her husband, and he ate.[1] Therefore . . . sin came into the world through one man and death through sin, and so death spread to all men because all men sinned.[2]

Behold, I was brought forth in iniquity, and in sin did my mother conceive me.[3] The wicked go astray from the womb, they err from their birth, speaking lies.[4] Who can bring a clean thing out of an unclean? There is not one.[5]

From within, out of the heart of man, come evil thoughts, fornication, theft, murder, adultery, coveting, wickedness, deceit, licentiousness, envy, slander, pride, foolishness. All these evil things come from within, and they defile a man.[6] Let no one say when he is tempted, I am tempted by God; for God cannot be tempted with evil, and He Himself tempts no one; but each person is tempted when he is lured and enticed by his own desire. Then desire when it has conceived gives birth to sin; and sin when it is full-grown brings forth death.[7]

**Rom. 7:14.* [1]*Gen. 3:6.* [2]*Rom. 5:12.* [3]*Ps. 51:5.* [4]*Ps. 58:3.* [5]*Job 14:4.* [6]*Mk. 7:21–23.* [7]*Jas. 1:13–15.*

MAY 15

*The people who know their God shall stand firm and take action**

All were amazed and perplexed, saying to one another, 'What does this mean?' But others mocking said, 'They are filled with new wine.' But Peter . . . lifted up his voice and addressed them . . . 'These men are not drunk, as you suppose . . . but this is what was spoken by the prophet Joel: "And in the last days it shall be, God declares, that I will pour out My Spirit upon all flesh".'[1]

Men of good repute, full of the Spirit and of wisdom.[2] Men who have turned the world upside down.[3] Men who have risked their lives for the sake of our Lord Jesus Christ.[4] Men of valor whose hearts God had touched.[5] They loved not their lives even unto death.[6]

Then flew one of the seraphim to me, having in his hand a burning coal which he had taken with tongs from the altar. And he touched my mouth, and said: 'Behold, this has touched your lips; your guilt is taken away, and your sin forgiven.' And I heard the voice of the Lord saying, 'Whom shall I send, and who will go for Us?' Then I said, 'Here I am! Send me.' And He said, 'Go . . .'[7]

**Dan. 11:32.* [1]*Acts 2:12–17.* [2]*Acts 6:3.* [3]*Acts 17:6.* [4]*Acts 15:26.* [5]*1 Sam. 10:26.* [6]*Rev. 12:11.* [7]*Isa. 6:6–9.*

*Bear one another's burdens**

Rejoice with those who rejoice, weep with those who weep.[1] Did not I weep for him whose day was hard? Was not my soul grieved for the poor?[2] A friend loves at all times, and a brother is born for adversity.[3] We who are strong ought to bear with the failings of the weak, and not to please ourselves.[4]

And they sat with Job on the ground seven days and seven nights, and no one spoke a word to him, for they saw that his suffering was very great.[5] If one member suffers, all suffer together; if one member is honored, all rejoice together.[6] Remember those who are in prison, as though in prison with them; and those who are ill-treated, since you also are in the body.[7]

I could strengthen you with my mouth, and the solace of my lips would assuage your pain.[8] Anxiety in a man's heart weighs him down, but a good word makes him glad.[9] Blessed be . . . the God . . . of all comfort, who comforts us in all our affliction, so that we may be able to comfort those who are in any affliction, with the comfort with which we ourselves are comforted by God.[10]

**Gal. 6:2.* [1]*Rom. 12:15.* [2]*Job 30:25.* [3]*Prov. 17:17.* [4]*Rom. 15:1.* [5]*Job 2:13.* [6]*1 Cor. 12:26.* [7]*Heb. 13:3.* [8]*Job 16:5.* [9]*Prov. 12:25.* [10]*2 Cor. 1:3, 4.*

MAY 17

*That this may be a sign among you**

And God said . . . 'When I bring clouds over the earth and the bow is seen in the clouds, I will remember My covenant which is between Me and you . . . and the waters shall never again become a flood to destroy all flesh.'[1] I am the Lord. The blood shall be a sign for you, upon the houses where you are; and when I see the blood, I will pass over you, and no plague shall fall upon you.[2] Joshua said . . . 'When your children ask . . . "What do these stones mean to you?" Then you shall tell them that the waters of the Jordan were cut off . . . So these stones shall be to the people of Israel a memorial for ever.'[3]

The Lord Jesus on the night when He was betrayed took bread, and when He had given thanks, He broke it, and said, 'This is My body which is for you. Do this in remembrance of Me.' In the same way also the cup, after supper, saying, 'This cup is the new covenant in My blood. Do this, as often as you drink it, in remembrance of Me.' . . . Whoever, therefore, eats the bread or drinks the cup of the Lord in an unworthy manner will be guilty of profaning the body and blood of the Lord. Let a man examine himself, and so eat of the bread and drink of the cup.[4]

**Josh. 4:6.* [1]*Gen. 9:12, 14, 15.* [2]*Ex. 12:12, 13.* [3]*Josh. 4:5–7.* [4]*1 Cor. 11:23–28.*

*We have our hope set on the living God**

Blessed be the God and Father of our Lord Jesus Christ! By His great mercy we have been born anew to a living hope through the resurrection of Jesus Christ from the dead, and to an inheritance which is imperishable, undefiled, and unfading, kept in heaven for you.[1] According to His promise we wait for new heavens and a new earth in which righteousness dwells.[2]

For you have need of endurance, so that you may do the will of God and receive what is promised.[3] Now hope that is seen is not hope. For who hopes for what he sees? But if we hope for what we do not see, we wait for it with patience.[4] Because we look not to the things that are seen but to the things that are unseen; for the things that are seen are transient, but the things that are unseen are eternal.[5]

Therefore gird up your minds, be sober, set your hope fully upon the grace that is coming to you at the revelation of Jesus Christ.[6] May the God of hope fill you with all joy and peace in believing, so that by the power of the Holy Spirit you may abound in hope.[7]

**1 Tim. 4:10.* [1]*1 Pet. 1:3, 4.* [2]*2 Pet. 3:13.* [3]*Heb. 10:36.* [4]*Rom. 8:24, 25.* [5]*2 Cor. 4:18.* [6]*1 Pet. 1:13.* [7]*Rom. 15:13.*

MAY 19

*Every one of you shall revere his mother and his father**

Honor your father and your mother, that your days may be long in the land which the Lord your God gives you.[1] Children, obey your parents in everything, for this pleases the Lord.[2] And Jesus went down with them and came to Nazareth, and was obedient to them.[3]

Hear, my son, your father's instruction, and reject not your mother's teaching; for they are a fair garland for your head, and pendants for your neck.[4] A wise son makes a glad father, but a foolish son is a sorrow to his mother.[5] Hearken to your father who begot you, and do not despise your mother when she is old . . . The father of the righteous will greatly rejoice . . . Let your father and mother be glad, let her who bore you rejoice.[6]

Fathers, do not provoke your children to anger, but bring them up in the discipline and instruction of the Lord.[7] Children ought not to lay up for their parents, but parents for their children.[8] If a widow has children or grandchildren, let them first learn their religious duty to their own family and make some return to their parents; for this is acceptable in the sight of God.[9]

**Lev. 19:3. [1]Ex. 20:12. [2]Col. 3:20. [3]Lk. 2:51. [4]Prov. 1:8, 9. [5]Prov. 10:1. [6]Prov. 23:22, 24, 25. [7]Eph. 6:4. [8]2 Cor. 12:14. [9]1 Tim. 5:4.*

*The word of God is living and active**

By faith we understand that the world was created by the word of God.[1] By the word of the Lord the heavens were made, and all their host by the breath of His mouth . . . For He spoke, and it came to be; He commanded, and it stood forth.[2]

For it is the God who said, 'Let light shine out of darkness,' who has shone in our hearts to give the light of the knowledge of the glory of God in the face of Christ.[3] I commend you to God and to the word of His grace, which is able to build you up and to give you the inheritance among all those who are sanctified.[4] Therefore . . . receive with meekness the implanted word, which is able to save your souls.[5]

For as the rain and the snow come down from heaven, and return not thither but water the earth, making it bring forth and sprout, giving seed to the sower and bread to the eater, so shall My word be that goes forth from My mouth; it shall not return to Me empty, but it shall accomplish that which I purpose, and prosper in the thing for which I sent it.[6]

**Heb. 4:12.* [1]*Heb. 11:3.* [2]*Ps. 33:6, 9.* [3]*2 Cor. 4:6.* [4]*Acts 20:32.* [5]*Jas. 1:21.* [6]*Is. 55:10, 11.*

MAY 21

*The purpose of the Lord**

In Him, according to the purpose of Him who accomplishes all things according to the counsel of His will, we who first hoped in Christ have been destined and appointed to live for the praise of His glory.[1] Whom I created for My glory.[2] So glorify God in your body.[3]

My chosen shall long enjoy the work of their hands. They shall not labor in vain, or bear children for calamity.[4] For we are His workmanship, created in Christ Jesus for good works, which God prepared beforehand, that we should walk in them.[5] As each has received a gift, employ it for one another, as good stewards of God's varied grace: . . . in order that in everything God may be glorified through Jesus Christ.[6]

For it was fitting that He, for whom and by whom all things exist, in bringing many sons to glory, should make the pioneer of their salvation perfect through suffering.[7] Therefore I endure everything for the sake of the elect, that they also may obtain the salvation which in Christ Jesus goes with eternal glory.[8] I do not run aimlessly.[9]

**Jas. 5:11.* [1]*Eph. 1:11, 12.* [2]*Is. 43:7.* [3]*1 Cor. 6:20.* [4]*Is. 65:22, 23.* [5]*Eph. 2:10.* [6]*1 Pet. 4:10, 11.* [7]*Heb. 2:10.* [8]*2 Tim. 2:10.* [9]*1 Cor. 9:26.*

*Think about these things**

The precious blood of Christ.[1] God . . . did not spare His own Son but gave Him up for us all.[2] In Him we have redemption through His blood, the forgiveness of our trespasses, according to the riches of His grace which He lavished upon us.[3] Truly no man can ransom himself, or give to God the price of his life, for the ransom of his life is costly.[4] To you therefore who believe, He is precious, but for those who do not believe, 'The very stone which the builders rejected has become the head of the corner.'[5]

How precious is Thy steadfast love, O God! The children of men take refuge in the shadow of Thy wings.[6] How precious to me are Thy thoughts, O God! How vast is the sum of them! If I would count them, they are more than the sand. When I awake, I am still with Thee.[7]

He has granted to us His precious and very great promises.[8] Not one of all the good promises which the Lord had made to the house of Israel had failed; all came to pass.[9] No distrust made Abraham waver concerning the promise of God, but he grew strong in his faith . . . fully convinced that God was able to do what He had promised.[10]

**Phil. 4:8. [1]1 Pet. 1:19. [2]Rom. 8:32. [3]Eph. 1:7, 8. [4]Ps. 49:7, 8. [5]1 Pet. 2:7. [6]Ps. 36:7. [7]Ps. 139:17, 18. [8]2 Pet. 1:4. [9]Josh. 21:45. [10]Rom. 4:20, 21.*

MAY 23

*That which is evil in Thy sight**

Teacher, which is the great commandment in the law? . . . You shall love the Lord your God with all your heart, and with all your soul, and with all your mind. . . . You shall love your neighbor as yourself.[1] A new commandment I give to you, that you love one another; even as I have loved you, that you also love one another.[2] Whoever knows what is right to do and fails to do it, for him it is sin.[3]

For the mind that is set on the flesh is hostile to God; it does not submit to God's law, indeed it cannot; and those who are in the flesh cannot please God.[4] Now the works of the flesh are plain: immorality, impurity, licentiousness, idolatry, sorcery, enmity, strife, jealousy, anger, selfishness, dissension, party spirit, envy, drunkenness, carousing, and the like. I warn you, as I warned you before, that those who do such things shall not inherit the kingdom of God.[5]

All wrongdoing is sin.[6] The devising of folly is sin.[7] Whatever does not proceed from faith is sin.[8] All these things I hate, says the Lord.[9] Against Thee, Thee only, have I sinned, and done that which is evil in Thy sight.[10]

**Ps. 51:4.* [1]*Mt. 22:36, 37, 39.* [2]*Jn. 13:34.* [3]*Jas. 4:17.* [4]*Rom. 8:7, 8.* [5]*Gal. 5:19–21.* [6]*1 Jn. 5:17.* [7]*Prov. 24:9.* [8]*Rom. 14:23.* [9]*Zech. 8:17.* [10]*Ps. 51:4.*

*The Lord God is my strength**

And behold, a young lion roared against Samson; and the Spirit of the Lord came mightily upon him, and he tore the lion asunder as one tears a kid.[1] They bound Samson with two new ropes . . . and the Spirit of the Lord came mightily upon him . . . and his bonds melted off his hands. And he found a fresh jawbone of an ass, and . . . with it he slew a thousand men.[2] Strong in the Lord and in the strength of His might.[3]

Delilah said to Samson, 'Please tell me wherein your great strength lies . . .'[4] And he said to her . . . If I be shaved, then my strength will leave me, and I shall become weak, and be like any other man.'[5] She made him sleep upon her knees; and she called a man, and had him shave off the seven locks of his head.[6] And the Philistines seized him.[7] Watch and pray that you may not enter into temptation; the spirit indeed is willing, but the flesh is weak.[8]

Then Samson called to the Lord and said, 'O Lord God, remember me, I pray Thee, and strengthen me, I pray Thee, only this once'.[9] On the day I called, Thou didst answer me, my strength of soul Thou didst increase.[10]

**Is. 12:2.* [1]*Judg. 14:5, 6.* [2]*Judg. 15:13–15.* [3]*Eph. 6:10.* [4]*Judg. 16:6.* [5]*Judg. 16:17.* [6]*Judg. 16:19.* [7]*Judg. 16:21.* [8]*Mt. 26:41.* [9]*Judg. 16:28.* [10]*Ps. 138:3.*

MAY 25

*The immeasurable riches of His grace**

The Lord your God turned the curse into a blessing for you, because the Lord your God loved you.[1] I will heal their faithlessness; I will love them freely, for My anger has turned from them.[2] I . . . blasphemed and persecuted and insulted Him; but . . . the grace of our Lord overflowed for me with the faith and love that are in Christ Jesus.[3]

Thou hast held back my life from the pit of destruction, for Thou hast cast all my sins behind Thy back.[4] For Thou hast delivered my soul from death, my eyes from tears, my feet from stumbling; I walk before the Lord in the land of the living.[5] Thou hast granted me life and steadfast love; and Thy care has preserved my spirit.[6]

Those who err in spirit will come to understanding, and those who murmur will accept instruction.[7] Let us then with confidence draw near to the throne of grace, that we may receive mercy and find grace to help in time of need.[8] For Thou, O Lord, art good and forgiving, abounding in steadfast love to all who call on Thee.[9]

**Eph.* 2:7. [1]*Deut.* 23:5. [2]*Hos.* 14:4. [3]*1 Tim.* 1:13, 14. [4]*Is.* 38:17. [5]*Ps.* 116:8, 9. [6]*Job* 10:12. [7]*Is.* 29:24. [8]*Heb.* 4:16. [9]*Ps.* 86:5.

*Our commonwealth is in heaven**

These all died in faith . . . having acknowledged that they were strangers and exiles on the earth. For people who speak thus make it clear that they are seeking a homeland . . . They desire a better country, that is, a heavenly one. Therefore God is not ashamed to be called their God, for He has prepared for them a city.[1] The city which has foundations, whose builder and maker is God.[2] For here we have no lasting city, but we seek the city which is to come.[3]

Do not lay up for yourselves treasures on earth, where moth and rust consume and where thieves break in and steal, but lay up for yourselves treasures in heaven . . . For where your treasure is, there will your heart be also.[4] If then you have been raised with Christ, seek the things that are above . . . Set your minds on things that are above, not on things that are on earth.[5]

Beloved, I beseech you as aliens and exiles to abstain from the passions of the flesh that wage war against your soul.[6] I do not pray that Thou shouldst take them out of the world, but that Thou shouldst keep them from the evil one. They are not of the world, even as I am not of the world.[7]

**Phil.* 3:20. [1]*Heb.* 11:13, 14, 16. [2]*Heb.* 11:10. [3]*Heb.* 13:14. [4]*Mt.* 6:19–21. [5]*Col.* 3:1, 2. [6]*1 Pet.* 2:11. [7]*Jn.* 17:15, 16.

MAY 27

*They cannot die any more**

The free gift of God is eternal life in Christ Jesus our Lord.[1] This is what He has promised us, eternal life.[2] And this life is in His Son. He who has the Son has life; he who has not the Son has not life.[3]

I am the resurrection and the life; he who believes in Me, though he die, yet shall he live, and whoever lives and believes in Me shall never die.[4] Because I live, you will live also.[5] And this is eternal life, that they know Thee the only true God, and Jesus Christ whom Thou hast sent.[6]

If we have died with Christ, we believe that we shall also live with Him.[7] You have died, and your life is hid with Christ in God. When Christ who is our life appears, then you also will appear with Him in glory.[8]

We know that if the earthly tent we live in is destroyed, we have a building from God, a house not made with hands, eternal in the heavens.[9] In Thy presence there is fullness of joy, in Thy right hand there are pleasures for evermore.[10] At home with the Lord.[11]

**Lk. 20:36. [1]Rom. 6:23. [2]1 Jn. 2:25. [3]1 Jn. 5:11, 12. [4]Jn. 11:25, 26. [5]Jn. 14:19. [6]Jn. 17:3. [7]Rom. 6:8. [8]Col. 3:3, 4. [9]2 Cor. 5:1. [10]Ps. 16:11. [11]2 Cor. 5:8.*

*The power of the Lord**

He was in the beginning with God; all things were made through Him, and without Him was not anything made that was made.[1] Upholding the universe by His word of power.[2] The men marveled, saying, 'What sort of man is this, that even winds and sea obey Him?'[3] With authority He commands even the unclean spirits, and they obey Him.[4] The blind receive their sight, the lame walk, lepers are cleansed, and the deaf hear, the dead are raised up.[5]

The reason the Son of God appeared was to destroy the works of the devil.[6] He disarmed the principalities and powers and made a public example of them, triumphing over them in Him.[7] Our Savior Christ Jesus, who abolished death and brought life and immortality to light through the gospel.[8] That through death He might destroy Him who has the power of death, that is, the devil, and deliver all those who through fear of death were subject to lifelong bondage.[9]

We did not follow cleverly devised myths when we made known to you the power and coming of our Lord Jesus Christ, but we were eye-witnesses of His majesty.[10]

**Lk. 5:17.* [1]*Jn. 1:2, 3.* [2]*Heb. 1:3.* [3]*Mt. 8:27.* [4]*Mk. 1:27.* [5]*Lk. 7:22.* [6]*1 Jn. 3:8.* [7]*Col. 2:15.* [8]*2 Tim. 1:10.* [9]*Heb. 2:14, 15.* [10]*2 Pet. 1:16.*

MAY 29

*Whoever loses his life for My sake will find it**

You know the grace of our Lord Jesus Christ, that though He was rich, yet for your sake He became poor, so that by His poverty you might become rich.[1] Though He was in the form of God, (He) did not count equality with God a thing to be grasped, but emptied Himself, taking the form of a servant, being born in the likeness of men.[2]

Jesus . . . said to him, 'One thing you still lack. Sell all that you have and distribute to the poor, and you will have treasure in heaven; and come, follow Me.' But when he heard this he became sad, for he was very rich.[3]

Peter began to say to Him, 'Lo, we have left everything and followed You.' Jesus said, 'Truly, I say to you, there is no one who has left house or brothers or sisters or mother or father or children or lands, for My sake and for the gospel, who will not receive a hundredfold now in this time . . . and in the age to come eternal life.'[4]

For His sake I have suffered the loss of all things, and count them as refuse, in order that I may gain Christ.[5] As poor, yet making many rich; as having nothing, and yet possessing everything.[6]

**Mt. 16:25.* [1]*2 Cor. 8:9.* [2]*Phil. 2:6, 7.* [3]*Lk. 18:22, 23.* [4]*Mk. 10:28–30.* [5]*Phil. 3:8.* [6]*2 Cor. 6:10.*

*Whoever speaks, as one who utters oracles of God**

As commissioned by God, in the sight of God we speak in Christ.[1] For what we preach is not ourselves, but Jesus Christ as Lord, with ourselves as your servants for Jesus' sake.[2] Not in plausible words of wisdom, but in demonstration of the Spirit and power, that your faith might not rest in the wisdom of men but in the power of God.[3]

In honor and dishonor, in ill repute and good repute.[4] Philip went down to a city of Samaria, and proclaimed to them the Christ. And the multitudes with one accord gave heed to what was said by Philip.[5] Up to this word they listened to Paul; then they lifted up their voices and said, 'Away with such a fellow from the earth! For he ought not to live.'[6]

As servants of God we commend ourselves in every way: . . . by . . . the Holy Spirit, genuine love, truthful speech, and the power of God.[7] Behold, I am making My words in your mouth a fire, and this people wood.[8] But we have this treasure in earthen vessels, to show that the transcendent power belongs to God and not to us.[9]

* *1 Pet. 4:11.* [1] *2 Cor. 2:17.* [2] *2 Cor. 4:5.* [3] *1 Cor. 2:4, 5.* [4] *2 Cor. 6:8.* [5] *Acts 8:5, 6.* [6] *Acts 22:22.* [7] *2 Cor. 6:4, 6, 7.* [8] *Jer. 5:14.* [9] *2 Cor. 4:7.*

MAY 31

*A time to die**

All the days of Methuselah were nine hundred and sixty-nine years; and he died.[1] No man has . . . authority over the day of death.[2] When Thou takest away their breath, they die and return to their dust.[3] And the dust returns to the earth as it was, and the spirit returns to God who gave it.[4]

As they were stoning Stephen, he prayed, 'Lord Jesus, receive my spirit.' . . . And when he had said this, he fell asleep.[5] To me to live is Christ, and to die is gain. . . . My desire is to depart and be with Christ, for that is far better.[6] Precious in the sight of the Lord is the death of His saints.[7] Even though I walk through the valley of the shadow of death, I fear no evil; for Thou art with me.[8]

But some one will ask, 'How are the dead raised? With what kind of body do they come?' You foolish man! What you sow does not come to life unless it dies. And what you sow is not the body which is to be, but a bare kernel, perhaps of wheat or of some other grain . . . So is it with the resurrection of the dead. What is sown is perishable, what is raised is imperishable. . . . It is sown a physical body, it is raised a spiritual body.[9]

Eccl. 3:2. [1]*Gen. 5:27.* [2]*Eccl. 8:8.* [3]*Ps. 104:29.* [4]*Eccl. 12:7.* [5]*Acts 7:59, 60.* [6]*Phil. 1:21, 23.* [7]*Ps. 116:15.* [8]*Ps. 23:4.* [9]*1 Cor. 15:35–37, 42, 44.*

JUNE 1

*God's Spirit dwells in you**

Do you not know that your body is a temple of the Holy Spirit within you, which you have from God?[1] Do you not realize that Jesus Christ is in you?[2] He yearns jealously over the spirit which He has made to dwell in us.[3] Do not quench the Spirit.[4] And do not grieve the Holy Spirit of God, in whom you were sealed for the day of redemption.[5]

If we live by the Spirit, let us also walk by the Spirit.[6] For God has not called us for uncleanness, but in holiness. Therefore whoever disregards this, disregards not man but God, who gives His Holy Spirit to you.[7] But the fruit of the Spirit is love, joy, peace, patience, kindness, goodness, faithfulness, gentleness, self-control; against such there is no law.[8]

May the God of hope fill you with all joy and peace in believing, so that by the power of the Holy Spirit you may abound in hope.[9] That according to the riches of His glory He may grant you to be strengthened with might through His Spirit in the inner man.[10]

* *1 Cor. 3:16.* [1] *1 Cor. 6:19.* [2] *2 Cor. 13:5.* [3] *Jas. 4:5.* [4] *1 Thess. 5:19.* [5] *Eph. 4:30.* [6] *Gal. 5:25.* [7] *1 Thess. 4:7, 8.* [8] *Gal. 5:22, 23.* [9] *Rom. 15:13.* [10] *Eph. 3:16.*

JUNE 2

*The cross of our Lord Jesus Christ**

If any man would come after Me, let him deny himself and take up his cross daily and follow Me.[1] He who does not take his cross and follow Me is not worthy of Me.[2] (He) cannot be My disciple.[3] For whoever is ashamed of Me and of My words, of him will the Son of man be ashamed when He comes in His glory.[4]

So they took Jesus, and He went out, bearing His own cross.[5] Despising the shame.[6] Obedient unto death, even death on a cross.[7] As they were marching out, they came upon a man of Cyrene, Simon by name; this man they compelled to carry His cross.[8] But far be it from me to glory except in the cross of our Lord Jesus Christ, by which the world has been crucified to me, and I to the world.[9]

I am not ashamed of the gospel: it is the power of God for salvation to every one who has faith.[10] For the word of the cross is folly to those who are perishing, but to us who are being saved it is the power of God.[11] We preach Christ crucified . . . the power of God and the wisdom of God.[12]

**Gal. 6:14.* [1]*Lk. 9:23.* [2]*Mt. 10:38.* [3]*Lk. 14:27.* [4]*Lk. 9:26.* [5]*Jn. 19:17.* [6]*Heb. 12:2.* [7]*Phil. 2:8.* [8]*Mt. 27:32.* [9]*Gal. 6:14.* [10]*Rom. 1:16.* [11]*1 Cor. 1:18.* [12]*1 Cor. 1:23, 24.*

*Praise the Lord!**

Blessed be the name of the Lord from this time forth and for evermore! From the rising of the sun to its setting the name of the Lord is to be praised![1] Praise the Lord from the heavens, praise Him in the heights! Praise Him, all His angels, praise Him, all His host![2] Young men and maidens together, old men and children! Let them praise the name of the Lord.[3] Let everything that breathes praise the Lord![4] Bless the Lord, O my soul; and all that is within me, bless His holy name![5]

Praise Him according to His exceeding greatness![6] The Lord is high above all nations, and His glory above the heavens.[7] O Lord, our Lord, how majestic is Thy name in all the earth![8] Power belongs to God.[9] Holiness befits Thy house, O Lord, for evermore.[10] A God of faithfulness and without iniquity, just and right is He.[11] None can compare with Thee![12]

Praise Him for His mighty deeds.[13] O Lord, how manifold are Thy works![14] Thou didst set the earth on its foundations, so that it should never be shaken.[15] It is He that made us, and we are His; we are His people and the sheep of His pasture.[16] He has wondrously shown His steadfast love to me.[17]

**Ps. 113:1.* [1]*Ps. 113:2, 3.* [2]*Ps. 148:1, 2.* [3]*Ps. 148:12, 13.* [4]*Ps. 150:6.* [5]*Ps. 103:1.* [6]*Ps. 150:2.* [7]*Ps. 113:4.* [8]*Ps. 8:1.* [9]*Ps. 62:11.* [10]*Ps. 93:5.* [11]*Deut. 32:4.* [12]*Ps. 40:5.* [13]*Ps. 150:2.* [14]*Ps. 104:24.* [15]*Ps. 104:5.* [16]*Ps. 100:3.* [17]*Ps. 31:21.*

JUNE 4

*Our fellowship is with the Father**

Therefore come out from them, and be separate . . . says the Lord . . . then I will welcome you, and I will be a father to you, and you shall be My sons and daughters.[1] Because you are sons, God has sent the Spirit of His Son into our hearts, crying, 'Abba! Father!'[2] Our Father who art in heaven.[3]

See what love the Father has given us, that we should be called children of God.[4] The Father Himself loves you, because you have loved Me and have believed that I came from the Father.[5] No one knows the Father except the Son and any one to whom the Son chooses to reveal Him.[6] So that whatever you ask the Father in My name, He may give it to you.[7] For your Father knows what you need before you ask Him.[8]

My son, do not regard lightly the discipline of the Lord . . . For the Lord disciplines him whom He loves, and chastises every son whom He receives.[9] We have had earthly fathers to discipline us and we respected them. Shall we not much more be subject to the Father of spirits and live?[10]

**1 Jn. 1:3. [1]2 Cor. 6:17, 18. [2]Gal. 4:6. [3]Mt. 6:9. [4]1 Jn. 3:1. [5]Jn. 16:27. [6]Mt. 11:27. [7]Jn. 15:16. [8]Mt. 6:8. [9]Heb. 12:5, 6. [10]Heb. 12:9.*

JUNE 5

*Shun immorality**

How can a young man keep his way pure? By guarding it according to Thy word.[1] For from within, out of the heart of man come evil thoughts . . . fornication . . . adultery.[2]

Every one who looks at a woman lustfully has already committed adultery with her in his heart.[3] I have made a covenant with my eyes.[4] Do not desire her beauty in your heart, and do not let her capture you with her eyelashes.[5] Give not your strength to women, your ways to those who destroy kings.[6] Let not your heart turn aside to her ways, do not stray into her paths.[7] I found more bitter than death the woman whose heart is snares and nets, and whose hands are fetters; he who pleases God escapes her.[8] Passion makes the bones rot.[9]

Abstain . . . from unchastity.[10] You shall not commit adultery.[11] How . . . can I do this great wickedness, and sin against God?[12]

Create in me a clean heart, O God.[13] The law of the Spirit of life in Christ Jesus has set me free from the law of sin and death.[14] I have laid up Thy word in my heart, that I might not sin against Thee.[15]

** 1 Cor. 6:18. [1]Ps. 119:9. [2]Mk. 7:21. [3]Mt. 5:28. [4]Job 31:1. [5]Prov. 6:25. [6]Prov. 31:3. [7]Prov. 7:25. [8]Eccl. 7:26. [9]Prov. 14:30. [10]Acts 15:20. [11]Ex. 20:14. [12]Gen. 39:9. [13]Ps. 51:10. [14]Rom. 8:2. [15]Ps. 119:11.*

JUNE 6

*Work out your own salvation**

From the day we heard of it, we have not ceased to pray for you, asking that you may be filled with the knowledge of His will in all spiritual wisdom and understanding, to lead a life worthy of the Lord, fully pleasing to Him, bearing fruit in every good work and increasing in the knowledge of God.[1]

Examine yourselves, to see whether you are holding to your faith. Test yourselves.[2] Yield yourselves to God as men who have been brought from death to life, and your members to God as instruments of righteousness.[3] Keep yourselves in the love of God.[4] Keep yourselves from idols.[5] Humble yourselves . . . under the mighty hand of God, that in due time He may exalt you.[6]

Therefore, my beloved . . . work out your own salvation with fear and trembling; for God is at work in you, both to will and to work for His good pleasure.[7] And I am sure that He who began a good work in you will bring it to completion at the day of Jesus Christ.[8]

**Phil. 2:12.* [1]*Col. 1:9, 10.* [2]*2 Cor. 13:5.* [3]*Rom. 6:13.* [4]*Jude 21.* [5]*1 Jn. 5:21.* [6]*1 Pet. 5:6.* [7]*Phil. 2:12, 13.* [8]*Phil. 1:6.*

*The light of life**

This is the message we have heard from Him and proclaim to you, that God is light and in Him is no darkness at all.[1] And we know that the Son of God has come and has given us understanding, to know Him who is true. . . . This is the true God and eternal life.[2] In Him was life, and the life was the light of men.[3]

Jesus said to them, 'The light is with you for a little longer. Walk while you have the light, lest the darkness overtake you; he who walks in the darkness does not know where he goes. While you have the light, believe in the light, that you may become sons of light.'[4] But you are a chosen race, a royal priesthood, a holy nation, God's own people, that you may declare the wonderful deeds of Him who called you out of darkness into His marvelous light.[5]

For with Thee is the fountain of life; in Thy light do we see light.[6] The light shines in the darkness, and the darkness has not overcome it.[7] Rejoice not over me, O my enemy; when I fall, I shall rise; when I sit in darkness, the Lord will be a light to me.[8]

Jn. 8:12. [1]1 Jn. 1:5. [2]1 Jn. 5:20. [3]Jn. 1:4. [4]Jn. 12:35, 36. [5]1 Pet. 2:9. [6]Ps. 36:9. [7]Jn. 1:5. [8]Mic. 7:8.

JUNE 8

*All things are possible to him who believes**

Jesus rebuked him, and the demon came out of him, and the boy was cured instantly. Then the disciples came to Jesus privately and said, 'Why could we not cast it out?' He said to them, 'Because of your little faith'.[1] Truly, truly, I say to you, he who believes in Me will also do the works that I do; and greater works than these will he do, because I go to the Father. Whatever you ask in My name, I will do it, that the Father may be glorified in the Son.[2]

For whatever is born of God overcomes the world; and this is the victory that overcomes the world, our faith.[3] Who through faith conquered kingdoms, enforced justice, received promises, stopped the mouths of lions, quenched raging fire, escaped the edge of the sword, won strength out of weakness, became mighty in war, put foreign armies to flight.[4]

Behold, I have given you authority to tread upon serpents and scorpions, and over all the power of the enemy; and nothing shall hurt you.[5] Therefore, brethren, since we have confidence to enter the sanctuary by the blood of Jesus . . . let us draw near with a true heart in full assurance of faith, with our hearts sprinkled clean from an evil conscience.[6]

**Mk. 9:23.* [1]*Mt. 17:18–20.* [2]*Jn. 14:12, 13.* [3]*1 Jn. 5:4.* [4]*Heb. 11:33, 34.* [5]*Lk. 10:19.* [6]*Heb. 10:19, 22.*

JUNE 9

*Present your bodies . . . to God**

I appeal to you therefore, brethren, by the mercies of God, to present your bodies as a living sacrifice, holy and acceptable to God.[1]

The body is not meant for immorality, but for the Lord, and the Lord for the body.[2] Do you not know that your body is a temple of the Holy Spirit within you?[3] Let not sin therefore reign in your mortal bodies, to make you obey their passions.[4]

Every athlete exercises self-control in all things. They do it to receive a perishable wreath, but we an imperishable. Well . . . I pommel my body and subdue it, lest after preaching to others I myself should be disqualified.[5] Shun immorality.[6] Shun youthful passions.[7] Do not get drunk with wine, for that is debauchery.[8] Love not sleep, lest you come to poverty.[9] For the drunkard and the glutton will come to poverty, and drowsiness will clothe a man with rags.[10]

May the God of peace Himself sanctify you wholly; and may your spirit and soul and body be kept sound and blameless at the coming of our Lord Jesus Christ. He who calls you is faithful, and He will do it.[11]

**Rom. 12:1.* [1]*Rom. 12:1.* [2]*1 Cor. 6:13.* [3]*1 Cor. 6:19.* [4]*Rom. 6:12.* [5]*1 Cor. 9:25–27.* [6]*1 Cor. 6:18.* [7]*2 Tim. 2:22.* [8]*Eph. 5:18.* [9]*Prov. 20:13.* [10]*Prov. 23:21.* [11]*1 Thess. 5:23, 24.*

JUNE 10

*The Lord your God will . . . have compassion upon you**

Jesus . . . said, 'I have compassion on the crowd, because they have been with Me now three days, and have nothing to eat; and I am unwilling to send them away hungry, lest they faint on the way.[1] The needy shall not always be forgotten, and the hope of the poor shall not perish for ever.[2]

As Jesus went ashore He saw a great throng; and He had compassion on them, and healed their sick.[3] In all their affliction He was afflicted, and the angel of His presence saved them.[4]

As Jesus drew near . . . behold, a man who had died was being carried out, the only son of his mother, and she was a widow . . . And when the Lord saw her, He had compassion on her, and said to her, 'Do not weep.'[5] Surely He has borne our griefs and carried our sorrows.[6]

When He saw the crowds, he had compassion for them, because they were harassed and helpless, like sheep without a shepherd.[7] He will feed His flock like a shepherd, He will gather the lambs in His arms, He will carry them in His bosom, and gently lead those that are with young.[8]

**Deut. 30:3. [1]Mt. 15:32. [2]Ps. 9:18. [3]Mt. 14:14. [4]Is. 63:9. [5]Lk. 7:12, 13. [6]Is. 53:4. [7]Mt. 9:36. [8]Is. 40:11.*

JUNE 11

*Full of the Holy Spirit and of faith**

Barnabas (which means, Son of encouragement) . . . sold a field which belonged to him, and brought the money and laid it at the apostles' feet.[1] God loves a cheerful giver.[2]

Barnabas took Paul, and brought him to the apostles, and declared to them how on the road he had seen the Lord, who spoke to him, and how at Damascus he had preached boldly in the name of Jesus.[3] Welcome one another, therefore, as Christ has welcomed you, for the glory of God.[4]

They sent Barnabas to Antioch. When he came and saw the grace of God, he was glad; and he exhorted them all to remain faithful to the Lord with steadfast purpose; for he was a good man, full of the Holy Spirit and of faith.[5] Let us consider how to stir up one another to love and good works.[6]

The Holy Spirit said, 'Set apart for Me Barnabas and Saul for the work to which I have called them.' Then after fasting and praying they laid their hands on them and sent them off.[7] Barnabas and Paul, men who have risked their lives for the sake of our Lord Jesus Christ.[8]

**Acts 11:24.* [1]*Acts 4:36, 37.* [2]*2 Cor. 9:7.* [3]*Acts 9:27.* [4]*Rom. 15:7.* [5]*Acts 11:22–24.* [6]*Heb. 10:24.* [7]*Acts 13:2, 3* [8]*Acts 15:25, 26.*

JUNE 12

*Let not your hearts be troubled**

Martha, Martha, you are anxious and troubled about many things.[1] He said to them, 'Why are you afraid, O men of little faith?' Then He rose and rebuked the winds and the sea; and there was a great calm.[2]

When you hear of wars and rumors of wars, do not be alarmed.[3] You will not fear the terror of the night, nor the arrow that flies by day, nor the pestilence that stalks in darkness, nor the destruction that wastes at noonday.[4] He is not afraid of evil tidings; his heart is firm, trusting in the Lord.[5] Cast all your anxieties on Him, for He cares about you.[6]

When the cares of my heart are many, Thy consolations cheer my soul.[7] God is not a God of confusion but of peace.[8] Be still before the Lord, and wait patiently for Him; fret not yourself.[9] In quietness and in trust shall be your strength.[10]

Thou dost keep him in perfect peace, whose mind is stayed on Thee, because he trusts in Thee. Trust in the Lord for ever, for the Lord God is an everlasting rock.[11] Be still, and know that I am God.[12]

**Jn. 14:1.* [1]*Lk. 10:41.* [2]*Mt. 8:26.* [3]*Mk. 13:7.* [4]*Ps. 91:5, 6.* [5]*Ps. 112:7.* [6]*1 Pet. 5:7.* [7]*Ps. 94:19.* [8]*1 Cor. 14:33.* [9]*Ps. 37:7.* [10]*Is. 30:15.* [11]*Is. 26:3, 4.* [12]*Ps. 46:10.*

*How can a man be just before God?**

If one wished to contend with Him, one could not answer Him once in a thousand times.[1] No human being will be justified in His sight by works of the law . . . Since all have sinned and fall short of the glory of God, they are justified by His grace as a gift, through . . . Christ Jesus.[2] One man's act of righteousness leads to acquittal and life for all men.[3]

Justified by His grace.[4] And this is not your own doing, it is the gift of God.[5] Out of the great love with which He loved us.[6]

Justified by His blood.[7] For Christ . . . died for sins once for all, the righteous for the unrighteous, that He might bring us to God.[8]

Justified by faith.[9] He believed the Lord; and He reckoned it to him as righteousness.[10] Not having a righteousness of my own, . . . but that which is through faith in Christ.[11]

Who shall bring any charge against God's elect? It is God who justifies; who is to condemn? Is it Christ Jesus, who died . . . who . . . intercedes for us?[12] He who vindicates me is near . . . Who will declare me guilty?[13]

**Job 9:2. [1]Job 9:3. [2]Rom. 3:20, 23, 24. [3]Rom. 5:18. [4]Tit. 3:7. [5]Eph. 2:8. [6]Eph. 2:4. [7]Rom. 5:9. [8]1 Pet. 3:18. [9]Rom. 5:1. [10]Gen. 15:6. [11]Phil. 3:9. [12]Rom. 8:33, 34. [13]Is. 50:8, 9.*

JUNE 14

*Put on the Lord Jesus Christ**

And the son said . . . 'Father, I have sinned against heaven and before you; I am no longer worthy to be called your son.' But the father said to his servants, 'Bring quickly the best robe, and put it on him; and put a ring on his hand, and shoes on his feet.'[1]

All our righteous deeds are like a polluted garment.[2] I will greatly rejoice in the Lord . . . for He has clothed me with the garments of salvation, He has covered me with the robe of righteousness.[3]

Put on . . . as God's chosen ones, holy and beloved, compassion, kindness, lowliness, meekness, and patience . . . And above all these put on love, which binds everything together in perfect harmony.[4] Clothe yourselves, all of you, with humility.[5] Put on your strength, O Zion.[6] The mantle of praise instead of a faint spirit.[7] The armor of light.[8]

Who are these, clothed in white robes? . . . These are they who have come out of the great tribulation; they have washed their robes and made them white in the blood of the Lamb. Therefore are they before the throne of God, and serve Him day and night within His temple.[9]

**Rom. 13:14.* [1]*Lk. 15:21, 22.* [2]*Is. 64:6.* [3]*Is. 61:10.* [4]*Col. 3:12, 14.* [5]*1 Pet. 5:5.* [6]*Is. 52:1.* [7]*Is. 61:3.* [8]*Rom. 13:12.* [9]*Rev. 7:13–15.*

*What is your life?**

The years of our life are threescore and ten, or even by reason of strength fourscore; yet their span is but toil and trouble; they are soon gone, and we fly away.[1] For you are a mist that appears for a little time and then vanishes.[2] So teach us to number our days that we may get a heart of wisdom.[3]

A man's life does not consist in the abundance of his possessions.[4] Man shall not live by bread alone, but by every word that proceeds from the mouth of God.[5] Therefore I tell you, do not be anxious about your life, what you shall eat or what you shall drink, nor about your body, what you shall put on. Is not life more than food, and the body more than clothing?[6]

Your life is hid with Christ in God.[7] None of us lives to himself, and none of us dies to himself. If we live, we live to the Lord, and if we die, we die to the Lord; so then, whether we live or whether we die, we are the Lord's.[8] To me to live is Christ, and to die is gain.[9] Making the most of the time, because the days are evil.[10]

**Jas. 4:14.* [1]*Ps. 90:10.* [2]*Jas. 4:14.* [3]*Ps. 90:12.* [4]*Lk. 12:15.* [5]*Mt. 4:4.* [6]*Mt. 6:25.* [7]*Col. 3:3.* [8]*Rom. 14:7, 8.* [9]*Phil. 1:21.* [10]*Eph. 5:16.*

JUNE 16

*Christ loved the church**

And God . . . has made Him the Head over all things for the church, which is His body, the fulness of Him who fills all in all.[1] For just as the body is one and has many members, and all the members of the body, though many, are one body, so it is with Christ. For by one Spirit we were all baptized into one body.[2]

Husbands, love your wives, as Christ loved the church and gave Himself up for her, that He might sanctify her, having cleansed her by the washing of water with the word, that the church might be presented before Him in splendor, without spot or wrinkle or any such thing, that she might be holy and without blemish.[3]

You are . . . God's building.[4] Built upon the foundation of the apostles and prophets, Christ Jesus Himself being the chief cornerstone, in whom the whole structure is joined together and grows into a holy temple in the Lord; in whom you also are built into it for a dwelling place of God in the Spirit.[5] For no other foundation can anyone lay than that which is laid, which is Jesus Christ.[6]

**Eph. 5:25.* [1]*Eph. 1:22, 23.* [2]*1 Cor. 12:12, 13.* [3]*Eph. 5:25–27.* [4]*1 Cor. 3:9.* [5]*Eph. 2:20–22.* [6]*1 Cor. 3:11.*

*When you pass through the waters I will be with you**

And the patriarchs, jealous of Joseph, sold him into Egypt; but God was with Him, and rescued him out of all his afflictions, and gave him favor and wisdom before Pharaoh, king of Egypt.[1] Those who wait for the Lord shall possess the land.[2]

So Peter was kept in prison; but earnest prayer for him was made to God by the church.[3] They cried to the Lord in their trouble, and . . . He brought them out of darkness and gloom, and broke their bonds asunder. Let them thank the Lord for His steadfast love . . . for He shatters the doors of bronze, and cuts in two the bars of iron.[4]

I am already on the point of being sacrificed; the time of my departure has come.[5] At my first defense no one took my part; all deserted me. May it not be charged against them! But the Lord stood by me and gave me strength to proclaim the word fully.[6] Even though I walk through the valley of the shadow of death, I fear no evil; for Thou art with me; Thy rod and Thy staff, they comfort me.[7] My presence will go with you, and I will give you rest.[8]

**Is.* 43:2. [1]*Acts* 7:9, 10. [2]*Ps.* 37:9. [3]*Acts* 12:5. [4]*Ps.* 107:13–16 [5]2 *Tim.* 4:6. [6]2 *Tim.* 4:16, 17. [7]*Ps.* 23:4. [8]*Ex.* 33:14.

JUNE 18

*Seek and you will find**

The kingdom of heaven is like treasure hidden in a field, which a man found and covered up; then in his joy he goes and sells all that he has and buys that field. Again, the kingdom of heaven is like a merchant in search of fine pearls, who, on finding one pearl of great value, went and sold all that he had and bought it.[1]

Seek the Lord while He may be found, call upon Him while He is near.[2] Philip . . . said to Nathanael, 'We have found Him of whom Moses in the law and also the prophets wrote, Jesus of Nazareth, the son of Joseph.' Nathanael said to him, 'Can anything good come out of Nazareth?' Philip said to him, 'Come and see.'[3]

Those who seek me diligently find me.[4] He who finds me finds life and obtains favor from the Lord.[5] Then you will understand the fear of the Lord and find the knowledge of God.[6]

I am the door; if any one enters by Me, he will be saved, and will go in and out and find pasture.[7] And you will find rest for your souls.[8]

**Mt. 7:7.* [1]*Mt. 13:44–46.* [2]*Is. 55:6.* [3]*Jn. 1:45, 46.* [4]*Prov. 8:17.* [5]*Prov. 8:35.* [6]*Prov. 2:5.* [7]*Jn. 10:9.* [8]*Mt. 11:29.*

*Jesus Christ—He is Lord of all**

He is before all things, and in Him all things hold together. He is the Head of the body, the church; He is the beginning, the first-born from the dead, that in everything He might be pre-eminent.[1] That at the name of Jesus every knee should bow, in heaven and on earth and under the earth, and every tongue confess that Jesus Christ is Lord, to the glory of God the Father.[2]

You call me Teacher and Lord; and you are right, for so I am.[3] Why do you call Me Lord, Lord, and not do what I tell you?[4] There came a voice to him, 'Rise, Peter; kill and eat.' But Peter said, 'No, Lord; for I have never eaten anything that is common or unclean.'[5] Another said, 'I will follow You, Lord; but let me first say farewell to those at my home.'[6]

His mother said to the servants, 'Do whatever He tells you.'[7] Therefore, as the Holy Spirit says, 'Today, when you hear His voice, do not harden your hearts.'[8] Therefore do not be foolish, but understand what the will of the Lord is.[9] And try to learn what is pleasing to the Lord.[10]

**Acts 10:36.* [1]*Col. 1:17, 18.* [2]*Phil. 2:10, 11.* [3]*Jn. 13:13.* [4]*Lk. 6:46.* [5]*Acts 10:13, 14.* [6]*Lk. 9:61.* [7]*Jn. 2:5.* [8]*Heb. 3:7, 8.* [9]*Eph. 5:17.* [10]*Eph. 5:10.*

JUNE 20

*My brethren, whom I love and long for**

God is faithful, by whom you were called into the fellowship of His Son, Jesus Christ our Lord.[1] For by one Spirit we were all baptized into one body—Jews or Greeks, slaves or free—and all were made to drink of one Spirit.[2] So then you are no longer strangers and sojourners, but you are fellow citizens with the saints and members of the household of God.[3]

When the day of Pentecost had come, they were all together in one place.[4] And they devoted themselves to the apostles' teaching and fellowship, to the breaking of bread and the prayers.[5] Now the company of those who believed were of one heart and soul . . . and great grace was upon them all.[6] On the second day we came to Puteoli. There we found brethren, and were invited to stay with them for seven days. And so we came to Rome.[7]

So if there is any encouragement in Christ, any incentive of love, any participation in the Spirit, any affection and sympathy, complete my joy by being of the same mind, having the same love, being in full accord and of one mind.[8] As for the saints in the land, they are the noble, in whom is all my delight.[9]

**Phil. 4:1.* [1]*1 Cor. 1:9.* [2]*1 Cor. 12:13.* [3]*Eph. 2:19.* [4]*Acts 2:1.* [5]*Acts 2:42.* [6]*Acts 4:32, 33.* [7]*Acts 28:13, 14.* [8]*Phil. 2:1, 2.* [9]*Ps. 16:3.*

*Make me to know Thy ways, O Lord; teach me Thy paths**

Thy word is a lamp to my feet and a light to my path.[1] This book of the law shall not depart out of your mouth, but you shall meditate on it day and night, . . . for then you shall make your way prosperous, and then you shall have good success.[2] Learn . . . to live according to scripture.[3]

And behold, . . . a minister of Candace the queen of the Ethiopians . . . was returning; seated in his chariot, he was reading the prophet Isaiah. And the Spirit said to Philip, 'Go up and join this chariot.' So Philip ran to him.[4] Now after these events Paul resolved in the Spirit to pass through Macedonia and Achaia and go to Jerusalem, saying, 'After I have been there, I must also see Rome.'[5] For all who are led by the Spirit of God are sons of God.[6]

Take delight in the Lord, and He will give you the desires of your heart. Commit your way to the Lord; trust in Him, and He will act.[7] I will instruct you and teach you the way you should go; I will counsel you with My eye upon you.[8]

**Ps. 25:4.* [1]*Ps. 119:105.* [2]*Josh. 1:8.* [3]*1 Cor. 4:6.* [4]*Acts 8:27–30.* [5]*Acts 19:21.* [6]*Rom. 8:14.* [7]*Ps. 37:4, 5.* [8]*Ps. 32:8.*

JUNE 22

*I AM WHO I AM**

Have you not known? Have you not heard? The Lord is the everlasting God, the Creator of the ends of the earth.[1] I am the Lord, your Holy One, the Creator of Israel.[2]

Thou, O Lord, art our Father.[3] Father of the fatherless and protector of widows is God in His holy habitation.[4] As a father pities his children, so the Lord pities those who fear Him.[5]

They remembered that God was their rock, the Most High God their Redeemer.[6] Their Redeemer is strong; the Lord of hosts is His name. He will surely plead their cause, that He may give rest to the earth.[7] Then all flesh shall know that I am the Lord your Savior, and your Redeemer, the Mighty One of Jacob.[8]

The heavens declare His righteousness, for God Himself is Judge![9] Shall not the Judge of all the earth do right?[10] O the depth of the riches and wisdom and knowledge of God! How unsearchable are His judgments and how inscrutable His ways![11]

The Lord is the true God; He is the living God and the everlasting King.[12] Now I . . . praise and extol and honor the King of heaven; for all His works are right and His ways are just.[13]

**Ex. 3:14.* [1]*Is. 40:28.* [2]*Is. 43:15.* [3]*Is. 63:16.* [4]*Ps. 68:5.* [5]*Ps. 103:13.* [6]*Ps. 78:35.* [7]*Jer. 50:34.* [8]*Is. 49:26.* [9]*Ps. 50:6.* [10]*Gen. 18:25.* [11]*Rom. 11:33.* [12]*Jer. 10:10.* [13]*Dan. 4:37.*

JUNE 23

*You wicked and slothful servant!**

How long will you lie there, O sluggard? When will you arise from your sleep? A little sleep, a little slumber, a little folding of the hands to rest, and poverty will come upon you like a vagabond, and want like an armed man.[1] The sluggard does not plow in the autumn; he will seek at harvest and have nothing.[2] Through sloth the roof sinks in, and through indolence the house leaks.[3] Go to the ant, O sluggard; consider her ways, and be wise.[4]

We desire each one of you to show the same earnestness in realizing the full assurance of hope until the end, so that you may not be sluggish, but imitators of those who through faith and patience inherit the promises.[5] How long will you be slack to go in and take possession of the land, which the Lord . . . has given you?[6]

It is full time now for you to wake from sleep. For salvation is nearer to us now than when we first believed; the night is far gone, the day is at hand. Let us then cast off the works of darkness and put on the armor of light.[7] Making the most of the time, because the days are evil.[8]

**Mt. 25:26.* [1]*Prov. 6:9–11.* [2]*Prov. 20:4.* [3]*Eccl. 10:18.* [4]*Prov. 6:6.* [5]*Heb. 6:11, 12.* [6]*Josh. 18:3.* [7]*Rom. 13:11, 12.* [8]*Eph. 5:16.*

JUNE 24

*There was a man sent from God, whose name was John**

Jesus began to speak to the crowds concerning John: 'What did you go out into the wilderness to behold? A reed shaken by the wind?'[1] John said therefore to the multitudes that came out to be baptized by him, 'You brood of vipers! Who warned you to flee from the wrath to come? Bear fruits that befit repentance.'[2]

Why then did you go out? To see a man clothed in soft raiment? Behold, those who wear soft raiment are in kings' houses.[3] Now John wore a garment of camel's hair, and a leather girdle around his waist; and his food was locusts and wild honey.[4]

Why then did you go out? To see a prophet? Yes, I tell you, and more than a prophet . . . There has risen no one greater than John the Baptist.[5] He was a burning and shining lamp.[6] The voice of one crying in the wilderness, 'Make straight the way of the Lord'.[7] And John looked at Jesus as He walked, and said, Behold, the Lamb of God![8] He who has the bride is the bridegroom; the friend of the bridegroom, who stands and hears him, rejoices greatly at the bridegroom's voice; therefore this joy of mine is now full. He must increase, but I must decrease.[9]

**Jn. 1:6.* [1]*Mt. 11:7.* [2]*Lk. 3:7, 8.* [3]*Mt. 11:8.* [4]*Mt. 3:4.* [5]*Mt. 11:9, 11.* [6]*Jn. 5:35.* [7]*Jn. 1:23.* [8]*Jn. 1:36.* [9]*Jn. 3:29, 30.*

*The time for . . . rewarding Thy servants**

The work of a man's hand comes back to him.[1] For we must all appear before the judgment seat of Christ, so that each one may receive good or evil, according to what he has done in the body.[2]

Each man's work will become manifest; for the Day will disclose it . . . and the fire will test what sort of work each one has done. If the work which any man has built on the foundation survives, he will receive a reward. If any man's work is burned up, he will suffer loss, though he himself will be saved, but only as through fire.[3]

Therefore do not pronounce judgment before the time, before the Lord comes, who will bring to light the things now hidden in darkness and will disclose the purposes of the heart.[4] Each of us shall give account of himself to God.[5]

Well done, good and faithful servant; you have been faithful over a little, I will set you over much; enter into the joy of your master.[6] And those who are wise shall shine like the brightness of the firmament; and those who turn many to righteousness, like the stars for ever and ever.[7]

**Rev. 11:18.* [1]*Prov. 12:14.* [2]*2 Cor. 5:10.* [3]*1 Cor. 3:13–15.* [4]*1 Cor. 4:5.* [5]*Rom. 14:12.* [6]*Mt. 25:21.* [7]*Dan. 12:3.*

JUNE 26

*Call upon Me in the day of trouble**

Hear my prayer, O Lord; let my cry come to Thee! Do not hide Thy face from me in the day of my distress! Incline Thy ear to me; answer me speedily in the day when I call![1]

And the king said to me, 'Why is your face sad, seeing you are not sick? This is nothing else but sadness of the heart . . . For what do you make request?' So I prayed to the God of heaven. And I said to the king, 'If it pleases the king . . . that you send me to Judah, to the city of my fathers' sepulchres, that I may rebuild it' . . . So it pleased the king to send me.[2] Then Jonah prayed to the Lord his God from the belly of the fish . . . And the Lord spoke to the fish, and it vomited out Jonah upon the dry land.[3] So Peter . . . walked on the water and came to Jesus; but when he saw the wind, he was afraid, and beginning to sink he cried out, Lord, save me. Jesus immediately reached out His hand and caught him.[4]

Let us then with confidence draw near to the throne of grace, that we may receive mercy and find grace to help in time of need.[5]

**Ps. 50:15.* [1]*Ps. 102:1, 2.* [2]*Neh. 2:2, 4–6.* [3]*Jon. 2:1, 10.* [4]*Mt. 14:29, 30, 31.* [5]*Heb. 4:16.*

*Each tree is known by its own fruit**

My beloved had a vineyard on a very fertile hill. He digged it and cleared it of stones, and planted it with choice vines; he built a watchtower in the midst of it, and hewed out a wine vat in it; and he looked for it to yield grapes, but it yielded wild grapes.[1]

But the fruit of the Spirit is love, joy, peace, patience, kindness, goodness, faithfulness, gentleness, self-control; against such there is no law.[2] We have not ceased to pray for you, asking that you may . . . lead a life worthy of the Lord, fully pleasing to Him, bearing fruit in every good work and increasing in the knowledge of God.[3] Instead of the thorn shall come up the cypress; instead of the brier shall come up the myrtle; and it shall be to the Lord for a memorial, for an everlasting sign which shall not be cut off.[4]

Abide in Me, and I in you. As the branch cannot bear fruit by itself, unless it abides in the vine, neither can you, unless you abide in Me . . . For apart from Me you can do nothing.[5] From Me comes your fruit.[6]

**Lk. 6:44.* [1]*Is. 5:1, 2.* [2]*Gal. 5:22, 23.* [3]*Col. 1:9, 10.* [4]*Is. 55:13.* [5]*Jn. 15:4, 5.* [6]*Hos. 14:8.*

JUNE 28

*Worthy of the kingdom**

Do you not know that the unrighteous will not inherit the kingdom of God?[1] Be sure of this, that no immoral or impure man, or one who is covetous (that is, an idolater), has any inheritance in the kingdom of Christ and of God.[2] I warn you, as I warned you before, that those who do such things shall not inherit the kingdom of God.[3] Jesus came into Galilee, preaching the gospel of God, and saying, The time is fulfilled, and the kingdom of God is at hand; repent, and believe in the gospel.[4]

Jesus answered him, 'Truly, truly, I say to you, unless one is born anew, he cannot see the kingdom of God.' Nicodemus said to Him, 'How can a man be born when he is old? Can he enter a second time into his mother's womb and be born?' Jesus answered, 'Truly, truly, I say to you, unless one is born of water and the Spirit, he cannot enter the kingdom of God. That which is born of the flesh is flesh, and that which is born of the Spirit is spirit. Do not marvel that I said to you, "You must be born anew".'[5] I tell you this, brethren: flesh and blood cannot inherit the kingdom of God.[6]

**2 Thess. 1:5.* [1]*1 Cor. 6:9.* [2]*Eph. 5:5.* [3]*Gal. 5:21.* [4]*Mk. 1:14, 15.* [5]*Jn. 3:3–7.* [6]*1 Cor. 15:50.*

*Simon Peter, a servant and apostle of Jesus Christ**

Jesus said to Simon, 'Put out into the deep and let down your nets for a catch.' And Simon answered, 'Master, we toiled all night and took nothing! But at Your word I will let down the nets.' And when they had done this, they enclosed a great shoal of fish . . . When Simon Peter saw it, he fell down at Jesus' knees, saying, 'Depart from me, for I am a sinful man, O Lord.'[1]

Jesus said to them, 'But who do you say that I am?' Simon Peter replied, 'You are the Christ, the Son of the living God.'[2] Jesus said to the twelve, 'Will you also go away?' Simon Peter answered Him, 'Lord, to whom shall we go? You have the words of eternal life.[3]

The bystanders came up and said to Peter, 'Certainly you are also one of them, for your accent betrays you.' Then he began to . . . swear, 'I do not know the man.' And immediately the cock crowed. And Peter remembered the saying of Jesus . . . and he went out and wept bitterly.[4]

Jesus said to him the third time, 'Simon, son of John, do you love Me?' Peter was grieved because He said to him the third time, 'Do you love Me?' And he said to Him, 'Lord, You know everything; You know that I love You.'[5]

**2 Pet. 1:1. [1]Lk. 5:4–6, 8. [2]Mt. 16:15, 16. [3]Jn. 6:67, 68. [4]Mt. 26:73–75. [5]Jn. 21:17.*

JUNE 30

*You have been born anew**

If any one is in Christ, he is a new creation; the old has passed away, behold, the new has come.[1] You shall . . . be turned into another man.[2]

They came to Jesus, and found the man from whom the demons had gone, sitting at the feet of Jesus, clothed and in his right mind.[3] And Zacchaeus stood and said to the Lord, 'Behold, Lord, the half of my goods I give to the poor; and if I have defrauded any one of anything, I restore it fourfold.'[4] And passing along by the Sea of Galilee, He saw Simon and Andrew the brother of Simon casting a net in the sea; for they were fishermen. And Jesus said to them, 'Follow Me and I will make you become fishers of men.'[5]

No one puts new wine into old wineskins; if he does, the wine will burst the skins, and the wine is lost, and so are the skins; but new wine is for fresh skins.[6] Put off your old nature which belongs to your former manner of life and is corrupt through deceitful lusts, and be renewed in the spirit of your minds, and put on the new nature, created after the likeness of God in true righteousness and holiness.[7]

**1 Pet. 1:23.* [1]*2 Cor. 5:17.* [2]*1 Sam. 10:6.* [3]*Lk. 8:35.* [4]*Lk. 19:8.* [5]*Mk. 1:16, 17.* [6]*Mk. 2:22.* [7]*Eph. 4:22–24.*

JULY 1

*Holiness befits Thy house, O Lord**

The Lord God . . . drove out the man; and at the east of the garden of Eden He placed the cherubim, and a flaming sword which turned every way, to guard the way to the tree of life.[1]

Your iniquities have made a separation between you and your God, and your sins have hid His face from you so that He does not hear.[2] When you spread forth your hands, I will hide My eyes from you; even though you make many prayers, I will not listen.[3] You cannot serve the Lord; for He is a holy God.[4]

The city has no need of sun or moon to shine upon it, for the glory of God is its light . . . But nothing unclean shall enter it, nor any one who practices abomination or falsehood, but only those who are written in the Lamb's book of life.[5]

Who is able to stand before the Lord, this holy God?[6] Who shall stand in His holy place?[7] O Lord, who shall . . . dwell on Thy holy hill? He who walks blamelessly, and does what is right, and speaks truth from his heart; who does not slander with his tongue, and does no evil to his friend.[8]

**Ps. 93:5. [1]Gen. 3:23, 24. [2]Is. 59:2. [3]Is. 1:15. [4]Josh. 24:19. [5]Rev. 21:23, 27. [6]1 Sam. 6:20. [7]Ps. 24:3. [8]Ps. 15:1–3.*

JULY 2

*My soul refuses to be comforted**

Out of the depths I cry to Thee, O Lord! Lord, hear my voice![1] Hide not Thy face from Thy servant; for I am in distress.[2] Turn Thou to me, and be gracious to me; for I am lonely and afflicted. Relieve the troubles of my heart, and bring me out of my distresses. Consider my affliction and my trouble, and forgive all my sins.[3]

But He knows the way that I take; when He has tried me, I shall come forth as gold.[4] Behold, I have refined you, but not like silver; I have tried you in the furnace of affliction.[5] Every branch that does bear fruit He prunes that it may bear more fruit.[6] Suffering produces endurance, and endurance produces character, and character produces hope.[7]

Blessed be the God and Father of our Lord Jesus Christ, the Father of mercies and God of all comfort, who comforts us in all our affliction, so that we may be able to comfort those who are in any affliction, with the comfort with which we ourselves are comforted by God.[8] Let not your heart faint, and be not fearful.[9]

**Ps. 77:2. [1]Ps. 130: 1, 2. [2]Ps. 69;17. [3]Ps. 25:16–18. [4]Job 23:10. [5]Is. 48:10. [6]Jn. 15:2. [7]Rom. 5:3, 4. [8]2 Cor. 1:3, 4. [9]Jer. 51:46.*

*Lord, teach us to pray**

And in the morning, a great while before day, Jesus rose and went out to a lonely place, and there He prayed.[1] In these days He went out into the hills to pray; and all night He continued in prayer to God. And when it was day, He called His disciples, and chose from them twelve, whom He named apostles.[2]

Now about eight days after these sayings He took with Him Peter and John and James, and went up on the mountain to pray. And as He was praying, the appearance of His countenance was altered, and His raiment became dazzling white.[3] And Jesus lifted up His eyes and said, 'Father, I thank Thee that Thou hast heard Me. I knew that Thou hearest Me always' . . . When He had said this, He cried with a loud voice, 'Lazarus, come out.'[4]

He withdrew from them about a stone's throw, and knelt down and prayed, 'Father, if Thou art willing, remove this cup from Me; nevertheless not My will, but Thine, be done.' . . And being in an agony He prayed more earnestly; and His sweat became like great drops of blood falling down upon the ground.[5] Then Jesus, crying with a loud voice, said, 'Father, into Thy hands I commit My spirit!' And having said this He breathed His last.[6]

**Lk. 11:1.* [1]*Mk. 1:35.* [2]*Lk. 6:12, 13.* [3]*Lk. 9:28, 29.* [4]*Jn. 11:41–43.* [5]*Lk. 22:41, 42, 44.* [6]*Lk. 23:46.*

JULY 4

*He ascended on high**

I go to the Father, and you will see Me no more.[1] As they were looking on, He was lifted up, and a cloud took Him out of their sight.[2] So then the Lord Jesus, after He had spoken to them, was taken up into heaven, and sat down at the right hand of God.[3]

Lift up your heads, O gates! and be lifted up, O ancient doors! that the King of glory may come in. Who is the King of glory?[4] Jesus Christ, who has gone into heaven and is at the right hand of God, with angels, authorities, and powers subject to Him.[5] He has put all things under His feet.[6]

Christ has entered . . . into heaven itself, now to appear in the presence of God on our behalf.[7] Jesus has gone as a forerunner on our behalf.[8] Who is at the right hand of God, who indeed intercedes for us.[9]

God, who is rich in mercy . . . made us alive together with Christ . . . and raised us up with Him, and made us sit with Him in the heavenly places.[10] If then you have been raised with Christ, seek the things that are above, where Christ is, seated at the right hand of God. Set your mind on things that are above, not on things that are on earth.[11]

**Eph. 4:8. [1]Jn. 16:10. [2]Acts 1:9. [3]Mk. 16:19. [4]Ps. 24:7, 8. [5]1 Pet. 3:21, 22. [6]Eph. 1:22. [7]Heb. 9:24. [8]Heb. 6:20. [9]Rom. 8:34. [10]Eph. 2:4–6. [11]Col. 3:1, 2.*

JULY 5

*Do you do well to be angry?**

Now his elder son was in the field; and as he came and drew near to the house, he heard music and dancing. And he called one of the servants and asked what this meant. And he said to him, 'Your brother has come, and your father has killed the fatted calf, because he has received him safe and sound.' But he was angry and refused to go in.[1] And James and John . . . said to Jesus, 'Grant us to sit, one on Your right hand and one at Your left, in Your glory' . . . And when the ten heard it, they began to be indignant at James and John.[2] Martha was distracted with much serving; and she went to Jesus and said, 'Lord, do You not care that my sister has left me to serve alone? Tell her then to help me.'[3]

Love is patient and kind; love is not jealous or boastful; it is not arrogant or rude. Love does not insist on its own way; it is not irritable or resentful; it does not rejoice at wrong, but rejoices in the right. Love bears all things, believes all things, hopes all things, endures all things.[4] Do not say, 'I will do to him as he has done to me; I will pay the man back for what he has done.'[5] Be kind to one another, tenderhearted, forgiving one another, as God in Christ forgave you.[6]

**Jon. 4:4.* [1]*Lk. 15:25–28.* [2]*Mk. 10:35, 37, 41.* [3]*Lk. 10:40.* [4]*1 Cor. 13:4–7.* [5]*Prov. 24:29.* [6]*Eph. 4:32.*

JULY 6

*Tell me all the great things that Elisha has done**

Elijah said to Elisha, 'Ask what I shall do for you, before I am taken from you.' And Elisha said, 'I pray you, let me inherit a double share of your spirit.'[1] Now when the sons of the prophets ... saw him ... they said, 'The spirit of Elijah rests on Elisha.'[2] And she said to her husband, 'Behold now, I perceive that this is a holy man of God, who is continually passing our way.'[3]

When Elisha came into the house, he saw the child lying dead on his bed. So he went in and ... prayed to the Lord. Then he went up and lay upon the child ... and as he stretched himself upon him, the flesh of the child became warm.[4] Put on then, as God's chosen ones, holy and beloved, compassion.[5] The prayer of a righteous man has great power in its effects.[6]

Elisha said, 'Fear not, for those who are with us are more than those who are with them.' Then Elisha prayed, and said, 'O Lord, I pray Thee, open his eyes that he may see.' So the Lord opened the eyes of the young man, and he saw; and behold, the mountain was full of horses and chariots of fire round about Elisha.[7] The angel of the Lord encamps around those who fear Him, and delivers them.[8]

**2 Kings 8:4.* [1]*2 Kings 2:9.* [2]*2 Kings 2:15.* [3]*2 Kings 4:9.* [4]*2 Kings 4:32–34.* [5]*Col. 3:12.* [6]*Jas. 5:16.* [7]*2 Kings 6:16, 17.* [8]*Ps. 34:7.*

*Who . . . gave Himself for me**

Isaac said to his father Abraham . . . 'Where is the lamb for a burnt offering?' Abraham said, 'God will provide Himself the lamb' . . . And Abraham lifted up his eyes . . . and behold . . . a ram, caught in a thicket . . . and Abraham . . . offered it up . . . instead of his son.[1] Behold, the Lamb of God, who takes away the sin of the world![2]

Christ Jesus, who gave Himself as a ransom for all.[3] So that by the grace of God He might taste death for every one.[4] He is the expiation for our sins, and not for ours only but also for the sins of the whole world.[5] Thou wast slain and by Thy blood didst ransom men for God from every tribe and tongue and people and nation.[6]

God . . . did not spare His own Son but gave Him up for us all.[7] For our sake He made Him to be sin who knew no sin.[8] Christ redeemed us from the curse of the law, having become a curse for us—for it is written, 'Cursed be every one who hangs on a tree.'[9] But He was wounded for our transgressions, He was bruised for our iniquities.[10] By His wounds you have been healed.[11]

**Gal. 2:20.* [1]*Gen. 22:7, 8, 13.* [2]*Jn. 1:29.* [3]*1 Tim. 2:5, 6.* [4]*Heb. 2:9.* [5]*1 Jn. 2:2.* [6]*Rev. 5:9.* [7]*Rom. 8:32.* [8]*2 Cor. 5:21.* [9]*Gal. 3:13.* [10]*Is. 53:5.* [11]*1 Pet. 2:24.*

JULY 8

*I have learned . . . to be content**

Let every one lead the life which the Lord has assigned to him, and in which God has called him.[1] I have learned, in whatever state I am, to be content. I know how to be abased, and I know how to abound; in any and all circumstances I have learned the secret of facing plenty and hunger, abundance and want.[2] There is great gain in godliness with contentment.[3]

Give me neither poverty nor riches; feed me with the food that is needful for me, lest I be full, and deny Thee, and say, 'Who is the Lord?' or lest I be poor, and steal, and profane the name of my God.[4] But if we have food and clothing, with these we shall be content.[5] And be content with your wages.[6] Better is a little that the righteous has than the abundance of many wicked.[7]

Keep your life free from love of money, and be content with what you have; for He has said, 'I will never fail you nor forsake you.'[8] Take delight in the Lord, and He will give you the desires of your heart.[9] The lines have fallen for me in pleasant places; yea, I have a goodly heritage.[10]

**Phil. 4:11. [1] 1 Cor. 7:17. [2] Phil. 4:11, 12. [3] 1 Tim. 6:6. [4] Prov. 30:8, 9. [5] 1 Tim. 6:8. [6] Lk. 3:14. [7] Ps. 37:16. [8] Heb. 13:5. [9] Ps. 37:4. [10] Ps. 16:6.*

*My chosen people**

Blessed be the God and Father of our Lord Jesus Christ, who . . . chose us in Him before the foundation of the world.[1] But we are bound to give thanks to God always for you, brethren beloved by the Lord, because God chose you from the beginning to be saved . . .[2] If you were of the world, the world would love its own; but because you are not of the world, but I chose you out of the world, therefore the world hates you.[3]

You are a chosen race . . . that you may declare the wonderful deeds of Him who called you out of darkness into His marvelous light.[4] For we are His workmanship, created in Christ Jesus for good works, which God prepared beforehand, that we should walk in them.[5] For those whom He foreknew He also predestined to be conformed to the image of His Son.[6] You did not choose Me, but I chose you and appointed you that you should go and bear fruit and that your fruit should abide.[7] He (Paul) is a chosen instrument of Mine to carry My name before the Gentiles and kings and the sons of Israel.[8] He is Lord of lords and King of kings, and those with Him are called and chosen and faithful.[9]

**Is. 43:20.* [1]*Eph. 1:3, 4.* [2]*2 Thess. 2:13.* [3]*Jn. 15:19.* [4]*1 Pet. 2:9.* [5]*Eph. 2:10.* [6]*Rom. 8:29.* [7]*Jn. 15:16.* [8]*Acts 9:15.* [9]*Rev. 17:14.*

JULY 10

*Not under law but under grace**

It is evident that no man is justified before God by the law.[1] For whoever keeps the whole law but fails in one point has become guilty of all of it.[2] A man is not justified by works of the law but through faith in Jesus Christ.[3]

Do we then overthrow the law by this faith? By no means! On the contrary, we uphold the law.[4] If it had not been for the law, I should not have known sin. I should not have known what it is to covet if the law had not said, 'You shall not covet' . . . Apart from the law sin lies dead.[5] Through the law comes knowledge of sin.[6] The law was our custodian until Christ came, that we might be justified by faith.[7]

The law of the Spirit of life in Christ Jesus has set me free from the law of sin and death.[8] For freedom Christ has set us free; stand fast therefore, and do not submit again to a yoke of slavery.[9] Only do not use your freedom as an opportunity for the flesh, but through love be servants of one another. For the whole law is fulfilled in one word, 'You shall love your neighbor as yourself.'[10] Love is the fulfilling of the law.[11]

**Rom. 6:14.* [1]*Gal. 3:11.* [2]*Jas. 2:10.* [3]*Gal. 2:16.* [4]*Rom. 3:31.* [5]*Rom. 7:7, 8.* [6]*Rom. 3:20.* [7]*Gal. 3:24.* [8]*Rom. 8:2.* [9]*Gal. 5:1.* [10]*Gal. 5:13, 14.* [11]*Rom. 13:10.*

*You were running well; who hindered you?**

When anyone hears the word of the kingdom and does not understand it, the evil one comes and snatches away what is sown in his heart; this is what was sown along the path.[1] For good news came to us just as to them; but the message which they heard did not benefit them, because it did not meet with faith in the hearers.[2] Take heed then how you hear.[3]

As for what was sown on rocky ground, this is he who hears the word and immediately receives it with joy; yet he has no root in himself, but endures for a while, and when tribulation or persecution arises on account of the word, immediately he falls away.[4] For fear of the Jews no one spoke openly of Him.[5] The fear of man lays a snare.[6]

As for what was sown among thorns, this is he who hears the word, but the cares of the world and the delight in riches choke the word, and it proves unfruitful.[7] Do not love the world or the things in the world. If any one loves the world, love for the Father is not in him.[8] Those who desire to be rich fall into . . . a snare.[9]

**Gal. 5:7. [1]Mt. 13:19. [2]Heb. 4:2. [3]Lk. 8:18. [4]Mt. 13:20, 21. [5]Jn. 7:13. [6]Prov. 29:25. [7]Mt. 13:22. [8]1 Jn. 2:15. [9]1 Tim. 6:9.*

JULY 12

*You shall love your neighbor as yourself**

You shall not kill. You shall not commit adultery. You shall not steal. You shall not bear false witness against your neighbor. You shall not covet your neighbor's house . . . or anything that is your neighbor's.[1] You shall not oppress your neighbor or rob him.[2] You shall not remove your neighbor's landmark, which the men of old have set.[3]

Who is my neighbor?[4] Do not neglect to show hospitality to strangers, for thereby some have entertained angels unawares. Remember those who are in prison, as though in prison with them; and those who are ill-treated, since you also are in the body.[5] Practice hospitality ungrudgingly to one another. As each has received a gift, employ it for one another, as good stewards of God's varied grace.[6] Blessed is he who considers the poor![7] She opens her hand to the poor, and reaches out her hands to the needy.[8] Visit orphans and widows in their affliction.[9] If your enemy is hungry, feed him; if he is thirsty, give him drink.[10]

**Lev. 19:18.* [1]*Ex. 20:13–17.* [2]*Lev. 19:13.* [3]*Deut. 19:14.* [4]*Lk. 10:29.* [5]*Heb. 13:2, 3.* [6]*1 Pet. 4:9, 10.* [7]*Ps. 41:1.* [8]*Prov. 31:20.* [9]*Jas. 1:27.* [10]*Rom. 12:20.*

*Not wishing that any should perish**

When Jesus drew near and saw the city He wept over it.[1] O Jerusalem, Jerusalem . . . ! How often would I have gathered your children together as a hen gathers her brood under her wings, and you would not![2] On that day . . . will I declare to them, 'I never knew you; depart from Me, you evildoers.'[3]

What will be the end of those who do not obey the gospel of God? And if the righteous man is scarcely saved, where will the impious and sinner appear?[4] They shall suffer the punishment of eternal destruction and exclusion from the presence of the Lord.[5] It is a fearful thing to fall into the hands of the living God.[6] Fear Him who can destroy both soul and body in hell.[7] There men will weep and gnash their teeth.[8] My servants shall sing for gladness of heart, but you shall cry out for pain of heart, and shall wail for anguish of spirit.[9]

Have I any pleasure in the death of the wicked, says the Lord God, and not rather that he should turn from his way and live?[10] God our Savior . . . desires all men to be saved and to come to the knowledge of the truth.[11] Not wishing that any should perish, but that all should reach repentance.[12]

**2 Pet. 3:9.* [1]*Lk. 19:41.* [2]*Mt. 23:37.* [3]*Mt. 7:22, 23.* [4]*1 Pet. 4:17, 18.* [5]*2 Thess. 1:9.* [6]*Heb. 10:31.* [7]*Mt. 10:28.* [8]*Mt. 13:42.* [9]*Is. 65:14.* [10]*Ezek. 18:23.* [11]*1 Tim. 2:3, 4.* [12]*2 Pet. 3:9.*

JULY 14

*Let Thy saints shout for joy**

When the Lord restored the fortunes of Zion, we were like those who dream. Then our mouth was filled with laughter, and our tongue with shouts of joy . . . The Lord has done great things for us; we are glad.[1] In the day of prosperity be joyful.[2]

And he commanded the chariot to stop, and they both went down into the water, Philip and the eunuch, and he baptized him. And when they came up out of the water, the Spirit of the Lord caught up Philip; and the eunuch saw him no more, and went on his way rejoicing.[3] The seventy returned with joy, saying, 'Lord, even the demons are subject to us in Your name!'[4] Blessed are you when men hate you, and when they exclude you and revile you, and cast out your name as evil, on account of the Son of man! Rejoice in that day, and leap for joy, for behold, your reward is great in heaven.[5]

And to keep me from being too elated by the abundance of revelations, a thorn was given me in the flesh, a messenger of Satan, to harass me, to keep me from being too elated.[6]

**Ps. 132:9.* [1]*Ps. 126:1–3.* [2]*Eccl. 7:14.* [3]*Acts 8:38, 39.* [4]*Lk. 10:17.* [5]*Lk. 6:22, 23.* [6]*2 Cor. 12:7.*

*Sons of the living God**

To all who received Him, who believed in His name, He gave power to become children of God; who were born, not of blood nor of the will of the flesh nor of the will of man, but of God.[1] For in Christ Jesus you are all sons of God, through faith.[2] For all who are led by the Spirit of God are sons of God . . . When we cry, 'Abba! Father!' it is the Spirit Himself bearing witness with our spirit that we are children of God, and if children, then heirs, heirs of God and fellow heirs with Christ.[3]

Do all things without grumbling or questioning, that you may be blameless and innocent, children of God without blemish in the midst of a crooked and perverse generation, among whom you shine as lights in the world.[4] See what love the Father has given us, that we should be called children of God; and so we are. . . . Beloved, we are God's children now; it does not yet appear what we shall be, but we know that when He appears we shall be like Him, for we shall see Him as He is. And every one who thus hopes in Him purifies himself as He is pure.[5]

**Hos. 1:10.* [1]*Jn. 1:12, 13.* [2]*Gal. 3:26.* [3]*Rom. 8:14–17.* [4]*Phil. 2:14, 15.* [5]*1 Jn. 3:1–3.*

JULY 16

*Men will be . . . ungrateful**

When the ass saw the angel of the Lord, she lay down under Balaam; and Balaam's anger was kindled, and he struck the ass with his staff. Then the Lord opened the mouth of the ass, and she said to Balaam, 'What have I done to you, that you have struck me these three times? . . . Am I not your ass, upon which you have ridden all your life long to this day?'[1]

Moses said, 'Honor your father and your mother'; and, 'He who speaks evil of father or mother, let him surely die'; but you say, 'If a man tells his father or his mother, "What you would have gained from me is Corban" (that is, given to God)—then you no longer permit him to do anything for his father or mother, thus making void the word of God through your tradition.'[2]

One of the lepers, when he saw that he was healed, turned back, praising God with a loud voice; and he fell on his face at Jesus' feet, giving Him thanks. Now he was a Samaritan. Then said Jesus, 'Were not ten cleansed? Where are the nine? Was no one found to return and give praise to God except this foreigner?'[3]

**2 Tim. 3:2. [1]Num. 22:27, 28, 30. [2]Mk. 7:10–13. [3]Lk. 17:15–18.*

*The living and abiding word of God**

Thy word is a lamp to my feet and a light to my path.[1] For the commandment is a lamp and the teaching a light, and the reproofs of discipline are the way of life.[2]

Is not My word like fire, says the Lord, and like a hammer which breaks the rock in pieces?[3] I was at ease, and He broke me asunder.[4]

The word of God is living and active, sharper than any two-edged sword, piercing to the division of soul and spirit . . . and discerning the thoughts and intentions of the heart.[5] The sword of the Spirit, which is the word of God.[6]

Man shall not live by bread alone, but by every word that proceeds from the mouth of God.[7] Thy words were found, and I ate them, and Thy words became to me a joy and the delight of my heart.[8]

But be doers of the word, and not hearers only, deceiving yourselves. For if any one is a hearer of the word and not a doer, he is like a man who observes his natural face in a mirror; for he observes himself and goes away and at once forgets what he was like.[9]

**1 Pet. 1:23. [1]Ps. 119:105. [2]Prov. 6:23. [3]Jer. 23:29. [4]Job 16:12. [5]Heb. 4:12. [6]Eph. 6:17. [7]Mt. 4:4. [8]Jer. 15:16. [9]Jas. 1:22–24.*

JULY 18

*He is able to help those who are tempted**

The Lord knows how to rescue the godly from trial.[1] No temptation has overtaken you that is not common to man. God is faithful, and He will not let you be tempted beyond your strength, but with the temptation will also provide the way of escape, that you may be able to endure it.[2] For sin will have no dominion over you, since you are not under law but under grace.[3]

Therefore take the whole armor of God, that you may be able to withstand in the evil day, and having done all, to stand.[4] Above all taking the shield of faith, with which you can quench all the flaming darts of the evil one.[5] And take . . . the sword of the Spirit, which is the word of God.[6]

The Lord, your God, is in your midst, a warrior who gives victory; He will rejoice over you with gladness, He will renew you in His love.[7] He who is in you is greater than he who is in the world.[8] I can do all things in Him who strengthens me.[9] I love Thee, O Lord, my strength.[10]

**Heb. 2:18.* [1]*2 Pet. 2:9.* [2]*1 Cor. 10:13.* [3]*Rom. 6:14.* [4]*Eph. 6:13.* [5]*Eph. 6:16.* [6]*Eph. 6:17.* [7]*Zeph. 3:17.* [8]*1 Jn. 4:4.* [9]*Phil. 4:13.* [10]*Ps. 18:1.*

*Serving the Lord**

Having gifts that differ according to the grace given to us, let us use them: if prophecy, in proportion to our faith; if service, in our serving; he who teaches, in his teaching; he who exhorts, in his exhortation; he who contributes, in liberality; he who gives aid, with zeal; he who does acts of mercy, with cheerfulness.[1] Now there are varieties of gifts, but the same Spirit; and there are varieties of service, but the same Lord; and there are varieties of working, but it is the same God who inspires them all in every one.[2]

Jesus said to them, 'Follow Me, and I will make you fishers of men.' Immediately they left their nets and followed Him.[3] Andrew . . . first found his brother Simon, and said to him, 'We have found the Messiah' (which means Christ). He brought him to Jesus.[4] And Jesus said to Simon, 'Do not be afraid; henceforth you will be catching men.'[5] Philip found Nathanael, and said to him . . . 'Come and see.'[6] The woman . . . went away into the city, and said to the people, 'Come, see a man who told me all that I ever did. Can this be the Christ?'[7]

**Acts 20:19. [1]Rom. 12:6–8. [2]1 Cor. 12:4–6. [3]Mt. 4:19, 20. [4]Jn. 1:40–42. [5]Lk. 5:10. [6]Jn. 1:45, 46. [7]Jn. 4:28, 29.*

JULY 20

*Your sins are forgiven**

Peter said to Jesus, 'You shall never wash my feet.' Jesus answered him, 'If I do not wash you, you have no part in Me.' Simon Peter said to Him, 'Lord, not my feet only but also my hands and my head!' Jesus said to him, 'He who has bathed does not need to wash, except for his feet, but he is clean all over.'[1]

The steps of a man are from the Lord, and He establishes him in whose way He delights; though he fall, he shall not be cast headlong, for the Lord is the stay of his hand.[2] For a righteous man falls seven times, and rises again.[3] Rejoice not over me, O my enemy; when I fall, I shall rise.[4]

If we walk in the light, as He is in the light, we have fellowship with one another, and the blood of Jesus His Son cleanses us from all sin . . . If we confess our sins, He is faithful and just, and will forgive our sins and cleanse us from all unrighteousness.[5]

O Lord, be gracious to me; heal me, for I have sinned against Thee![6] The Lord also has put away your sin.[7] Blessed is he whose transgression is forgiven, whose sin is covered.[8]

**Lk. 7:48.* [1]*Jn. 13:8–10.* [2]*Ps. 37:23, 24.* [3]*Prov. 24:16.* [4]*Mic. 7:8.* [5]*1 Jn. 1:7, 9.* [6]*Ps. 41:4.* [7]*2 Sam. 12:13.* [8]*Ps. 32:1.*

*Now Samuel died; and all Israel assembled and mourned for him**

Now Samuel did not yet know the Lord, and the word of the Lord had not yet been revealed to him . . . And the Lord came and stood forth, calling as at other times, 'Samuel! Samuel!' And Samuel said, 'Speak, for Thy servant hears.'[1]

And Samuel grew, and the Lord was with him and let none of his words fall to the ground. And all Israel . . . knew that Samuel was established as a prophet of the Lord. And the Lord appeared again at Shiloh, for the Lord revealed Himself to Samuel at Shiloh by the word of the Lord.[2] Then Samuel said to all the house of Israel, 'If you are returning to the Lord with all your heart, then put away the foreign gods . . . from among you, and direct your heart to the Lord, and serve Him only.'[3]

Then Samuel said, 'Gather all Israel at Mizpah, and I will pray to the Lord for you.'[4] And the people of Israel said to Samuel, 'Do not cease to cry to the Lord our God for us, that He may save us from the hand of the Philistines.'[5] And Samuel said to the people . . . 'As for me, far be it from me that I should sin against the Lord by ceasing to pray for you; and I will instruct you in the good and the right way.'[6]

* *1 Sam. 25:1.* [1] *1 Sam. 3:7, 10.* [2] *1 Sam. 3:19–21.* [3] *1 Sam. 7:3.* [4] *1 Sam. 7:5.* [5] *1 Sam. 7:8.* [6] *1 Sam. 12:20, 23.*

JULY 22

*Looking to Jesus**

So Moses made a bronze serpent, and set it on a pole; and if a serpent bit any man, he would look at the bronze serpent and live.[1] As Moses lifted up the serpent in the wilderness, so must the Son of man be lifted up, that whoever believes in Him may have eternal life.[2] Turn to Me and be saved, all the ends of the earth! For I am God, and there is no other.[3]

Let us run with perseverance the race that is set before us, looking to Jesus the pioneer and perfecter of our faith.[4] To Thee I lift up my eyes, O Thou who art enthroned in the heavens![5] Let me see your face, let me hear your voice.[6] My eyes are ever toward the Lord, for He will pluck my feet out of the net.[7]

Look to Him, and be radiant.[8] We all, with unveiled face, beholding the glory of the Lord, are being changed into His likeness from one degree of glory to another; for this comes from the Lord who is the Spirit.[9] And gazing at Stephen, all who sat in the council saw that his face was like the face of an angel.[10]

**Heb. 12:2. [1]Num. 21:9. [2]Jn. 3:14, 15. [3]Is. 45:22. [4]Heb. 12:1, 2. [5]Ps. 123:1. [6]Song of Sol. 2:14. [7]Ps. 25:15. [8]Ps. 34:5. [9]2 Cor. 3:18. [10]Acts 6:15.*

*The work of ministry**

We beseech you, brethren, to respect those who labor among you and are over you in the Lord and admonish you, and to esteem them very highly in love because of their work.[1] I urge you to be subject to such men and to every fellow worker and laborer.[2] Remember your leaders, those who spoke to you the word of God; consider the outcome of their life, and imitate their faith.[3] Obey your leaders and submit to them; for they are keeping watch over your souls, as men who will have to give account.[4]

So I exhort the elders among you . . . Tend the flock of God that is your charge, not by constraint but willingly, not for shameful gain but eagerly, not as domineering over those in your charge but being examples to the flock. And when the chief Shepherd is manifested you will obtain the unfading crown of glory.[5] And . . . Paul . . . called to him the elders of the church. And . . . he said to them . . . 'Take heed to yourselves and to all the flock, in which the Holy Spirit has made you guardians, to feed the church of the Lord which He obtained with His own blood.'[6]

**Eph. 4:12.* [1]*1 Thess. 5:12, 13.* [2]*1 Cor. 16:16.* [3]*Heb. 13:7.* [4]*Heb. 13:17.* [5]*1 Pet. 5:1–4.* [6]*Acts 20:17, 18, 28.*

JULY 24

*Will you also go away?**

Many of His disciples drew back and no longer went about with Him. Jesus said to the twelve, 'Will you also go away?'[1] No one who puts his hand to the plow and looks back is fit for the kingdom of God.[2] You were running well; who hindered you from obeying the truth?[3]

Be appalled, O heavens, at this, be shocked, be utterly desolate, says the Lord, for My people have committed two evils: they have forsaken Me, the fountain of living waters, and hewed out cisterns for themselves, broken cisterns, that can hold no water.[4] There is severe discipline for him who forsakes the way.[5] All who forsake Thee shall be put to shame.[6]

Thou hast chastened me, and I was chastened, like an untrained calf; bring me back that I may be restored, for Thou art the Lord my God. For after I had turned away I repented.[7] Restore to me the joy of Thy salvation.[8] And . . . they . . . sought Him with their whole desire, and He was found by them, and the Lord gave them rest round about.[9] I will heal their faithlessness; I will love them freely.[10]

**Jn. 6:67.* [1]*Jn. 6:66, 67.* [2]*Lk. 9:62.* [3]*Gal. 5:7.* [4]*Jer. 2:12, 13.* [5]*Prov. 15:10.* [6]*Jer. 17:13.* [7]*Jer. 31:18, 19.* [8]*Ps. 51:12.* [9]*2 Chron. 15:15.* [10]*Hos. 14:4.*

*Be not proud**

Thus says the Lord: 'Let not the wise man glory in his wisdom, let not the mighty man glory in his might, let not the rich man glory in his riches: but let him who glories glory in this, that he understands and knows Me.'[1] For . . . what have you that you did not receive? If then you received it, why do you boast as if it were not a gift?[2] Every good endowment and every perfect gift is from above, coming down from the Father.[3]

The Pharisee stood and prayed thus with himself, 'God, I thank Thee that I am not like other men . . .'[4] But when they . . . compare themselves with one another, they are without understanding.[5] For it is not the man who commends himself that is accepted, but the man whom the Lord commends.[6]

God chose what is foolish in the world to shame the wise, God chose what is weak in the world to shame the strong . . . so that no human being might boast in the presence of God.[7] For by grace you have been saved through faith; and this is not your own doing, it is the gift of God—not because of works, lest any man should boast.[8] Let him who boasts, boast of the Lord.[9]

**Jer. 13:15.* [1]*Jer. 9:23, 24.* [2]*1 Cor. 4:7.* [3]*Jas. 1:17.* [4]*Lk. 18:11.* [5]*2 Cor. 10:12.* [6]*2 Cor. 10:18.* [7]*1 Cor. 1:27–29.* [8]*Eph. 2:8, 9.* [9]*2 Cor. 10:17.*

JULY 26

*That ancient serpent . . . the Devil**

The Lord God said to the serpent, 'Because you have done this, cursed are you above all cattle, and above all wild animals; upon your belly you shall go, and dust you shall eat all the days of your life. I will put enmity between you and the woman, and between your seed and her seed; he shall bruise your head, and you shall bruise his heel.'[1]

The God of peace will soon crush Satan under your feet.[2] Now is the judgment of this world, now shall the ruler of this world be cast out.[3] The reason the Son of God appeared was to destroy the works of the devil.[4] That through death He might destroy him who has the power of death, that is, the devil, and deliver all those who through fear of death were subject to lifelong bondage.[5]

And the great dragon was thrown down, that ancient serpent, who is called the Devil and Satan, the deceiver of the whole world—he was thrown down to the earth, and his angels were thrown down with him.[6] And the devil . . . was thrown into the lake of fire and brimstone.[7] And death shall be no more, neither shall there be mourning nor crying nor pain any more.[8]

**Rev. 12:9.* [1]*Gen. 3:14, 15.* [2]*Rom. 16:20.* [3]*Jn. 12:31.* [4]*1 Jn. 3:8.* [5]*Heb. 2:14, 15.* [6]*Rev. 12:9.* [7]*Rev. 20:10.* [8]*Rev. 21:4.*

*The work of our hands**

I stretch out my hands to Thee; my soul thirsts for Thee like a parched land.[1] If you set your heart aright, you will stretch out your hands toward Him. If iniquity is in your hand, put it far away, and let not wickedness dwell in your tents.[2] Therefore the Lord has recompensed me . . . according to the cleanness of my hands in His sight.[3]

If your right hand causes you to sin, cut it off and throw it away; it is better that you lose one of your members than that your whole body go into hell.[4] Let the thief no longer steal, but rather let him labor, doing honest work with his hands, so that he may be able to give to those in need.[5] The sluggard buries his hand in the dish; it wears him out to bring it back to his mouth.[6]

A slack hand causes poverty, but the hand of the diligent makes rich.[7] Whatever your hand finds to do, do it with your might.[8] In the morning sow your seed, and at evening withhold not your hand; for you do not know which will prosper, this or that, or whether both alike will be good.[9] The work of a man's hand comes back to him.[10]

**Ps. 90:17.* [1]*Ps. 143:6.* [2]*Job 11:13, 14.* [3]*Ps. 18:24.* [4]*Mt. 5:30.* [5]*Eph. 4:28.* [6]*Prov. 26:15.* [7]*Prov. 10:4.* [8]*Eccl. 9:10.* [9]*Eccl. 11:6.* [10]*Prov. 12:14.*

JULY 28

*Be strong and very courageous**

While Jesus was in one of the cities, there came a man full of leprosy; and when he saw Jesus, he fell on his face and besought Him, 'Lord, if You will, You can make me clean.' And He stretched out His hand, and touched him, saying, 'I will; be clean.'[1] In the temple He found those who were selling oxen and sheep and pigeons, and the money-changers at their business. And making a whip of cords, He drove them all, with the sheep and oxen, out of the temple; and He poured out the coins of the money-changers and overturned their tables.[2]

So Judas, procuring a band of soldiers and some officers from the chief priests and the Pharisees, went there with lanterns and torches and weapons. Then Jesus, knowing all that was to befall Him, came forward and said to them, 'Whom do you seek?'[3] And they brought Him to the place . . . Golgotha (which means the place of a skull). And they offered Him wine mingled with myrrh; but He did not take it. And they crucified Him.[4]

Looking to Jesus the pioneer and perfecter of our faith, who for the joy that was set before Him endured the cross, despising the shame, and is seated at the right hand of the throne of God. Consider Him who endured from sinners such hostility against Himself, so that you may not grow weary or fainthearted.[5]

**Josh.* 1:7. [1]*Lk.* 5:12, 13. [2]*Jn.* 2:14, 15. [3]*Jn.* 18:3, 4. [4]*Mk.* 15:22–24. [5]*Heb.* 12:2, 3.

*The lips of the righteous feed many**

And all spoke well of Jesus, and wondered at the gracious words which proceeded out of His mouth.[1] You are the fairest of the sons of men; grace is poured upon Your lips; therefore God has blessed You for ever.[2] No man ever spoke like this man![3]

Let no evil talk come out of your mouths, but only such as is good for edifying, as fits the occasion, that it may impart grace to those who hear.[4] Let your speech always be gracious, seasoned with salt, so that you may know how you ought to answer every one.[5] Do not return . . . reviling for reviling; but on the contrary bless, for to this you have been called, that you may obtain a blessing. For he that would love life and see good days, let him keep his tongue from evil and his lips from speaking guile.[6] A soft answer turns away wrath, but a harsh word stirs up anger.[7]

The tongue of the righteous is choice silver.[8] The mouth of the righteous brings forth wisdom.[9] The lips of the righteous know what is acceptable.[10]

**Prov. 10:21.* [1]*Lk. 4:22.* [2]*Ps. 45:2.* [3]*Jn. 7:46.* [4]*Eph. 4:29.* [5]*Col. 4:6.* [6]*1 Pet. 3:9, 10.* [7]*Prov. 15:1.* [8]*Prov. 10:20.* [9]*Prov. 10:31.* [10]*Prov. 10:32.*

JULY 30

*The riches of His glorious inheritance**

Blessed be the God and Father of our Lord Jesus Christ! By His great mercy we have been born anew to a living hope through the resurrection of Jesus Christ from the dead, and to an inheritance which is imperishable, undefiled and unfading, kept in heaven for you.[1] Giving thanks to the Father, who has qualified us to share in the inheritance of the saints in light.[2]

You ... were sealed with the promised Holy Spirit, which is the guarantee of our inheritance until we acquire possession of it, to the praise of His glory.[3] It is the Spirit Himself bearing witness with our spirit that we are children of God, and if children, then heirs, heirs of God and fellow heirs with Christ, provided we suffer with Him in order that we may also be glorified with Him.[4] And every one who has left houses or brothers or sisters or father or mother or children or lands, for My name's sake, will receive a hundredfold, and inherit eternal life.[5]

Then the King will say to those at His right hand, 'Come, O blessed of My Father, inherit the kingdom prepared for you from the foundation of the world.'[6] O how abundant is Thy goodness, which Thou hast laid up for those who fear Thee![7]

**Eph. 1:18.* [1]*1 Pet. 1:3, 4.* [2]*Col. 1:12.* [3]*Eph. 1:13, 14.* [4]*Rom. 8:16, 17.* [5]*Mt. 19:29.* [6]*Mt. 25:34.* [7]*Ps. 31:19.*

*Who is a teacher like Him?**

Nicodemus, a ruler of the Jews . . . came to Jesus by night and said to Him, 'Rabbi, we know that You are a teacher come from God.'[1] And when Jesus finished these sayings, the crowds were astonished at His teaching, for He taught them as one who had authority, and not as their scribes.[2] The officers answered, 'No man ever spoke like this man!'[3] All the people hung upon His words.[4]

Then the disciples came and said to Him, 'Why do You speak to them in parables?' And He answered them, 'To you it has been given to know the secrets of the kingdom of heaven, but to them it has not been given.'[5] He did not speak to them without a parable, but privately to His own disciples He explained everything.[6] 'Have you understood all this?' They said to Him, 'Yes.'[7]

A disciple is not above his teacher, but every one when he is fully taught will be like his teacher.[8] You have one teacher, and you are all brethren.[9] And they shall not teach every one his fellow or every one his brother, saying, 'Know the Lord,' for all shall know Me, from the least of them to the greatest.[10]

Job 36:22. [1]Jn. 3:1, 2. [2]Mt. 7:28, 29. [3]Jn. 7:46. [4]Lk. 19:48. [5]Mt. 13:10, 11. [6]Mk. 4:34. [7]Mt. 13:51. [8]Lk. 6:40. [9]Mt. 23:8. [10]Heb. 8:11.

AUGUST 1

*The Lord of glory**

Father, glorify . . . Me in Thy own presence with the glory which I had with Thee before the world was made.[1] When the morning stars sang together, and all the sons of God shouted for joy.[2] We were eye-witnesses of His majesty. For when He received honor and glory from God . . . we were with Him on the holy mountain.[3] We have beheld His glory, glory as of the only Son from the Father.[4]

You know the grace of our Lord Jesus Christ, that though He was rich, yet for your sake He became poor.[5] Who for the joy that was set before Him endured the cross, despising the shame, and is seated at the right hand of the throne of God.[6] We see Jesus, who for a little while was made lower than the angels, crowned with glory and honor because of the suffering of death.[7]

Was it not necessary that the Christ should suffer these things and enter into His glory?[8] Lift up your heads, O gates! and be lifted up, O ancient doors! that the King of glory may come in.[9] Worthy is the Lamb who was slain, to receive power and wealth and wisdom and might and honor and glory and blessing![10]

**Jas. 2:1.* [1]*Jn. 17:5.* [2]*Job 38:7.* [3]*2 Pet. 1:16–18.* [4]*Jn. 1:14.* [5]*2 Cor. 8:9.* [6]*Heb. 12:2.* [7]*Heb. 2:9.* [8]*Lk. 24:26.* [9]*Ps. 24:7.* [10]*Rev. 5:12.*

*The people in whose heart is My law**

Oh, how I love Thy law! It is my meditation all the day.[1] This book of the law shall not depart out of your mouth, but you shall meditate on it day and night, that you may be careful to do according to all that is written in it.[2] Let the word of Christ dwell in you richly, as you teach and admonish one another in all wisdom.[3]

I have laid up Thy word in my heart, that I might not sin against Thee.[4] How can a young man keep his way pure? By guarding it according to Thy word.[5] The law of his God is in his heart; his steps do not slip.[6]

I have more understanding than all my teachers, for Thy testimonies are my meditation. I understand more than the aged, for I keep Thy precepts.[7] The unfolding of Thy words gives light; it imparts understanding to the simple.[8] From childhood you have been acquainted with the sacred writings which are able to instruct you for salvation through faith in Christ Jesus. All scripture is inspired by God and profitable for teaching . . . that the man of God may be complete, equipped for every good work.[9]

**Is. 51:7. [1]Ps. 119:97. [2]Josh. 1:8. [3]Col. 3:16. [4]Ps. 119:11. [5]Ps. 119:9. [6]Ps. 37:31. [7]Ps. 119:99, 100. [8]Ps. 119:130. [9]2 Tim. 3:15–17.*

AUGUST 3

*Love covers a multitude of sins**

Peter . . . said to Him, 'Lord, how often shall my brother sin against me, and I forgive him? As many as seven times?' Jesus said to him, 'I do not say to you seven times, but seventy times seven.'[1] I forgave you all that debt because you besought me; and should not you have had mercy on your fellow servant, as I had mercy on you?[2] Be kind to one another . . . forgiving one another, as God in Christ forgave you.[3] But if you do not forgive men their trespasses, neither will your Father forgive your trespasses.[4] Therefore I tell you . . . whenever you stand praying, forgive, if you have anything against any one.[5]

Do not return evil for evil or reviling for reviling; but on the contrary bless, for to this you have been called.[6] If you see the ass of one who hates you lying under its burden, you shall refrain from leaving him with it, you shall help him to lift it up.[7] Do not rejoice when your enemy falls, and let not your heart be glad when he stumbles.[8] Love . . . does not rejoice at wrong, but rejoices in the right.[9] Hatred stirs up strife, but love covers all offenses.[10]

**1 Pet. 4:8. [1]Mt. 18:21, 22. [2]Mt. 18:32, 33. [3]Eph. 4:32. [4]Mt. 6:15. [5]Mk. 11:24, 25. [6]1 Pet. 3:9. [7]Ex. 23:5. [8]Prov. 24:17. [9]1 Cor. 13:5, 6. [10]Prov. 10:12.*

*They know Me not**

Behold, this alone I found, that God made man upright, but they have sought out many devices.[1] The Lord saw that the wickedness of man was great in the earth, and that every imagination of the thoughts of his heart was only evil continually.[2] The whole head is sick, and the whole heart faint.[3] They are a people who err in heart, and they do not regard My ways.[4]

We ourselves were once foolish, disobedient, led astray, slaves to various passions and pleasures, passing our days in malice and envy.[5] Following the course of this world, following the prince of the power of the air, the spirit that is now at work in the sons of disobedience.[6] But when the goodness and loving kindness of God our Savior appeared, He saved us . . . so that we might be justified by His grace.[7]

Therefore, if any one is in Christ, he is a new creation.[8] I will put My laws into their minds, and write them on their hearts, and I will be their God . . . All shall know Me, from the least of them to the greatest. For I will be merciful toward their iniquities, and I will remember their sins no more.[9]

**Jer. 4:22.* [1]*Eccl. 7:29.* [2]*Gen. 6:5.* [3]*Is. 1:5.* [4]*Ps. 95:10.* [5]*Tit. 3:3.* [6]*Eph. 2:2.* [7]*Tit. 3:4, 5, 7.* [8]*2 Cor. 5:17.* [9]*Heb. 8:10–12.*

AUGUST 5

*A lying tongue**

When the devil lies, he speaks according to his own nature, for he is a liar and the father of lies.[1] (The Lord God said) Of the tree of the knowledge of good and evil you shall not eat, for in the day that you eat of it you shall die.[2] But the serpent said to the woman, 'You will not die.'[3]

But Sarah denied, saying, 'I did not laugh;' for she was afraid. He said, 'No, but you did laugh.'[4] Then a maid, seeing Peter as he sat in the light and gazing at him, said, 'This man also was with Jesus.' But he denied it, saying, 'Woman, I do not know Him.'[5] But Peter said, 'Ananias . . . how is it that you have contrived this deed in your heart? You have not lied to men but to God.'[6]

Let every one speak the truth with his neighbor.[7] O Lord, who shall sojourn in Thy tent? . . . He who . . . speaks truth from his heart.[8] Hear, for I will speak noble things, and from my lips will come what is right; for my mouth will utter truth; wickedness is an abomination to my lips. All the words of my mouth are righteous; there is nothing twisted or crooked in them.[9] Buy truth, and do not sell it.[10]

**Prov.* 6:17. [1]*Jn.* 8:44. [2]*Gen.* 2:17. [3]*Gen.* 3:4. [4]*Gen.* 18:15. [5]*Lk.* 22:56, 57. [6]*Acts* 5:3, 4. [7]*Eph.* 4:25. [8]*Ps.* 15:1, 2. [9]*Prov.* 8:6–8. [10]*Prov.* 23:23.

*Fight the good fight of the faith**

Your adversary the devil.[1] For we are not contending against flesh and blood, but against principalities, against the powers, against the world rulers of this present darkness, against the spiritual hosts of wickedness in the heavenly places. Therefore take the whole armor of God, that you may be able to withstand in the evil day, and having done all, to stand.[2] That . . . you may wage the good warfare.[3]

For though we live in the world we are not carrying on a worldly war, for the weapons of our warfare are not worldly but have divine power to destroy strongholds.[4] Blessed be the Lord, my rock, who trains my hands for war, and my fingers for battle.[5]

For the Lord has driven out before you great and strong nations; and as for you, no man has been able to withstand you to this day. One man of you puts to flight a thousand, since it is the Lord your God who fights for you, as He promised you. Take good heed to yourselves, therefore, to love the Lord your God.[6] You shall not fear them; for it is the Lord your God who fights for you.[7] I have fought the good fight.[8]

* [1] *Tim. 6:12.* [1] *1 Pet. 5:8.* [2] *Eph. 6:12, 13.* [3] *1 Tim. 1:18.* [4] *2 Cor. 10:3, 4* [5] *Ps. 144: 1.* [6] *Josh. 23: 9–11.* [7] *Deut. 3:22.* [8] *2 Tim. 4: 7.*

AUGUST 7

*Everything created by God is good**

And God saw everything that He had made, and behold, it was very good.[1] God . . . richly furnishes us with everything to enjoy.[2] Upon whom does His light not arise?[3] He makes His sun rise on the evil and on the good, and sends rain on the just and on the unjust.[4] Thou dost cause the grass to grow for the cattle, and plants for man to cultivate, that he may bring forth food from the earth, and wine to gladden the heart of man, oil to make his face shine, and bread to strengthen man's heart.[5]

Let the faithful exult in glory; let them sing for joy on their couches.[6] Let them thank the Lord for His steadfast love, for His wonderful works to the sons of men! . . . Offer sacrifices of thanksgiving, and tell of His deeds in songs of joy![7]

What shall I render to the Lord for all His bounty to me? I will lift up the cup of salvation and call on the name of the Lord, I will pay my vows to the Lord in the presence of all His people.[8] Bless the Lord, O my soul, and forget not all His benefits.[9] For from Him and through Him and to Him are all things. To Him be glory forever. Amen.[10]

**1 Tim. 4:4. [1]Gen. 1:31. [2]1 Tim. 6:17. [3]Job 25:3. [4]Mt. 5:45. [5]Ps. 104: 14, 15. [6]Ps. 149:5. [7]Ps. 107:21, 22. [8]Ps. 116:12–14. [9]Ps. 103:2. [10]Rom. 11:36.*

*God has made me fruitful in the land of my affliction**

Now Israel loved Joseph more than any other of his children . . . and he made him a long robe with sleeves. But when his brothers saw that their father loved him more than all his brothers, they hated him, and could not speak peaceably to him.[1] And the patriarchs, jealous of Joseph, sold him into Egypt; but God was with him.[2]

And he became a successful man, . . . and his master saw that the Lord was with him.[3] Now Joseph was handsome and good-looking. And . . . his master's wife cast her eyes upon Joseph, and said, 'Lie with me.' But he refused and said . . . 'How . . . can I do this great wickedness, and sin against God?'[4] His master came home, and she told him the same story, saying, 'The Hebrew servant . . . came in to me to insult me.'[5] And Joseph's master . . . put him into the prison . . But the Lord was with Joseph and showed him steadfast love.[6]

So Pharaoh said to Joseph, 'Since God has shown you all this, there is none so discreet and wise as you are; you shall be . . . over all the land of Egypt.'[7] His brothers also came and fell down before him . . . But Joseph said to them . . . 'You meant evil against me; but God meant it for good.'[8] We know that in everything God works for good with those who love Him.[9]

**Gen. 41:52.* [1]*Gen. 37:3, 4.* [2]*Acts 7:9.* [3]*Gen. 39:2, 3.* [4]*Gen. 39:6–9.* [5]*Gen. 39:16, 17.* [6]*Gen. 39:20, 21.* [7]*Gen. 41:39–41.* [8]*Gen. 50:18–20.* [9]*Rom. 8:28.*

AUGUST 9

*Jesus said, 'Come'**

Incline your ear, and come to Me; hear, that your soul may live.[1] Come to Me, all who labor and are heavy laden, and I will give you rest.[2] If any one thirst, let him come to Me and drink.[3] All that the Father gives Me will come to Me; and him who comes to Me I will not cast out.[4]

People came to Him from every quarter.[5] There was a man of the Pharisees, named Nicodemus, a ruler of the Jews. This man came to Jesus by night.[6] And there was a man named Zacchaeus; he was a chief tax collector, and rich. And he sought to see who Jesus was . . . and climbed up into a sycamore tree to see Him . . . When Jesus came to the place, He looked up and said to him, 'Zacchaeus, make haste and come down; for I must stay at your house today.' So he made haste and came down, and received Him joyfully.[7] And behold, a woman who had suffered a hemorrhage for twelve years came up behind Him and touched the fringe of His garment; for she said to herself, 'If I only touch His garment, I shall be made well.'[8]

You search the scriptures, because you think that in them you have eternal life; and it is they that bear witness to Me; yet you refuse to come to Me that you may have life.[9] Behold, we come to Thee; for Thou art the Lord our God.[10]

**Mt.* 14:29. [1]*Is.* 55:3. [2]*Mt.* 11:28. [3]*Jn.* 7:37. [4]*Jn.* 6:37. [5]*Mk.* 1:45. [6]*Jn.* 3:1,2. [7]*Lk.* 19:2–6. [8]*Mt.* 9:20, 21. [9]*Jn.* 5:39, 40. [10]*Jer.* 3:22.

*Who gave Himself for our sins**

He was oppressed, and He was afflicted, yet He opened not His mouth; like a lamb that is led to the slaughter, and like a sheep that before its shearers is dumb, so He opened not His mouth . . . They made His grave with the wicked and with a rich man in His death, although He had done no violence, and there was no deceit in His mouth.[1]

And Pilate said . . . 'I find no crime in this man.'[2] One of the criminals . . . railed at Jesus . . . But the other rebuked him, saying . . . 'This man has done nothing wrong.'[3] When the centurion saw what had taken place, he praised God, and said, 'Certainly this man was innocent!'[4] Judas . . . repented . . . saying, 'I have sinned in betraying innocent blood.'[5] He committed no sin; no guile was found on His lips.[6] In Him there is no sin.[7] Who knew no sin.[8]

Yet it was the will of the Lord to bruise Him; He has put Him to grief; when He makes Himself an offering for sin . . . He shall see the fruit of the travail of His soul and be satisfied.[9] Lo, I have come to do Thy will, O God.[10] Shall I not drink the cup which the Father has given Me?[11] Obedient unto death.[12]

**Gal. 1:4.* [1]*Is. 53:7, 9.* [2]*Lk. 23:4.* [3]*Lk. 23:39–41.* [4]*Lk. 23:47.* [5]*Mt. 27:3, 4.* [6]*1 Pet. 2:22.* [7]*1 Jn. 3:5.* [8]*2 Cor. 5:21.* [9]*Is. 53:10, 11.* [10]*Heb. 10:7.* [11]*Jn. 18:11.* [12]*Phil. 2:8.*

AUGUST 11

*For this is the will of God, your sanctification**

I have been crucified with Christ; it is no longer I who live, but Christ who lives in me; and the life I now live in the flesh I live by faith in the Son of God, who loved me and gave Himself for me[1]. For if we have been united with Him in a death like His, we shall certainly be united with Him in a resurrection like His.[2]

Put to death therefore what is earthly in you: immorality, impurity, passion, evil desire, and covetousness, which is idolatry . . . In these you once walked . . . But now put them all away: anger, wrath, malice, slander, and foul talk from your mouth.[3] Put off your old nature.[4]

Put on the new nature, created after the likeness of God in true righteousness and holiness.[5] Put on the Lord Jesus Christ, and make no provision for the flesh, to gratify its desires.[6] Put on then, as God's chosen ones, holy and beloved, compassion, kindness, lowliness, meekness, and patience . . . And above all these put on love, which binds everything together in perfect harmony.[7]

**1 Thess. 4:3.* [1]*Gal. 2:20.* [2]*Rom. 6:5.* [3]*Col. 3:5, 7, 8.* [4]*Eph. 4:22.* [5]*Eph. 4:24.* [6]*Rom. 13:14.* [7]*Col. 3:12, 14.*

*Let us come into His presence with thanksgiving**

Then one of them, when he saw that he was healed, turned back . . and he fell on his face at Jesus' feet, giving Him thanks. Now he was a Samaritan. Then said Jesus, 'Were not ten cleansed? Where are the nine? Was no one found to return and give praise to God except this foreigner?'[1] They are without excuse; for although they knew God they did not honor Him as God or give thanks to Him.[2]

Thine, O Lord, is the greatness, and the power . . . and the victory, and the majesty; for all that is in the heavens and in the earth is Thine; Thine is the kingdom, O Lord, and Thou art exalted as Head above all. Both riches and honor come from Thee, and Thou rulest over all. In Thy hand are power and might; and in Thy hand it is to make great and to give strength to all. And now we thank Thee, our God, and praise Thy glorious name.[3]

Daniel . . . gave thanks before his God.[4] Jesus said, 'Father, I thank Thee that Thou hast heard Me.'[5] Paul took bread and giving thanks to God . . . began to eat.[6] They shall stand every morning, thanking and praising the Lord, and likewise at evening.[7] Always and for everything giving thanks in the name of our Lord Jesus Christ to God the Father.[8]

**Ps. 95:2.* [1]*Lk. 17:15–18.* [2]*Rom. 1:20, 21.* [3]*1 Chron. 29: 11–13.* [4]*Dan. 6:10.* [5]*Jn. 11:41.* [6]*Acts 27:35.* [7]*1 Chron. 23:30.* [8]*Eph. 5:20.*

AUGUST 13

*In Thee they trusted, and were not disappointed**

After this many of His disciples drew back and no longer went about with Him.[1] And Jesus came to the disciples and found them sleeping; and He said to Peter, 'So could you not watch with Me one hour?'[2] Then all the disciples forsook Him and fled.[3]

It is not an enemy who taunts me—then I could bear it; it is not an adversary who deals insolently with me—then I could hide from him. But it is you, my equal, my companion, my familiar friend.[4] Even my bosom friend in whom I trusted, who ate of my bread, has lifted his heel against me.[5] Those whom I loved have turned against me.[6] Demas . . . has deserted me.[7] At my first defense no one took my part.[8]

Put not your trust in princes, in a son of man, in whom there is no help.[9] Trust in a faithless man in time of trouble is like a bad tooth or a foot that slips.[10] It is better to take refuge in the Lord than to put confidence in man. It is better to take refuge in the Lord than to put confidence in princes.[11] O grant us help against the foe, for vain is the help of man![12]

**Ps. 22:5. [1]Jn. 6:66. [2]Mt. 26:40. [3]Mt. 26:56. [4]Ps. 55:12, 13. [5]Ps. 41:9. [6]Job 19:19. [7]2 Tim. 4:10. [8]2 Tim. 4:16. [9]Ps. 146:3. [10]Prov. 25:19. [11]Ps. 118:8, 9. [12]Ps. 60:11.*

*They have not all heeded the gospel**

For good news came to us just as to them, but the message which they heard did not benefit them, because it did not meet with faith in the hearers.[1] The word of the cross is folly to those who are perishing, but to us who are being saved it is the power of God.[2] When they heard of the resurrection of the dead, some mocked.[3] Though He had done so many signs before them, yet they did not believe in Him.[4]

They all alike began to make excuses. . . . 'I have bought a field' . . . 'I have bought five yoke of oxen' . . . 'I have married a wife.'[5] You . . . judge yourselves unworthy of eternal life.[6] They refused to love the truth and so be saved.[7] You refuse to come to Me that you may have life.[8]

The seed along the path are those who have heard; then the devil comes and takes away the word from their hearts, that they may not believe and be saved.[9] God may perhaps grant that they will repent and come to know the truth, and . . . escape from the snare of the devil, after being captured by him to do his will.[10]

**Rom. 10:16.* [1]*Heb. 4:2.* [2]*1 Cor. 1:18.* [3]*Acts 17:32.* [4]*Jn. 12:37.* [5]*Lk. 14:18–20.* [6]*Acts 13:46.* [7]*2 Thess. 2:10.* [8]*Jn. 5:40.* [9]*Lk. 8:12.* [10]*2 Tim. 2:25, 26.*

AUGUST 15

*Keep yourselves from idols**

For they themselves report concerning us what a welcome we had among you, and how you turned to God from idols, to serve a living and true God.[1] Put to death therefore what is earthly in you: immorality, impurity, passion, evil desire, and covetousness, which is idolatry.[2]

Do not love the world or the things in the world.[3] And the world passes away, and the lust of it.[4] For the love of money is the root of all evils; it is through this craving that some have wandered away from the faith and pierced their hearts with many pangs.[5] The cares of the world and the delight in riches choke the word, and it proves unfruitful.[6]

Therefore, my beloved, shun the worship of idols.[7] What agreement has the temple of God with idols?[8] O Ephraim, what have I to do with idols? It is I who answer and look after you. I am like an evergreen cypress, from Me comes your fruit.[9] And from all your idols I will cleanse you.[10] They shall not defile themselves any more with their idols.[11]

** 1 Jn. 5:21. [1] 1 Thess. 1:9. [2] Col. 3:5. [3] 1 Jn. 2:15. [4] 1 Jn. 2:17. [5] 1 Tim. 6:10. [6] Mt 13:22. [7] 1 Cor. 10:14. [8] 2 Cor. 6:16. [9] Hos. 14:8. [10] Ezek. 36:25. [11] Ezek. 37:23.*

*God is treating you as sons**

For the Lord disciplines him whom He loves, and chastises every son whom He receives. It is for discipline that you have to endure. God is treating you as sons; for what son is there whom his father does not discipline? . . . For they disciplined us for a short time at their pleasure, but He disciplines us for our good, that we may share His holiness.[1] Every branch of Mine . . . that does bear fruit He prunes, that it may bear more fruit.[2]

Although Jesus was a Son, He learned obedience through what He suffered.[3] Since therefore Christ suffered in the flesh, arm yourselves with the same thought, for whoever has suffered in the flesh has ceased from sin, so as to live for the rest of the time in the flesh no longer by human passions but by the will of God.[4]

For the sake of Christ, then, I am content with weaknesses, insults, hardships, persecutions, and calamities; for when I am weak, then I am strong.[5] The Lord has chastened me sorely, but He has not given me over to death.[6] For the moment all discipline seems painful rather than pleasant; later it yields the peaceful fruit of righteousness to those who have been trained by it.[7]

**Heb. 12:7.* [1]*Heb. 12:6, 7, 10.* [2]*Jn. 15:2.* [3]*Heb. 5:8.* [4]*1 Pet. 4:1, 2.* [5]*2 Cor. 12:10.* [6]*Ps. 118:18.* [7]*Heb. 12:11.*

AUGUST 17

*The meekness and gentleness of Christ**

Learn from Me; for I am gentle and lowly in heart.[1] I am among you as one who serves.[2] When He was reviled, He did not revile in return; when He suffered, He did not threaten; but He trusted to Him who judges justly.[3]

When He had said this, one of the officers standing by struck Jesus with his hand, saying, 'Is that how You answer the high priest?' Jesus answered him, 'If I have spoken wrongly, bear witness to the wrong; but if I have spoken rightly, why do you strike Me?'[4] And they stripped Him and put a scarlet robe upon Him, and plaiting a crown of thorns they put it on His head, and put a reed in His right hand. And kneeling before Him they mocked Him, saying, 'Hail, King of the Jews!'[5]

But I say to you, 'Do not resist one who is evil. But if any one strikes you on the right cheek, turn to him the other also. . . . If any one forces you to go one mile, go with him two miles.'[6] Behold, I send you out as sheep in the midst of wolves; so be wise as serpents and innocent as doves.[7]

**2 Cor. 10:1.* [1]*Mt. 11:29.* [2]*Lk. 22:27.* [3]*1 Pet. 2:23.* [4]*Jn. 18:22, 23.* [5]*Mt. 27:28, 29.* [6]*Mt. 5:39, 41.* [7]*Mt. 10:16.*

*The Lord was with Joshua; and his fame was in all the land**

The Lord said to Joshua . . . 'Moses My servant is dead; now therefore arise, go over this Jordan, you and all this people, into the land which I am giving to them.[1] No man shall be able to stand before you all the days of your life; as I was with Moses, so I will be with you; I will not fail you or forsake you. Be strong and of good courage.[2] With God we shall do valiantly; it is He who will tread down our foes.[3] More than conquerors through Him who loved us.[4]

When Joshua was by Jericho . . . a man stood before him with his drawn sword in his hand; and Joshua . . . said to him, 'Are you for us, or for our adversaries?' And he said, 'No; but as commander of the army of the Lord I have now come.' And Joshua fell on his face to the earth, and worshiped, and said to him, 'What does my Lord bid his servant?'[5]

Now therefore fear the Lord, and serve Him in sincerity and in faithfulness; put away the gods which your fathers served beyond the River, and in Egypt, and serve the Lord. And if you be unwilling to serve the Lord, choose this day whom you will serve . . . but as for me and my house, we will serve the Lord.[6]

**Josh. 6:27.* [1]*Josh. 1:1, 2.* [2]*Josh. 1:5, 6.* [3]*Ps. 60:12.* [4]*Rom. 8:37.* [5]*Josh. 5:13, 14.* [6]*Josh. 24:14, 15.*

AUGUST 19

*Continue in the faith**

What shall we say then? Are we to continue in sin that grace may abound? By no means! How can we who died to sin still live in it?[1] Let not your heart envy sinners, but continue in the fear of the Lord all the day.[2]

Jesus . . . said to the Jews who had believed in Him, 'If you continue in My word, you are truly My disciples, and you will know the truth, and the truth will make you free.'[3] Provided that you continue in the faith, stable and steadfast, not shifting from the hope of the gospel which you heard.[4] Continue in what you have learned and have firmly believed.[5]

Continue steadfastly in prayer, being watchful in it with thanksgiving.[6] Seek the Lord and His strength, seek His presence continually![7] I will bless the Lord at all times; His praise shall continually be in my mouth.[8] She who . . . has set her hope on God and continues in supplications and prayers night and day.[9]

And when the meeting . . . broke up, many Jews . . . followed Paul and Barnabas, who spoke to them and urged them to continue in the grace of God.[10]

**Col. 1:23. [1]Rom. 6:1, 2. [2]Prov. 23:17. [3]Jn. 8:31, 32. [4]Col. 1:23. [5]2 Tim. 3:14. [6]Col. 4:2. [7]1 Chron. 16:11. [8]Ps. 34:1. [9]1 Tim. 5:5. [10]Acts 13:43.*

*I know my transgressions, and my sin is ever before me**

Hide Thy face from my sins, and blot out all my iniquities. Create in me a clean heart, O God, and put a new and right spirit within me.[1] I do not understand my own actions. For I do not do what I want, but I do the very thing I hate.[2] Wretched man that I am! Who will deliver me from this body of death?[3]

But when he came to himself he said, 'How many of my father's hired servants have bread enough and to spare, but I perish here with hunger! I will arise and go to my father, and I will say to him, "Father, I have sinned against heaven and before you." '[4] Now when they heard this they were cut to the heart, and said to Peter and the rest of the apostles, 'Brethren, what shall we do?' And Peter said to them, 'Repent, and be baptized every one of you in the name of Jesus Christ for the forgiveness of your sins; and you shall receive the gift of the Holy Spirit.'[5]

The sacrifice acceptable to God is a broken spirit; a broken and contrite heart, O God, Thou wilt not despise.[6]

**Ps. 51:3.* [1]*Ps. 51:9, 10.* [2]*Rom. 7:15.* [3]*Rom. 7:24.* [4]*Lk. 15:17, 18.* [5]*Acts 2:37, 38.* [6]*Ps. 51:17.*

AUGUST 21

*Multitudes, in the valley of decision!**

Elijah came near to all the people, and said, 'How long will you go limping with two different opinions? If the Lord is God, follow Him; but if Baal, then follow him.'[1] Then Moses stood in the gate of the camp, and said, 'Who is on the Lord's side? Come to me.' And all the sons of Levi gathered themselves together to him.[2]

Nicodemus said to Jesus, 'How can this be?'[3] The woman . . . said . . . 'Can this be the Christ?'[4] Nathanael said to Philip, 'Can anything good come out of Nazareth?'[5] And who is He, sir, that I may believe in Him?[6] Thomas said to Him, 'Lord . . . how can we know the way?'[7] And Saul fell to the ground and heard a voice saying to him, 'Saul, Saul, why do you persecute Me?' And he said, 'Who are You, Lord?'[8]

Turn to Me and be saved, all the ends of the earth.[9] You will seek Me and find Me; when you seek Me with all your heart, I will be found by you.[10]

Thomas answered Him, 'My Lord and my God!'[11] Nicodemus also, who had at first come to Him by night, came bringing a mixture of myrrh and aloes.[12] And in the synagogues immediately Paul proclaimed Jesus, saying, 'He is the Son of God.'[13]

**Joel 3:14.* [1]*1 Kings 18:21.* [2]*Ex. 32:26.* [3]*Jn. 3:9.* [4]*Jn. 4:28, 29.* [5]*Jn. 1:46.* [6]*Jn. 9:36.* [7]*Jn. 14:5.* [8]*Acts 9:4, 5.* [9]*Is. 45:22.* [10]*Jer. 29:13, 14.* [11]*Jn. 20:28.* [12]*Jn. 19:39.* [13]*Acts 9:20.*

*How are they to hear without a preacher?**

If I say to the wicked, 'You shall surely die,' and you give him no warning, nor speak to warn the wicked from his wicked way, in order to save his life, that wicked man shall die in his iniquity; but his blood I will require at your hand.[1]

Restore to me the joy of Thy salvation . . . then I will teach transgressors Thy ways, and sinners will return to Thee.[2] Come and hear, all you who fear God, and I will tell what He has done for me.[3] Telling all Thy wondrous deeds.[4]

Let him know that whoever brings back a sinner from the error of his way will save his soul from death and will cover a multitude of sins.[5] And those who are wise shall shine like the brightness of the firmament; and those who turn many to righteousness, like the stars for ever and ever.[6]

The Lord gives the command; great is the host of those who bore the tidings.[7] And Jesus came and said to them, 'All authority in heaven and on earth has been given to Me. Go therefore and make disciples of all nations . . . teaching them to observe all that I have commanded you.'[8]

**Rom.* *10:14.* [1]*Ezek. 3:18.* [2]*Ps. 51:12, 13.* [3]*Ps. 66:16.* [4]*Ps. 26:7.* [5]*Jas. 5:20.* [6]*Dan. 12:3.* [7]*Ps. 68:11.* [8]*Mt. 28:18–20.*

AUGUST 23

*I Myself will be the Shepherd**

Tend the flock of God that is your charge . . . And when the chief Shepherd is manifested you will obtain the unfading crown of glory.[1] Prophesy against the shepherds of Israel . . . 'The weak you have not strengthened, the sick you have not healed . . . the lost you have not sought.'[2] He who is a hireling . . . sees the wolf coming and leaves the sheep and flees. . . . He flees because he . . . cares nothing for the sheep.[3] My sheep hear My voice, and I know them, and they follow Me; and I give them eternal life, and they shall never perish, and no one shall snatch them out of My hand.[4]

Our Lord Jesus, the great Shepherd of the sheep.[5] As a shepherd seeks out his flock . . . so will I seek out My sheep; and I will rescue them from all places where they have been scattered.[6]

I am the good Shepherd. The good Shepherd lays down His life for the sheep.[7] I will bring back the strayed, and I will bind up the crippled, and I will strengthen the weak, and the fat and the strong I will watch over.[8] I am the good Shepherd; I know My own and My own know Me.[9]

**Ezek. 34:15. [1]Pet. 5: 2, 4. [2]Ezek. 34:2, 4. [3]Jn. 10:12, 13. [4]Jn. 10:27, 28. [5]Heb. 13:20. [6]Ezek. 34:12. [7]Jn. 10:11. [8]Ezek. 34:16. [9]Jn. 10:14.*

*Let the peace of Christ rule in your hearts**

He who dwells in the shelter of the Most High, who abides in the shadow of the Almighty, will say to the Lord, 'My refuge and my fortress; my God, in whom I trust.'[1] Thou dost keep him in perfect peace, whose mind is stayed on Thee, because he trusts in Thee.[2]

I pour out my complaint before Him, I tell my trouble before Him.[3] Have no anxiety about anything, but in everything . . . let your requests be made known to God. And the peace of God, which passes all understanding, will keep your hearts and your minds in Christ Jesus.[4]

In peace I will both lie down and sleep; for Thou alone, O Lord, makest me dwell in safety.[5] You shall know that your tent is safe, and you shall inspect your fold and miss nothing.[6] He restores my soul.[7]

Now may the Lord of peace Himself give you peace at all times in all ways.[8] Peace I leave with you; My peace I give to you; not as the world gives do I give to you. Let not your heart be troubled, neither let them be afraid.[9]

**Col. 3:15.* [1]*Ps. 91:1, 2.* [2]*Isa. 26:3.* [3]*Ps. 142:2.* [4]*Phil. 4:6, 7.* [5]*Ps. 4:8.* [6]*Job 5:24.* [7]*Ps. 23:3.* [8]*2 Thess. 3:16.* [9]*Jn. 14:27.*

AUGUST 25

*Walking in all the commandments**

If we walk in the light, as He is in the light, we have fellowship with one another, and the blood of Jesus His Son cleanses us from all sin.[1] Again Jesus spoke to them, saying, 'I am the light of the world; he who follows Me will not walk in darkness, but will have the light of life.'[2] If any one walks in the day, he does not stumble, because he sees the light of this world. But if any one walks in the night, he stumbles, because the light is not in him.[3] For once you were darkness, but now you are light in the Lord; walk as children of light.[4] O house of Jacob, come, let us walk in the light of the Lord.[5]

Walk in love, as Christ loved us, and gave Himself up for us.[6] A new commandment I give to you, that you love one another; even as I have loved you, that you also love one another. By this all men will know that you are My disciples, if you have love for one another.[7] Whoever keeps His word, in him truly love for God is perfected. By this we may be sure that we are in Him: he who says he abides in Him ought to walk in the same way in which He walked.[8]

**Lk.* 1:6. [1]*1 Jn.* 1:7. [2]*Jn.* 8:12. [3]*Jn.* 11:9, 10. [4]*Eph.* 5:8. [5]*Is.* 2:5. [6]*Eph.* 5:2. [7]*Jn.* 13:34, 35. [8]*1 Jn.* 2:5, 6.

*Behold, I make all things new**

If any one is in Christ, he is a new creation; the old has passed away, behold, the new has come.[1] As Christ was raised from the dead by the glory of the Father, we too might walk in newness of life.[2] A new heart I will give you, and a new spirit I will put within you; and I will take out of your flesh the heart of stone and give you a heart of flesh. And I will put My Spirit within you, and cause you to walk in My statutes and be careful to observe My ordinances.[3] Be renewed in the spirit of your minds, and put on the new nature, created after the likeness of God in true righteousness and holiness.[4]

I waited patiently for the Lord; He inclined to me and heard my cry. He drew me up from the desolate pit, out of the miry bog, and set my feet upon a rock, making my steps secure. He put a new song in my mouth, a song of praise to our God. Many will see and fear, and put their trust in the Lord.[5] O sing to the Lord a new song.[6]

A new commandment I give to you, that you love one another; even as I have loved you, that you also love one another.[7]

**Rev. 21:5.* [1]*2 Cor. 5:17.* [2]*Rom. 6:4.* [3]*Ezek. 36:26, 27.* [4]*Eph. 4:23, 24.* [5]*Ps. 40:1–3.* [6]*Ps. 96:1.* [7]*Jn. 13:34.*

AUGUST 27

*I am with you**

When I awake, I am still with Thee.[1] Lo, I am with you always, to the close of the age.[2] I keep the Lord always before me; because He is at my right hand, I shall not be moved. Therefore my heart is glad, and my soul rejoices; my body also dwells secure.[3]

For He has said, 'I will never fail you nor forsake you.' Hence we can confidently say, 'The Lord is my helper, I will not be afraid; what can man do to me?'[4] Even though I walk through the valley of the shadow of death, I fear no evil; for Thou art with me; Thy rod and Thy staff, they comfort me.[5]

Whither shall I go from Thy Spirit? Or whither shall I flee from Thy presence? . . . If I take the wings of the morning and dwell in the uttermost parts of the sea, even there Thy hand shall lead me, and Thy right hand shall hold me.[6] Have I not commanded you? Be strong and of good courage; be not frightened, neither be dismayed; for the Lord your God is with you wherever you go.[7]

**Isa. 41:10.* [1]*Ps. 139:18.* [2]*Mt. 28:20.* [3]*Ps. 16:8, 9.* [4]*Heb. 13:5, 6.* [5]*Ps. 23:4.* [6]*Ps. 139:7, 9, 10.* [7]*Josh. 1:9.*

*Rejected by men**

When they heard this, all in the synagogue were filled with wrath. And they rose up and put Him out of the city, and led Him to the brow of the hill . . . that they might throw Him down headlong.[1] And behold, all the city came out to meet Jesus; and when they saw Him, they begged Him to leave their neighborhood.[2] And He sent messengers ahead of Him . . . to make ready for Him; but the people would not receive Him.[3] Even His brothers did not believe in Him.[4] And when they came to the place which is called The Skull, there they crucified Him.[5]

Consider Him who endured from sinners such hostility against Himself, so that you may not grow weary or faint-hearted.[6] He was despised and rejected by men; a man of sorrows, and acquainted with grief; and as one from whom men hide their faces He was despised, and we esteemed Him not.[7]

If the world hates you, know that it has hated Me before it hated you. . . . A servant is not greater than his master. If they persecuted Me, they will persecute you; if they kept My word, they will keep yours also.[8]

**Is. 53:3.* [1]*Lk. 4:28, 29.* [2]*Mt. 8:34.* [3]*Lk. 9:51–53.* [4]*Jn. 7:5.* [5]*Lk. 23:33.* [6]*Heb. 12:3.* [7]*Is. 53:3.* [8]*Jn. 15:18, 20.*

AUGUST 29

*Not having a righteousness of my own**

Jesus . . . told this parable to some who trusted in themselves that they were righteous and despised others: 'Two men went up into the temple to pray, one a Pharisee and the other a tax collector. The Pharisee stood and prayed thus with himself, "God, I thank Thee that I am not like other men, extortioners, unjust, adulterers, or even like this tax collector." '[1] He said to them, 'You are those who justify yourselves before men, but God knows your hearts; for what is exalted among men is an abomination in the sight of God.'[2] Truly I know that it is so: but how can a man be just before God?[3]

Being ignorant of the righteousness that comes from God, and seeking to establish their own, they did not submit to God's righteousness.[4] If any other man thinks he has reason for confidence in the flesh, I have more: circumcised on the eighth day . . . as to righteousness under the law blameless . . . For His sake I have suffered the loss of all things . . . in order that I may gain Christ and be found in Him, not having a righteousness of my own, based on law, but that which is through faith in Christ, the righteousness from God that depends on faith.[5]

**Phil. 3:9. [1]Lk. 18:9–11. [2]Lk. 16:15. [3]Job 9:2. [4]Rom. 10:3. [5]Phil. 3:4, 5, 6, 8, 9.*

*Why is the house of God forsaken?**

I was glad when they said to me, 'Let us go to the house of the Lord!'[1] Come, let us go up to the mountain of the Lord, to the house of the God of Jacob; that He may teach us His ways and that we may walk in His paths.[2] These I will bring . . . and make them joyful in My house of prayer . . . for My house shall be called a house of prayer for all peoples.[3]

And Jesus came to Nazareth, where He had been brought up; and He went to the synagogue, as His custom was, on the sabbath day. And He stood up to read; and there was given to Him the book of the prophet Isaiah.[4] And on the sabbath day we went outside the gate to the riverside, where we supposed there was a place of prayer; and we sat down and spoke to the women who had come together.[5] On the first day of the week, when we were gathered together to break bread, Paul talked with them . . . and he prolonged his speech until midnight.[6]

Let us hold fast the confession of our hope without wavering . . . not neglecting to meet together, as is the habit of some, but encouraging one another, and all the more as you see the Day drawing near.[7]

**Neh. 13:11. [1]Ps. 122:1. [2]Is. 2:3. [3]Is. 56:7. [4]Lk. 4:16, 17. [5]Acts 16:13. [6]Acts 20:7. [7]Heb. 10:23, 25.*

AUGUST 31

*Be filled with the Spirit**

On the last day of the feast, the great day, Jesus stood up and proclaimed, 'If any one thirst, let him come to Me and drink. He who believes in Me, as the scripture has said, Out of his heart shall flow rivers of living water.' Now this He said about the Spirit, which those who believed in Him were to receive.[1] You are not in the flesh, you are in the Spirit, if the Spirit of God really dwells in you. Any one who does not have the Spirit of Christ does not belong to Him.[2] Be aglow with the Spirit.[3]

They were all filled with the Holy Spirit and spoke the word of God with boldness.[4] Barnabas was a good man, full of the Holy Spirit and of faith.[5] And the disciples were filled with joy and with the Holy Spirit.[6]

That you may know . . . what are the riches of His glorious inheritance in the saints, and what is the immeasurable greatness of His power in us who believe.[7] That you may be filled with all the fullness of God.[8] If you then, who are evil, know how to give good gifts to your children, how much more will the heavenly Father give the Holy Spirit to those who ask Him?[9]

**Eph.* 5:18. [1]*Jn.* 7:37–39. [2]*Rom.* 8:9. [3]*Rom.* 12:11. [4]*Acts* 4:31. [5]*Acts* 11:24. [6]*Acts* 13:52. [7]*Eph.* 1:18, 19. [8]*Eph.* 3:19. [9]*Lk.* 11:13.

*The word of our God will stand for ever**

The living and abiding word of God; for . . . the grass withers, and the flower falls, but the word of the Lord abides for ever. That word is the good news which was preached to you.[1] Think not that I have come to abolish the law and the prophets; I have come not to abolish them but to fulfil them. For truly, I say to you, till heaven and earth pass away, not an iota, not a dot, will pass from the law until all is accomplished.[2] Heaven and earth will pass away, but My words will not pass away.[3]

God is not man, that He should lie, or a son of man, that He should repent. Has He said, and will He not do it? Or has He spoken, and will He not fulfil it?[4] Then the Lord said to me, 'You have seen well, for I am watching over My word to perform it.'[5] And the Lord said to Moses, 'Is the Lord's hand shortened? Now you shall see whether My word will come true for you or not.'[6] The Glory of Israel will not lie or repent; for He is not a man, that He should repent.[7]

**Is. 40:8.* [1]*1 Pet. 1:23–25.* [2]*Mt. 5:17, 18.* [3]*Mt. 24:35.* [4]*Num. 23:19.* [5]*Jer. 1:12.* [6]*Num. 11:23.* [7]*1 Sam. 15:29.*

SEPTEMBER 2

*Every man mature in Christ**

Let us leave the elementary doctrines of Christ and go on to maturity.[1] So that we may no longer be children, tossed to and fro and carried about with every wind of doctrine, by the cunning of men, by their craftiness in deceitful wiles.[2] Brethren, do not be children in your thinking; be babes in evil, but in thinking be mature.[3]

But solid food is for the mature, for those who have their faculties trained by practice to distinguish good from evil.[4] So shun youthful passions and aim at righteousness, faith, love, and peace, along with those who call upon the Lord from a pure heart.[5] May the God of peace Himself sanctify you wholly.[6] Grow up . . . into Christ.[7]

Let those of us who are mature be thus minded; and if in anything you are otherwise minded, God will reveal that also to you. Only let us hold true to what we have attained.[8] Until we all attain to the unity of the faith and of the knowledge of the Son of God, to mature manhood, to the measure of the stature of the fullness of Christ.[9]

**Col. 1:28.* [1]*Heb. 6:1.* [2]*Eph. 4:14.* [3]*1 Cor. 14:20.* [4]*Heb. 5:14.* [5]*2 Tim. 2:22.* [6]*1 Thess. 5:23.* [7]*Eph. 4:15.* [8]*Phil. 3:15, 16.* [9]*Eph. 4:13.*

*One thing I do**

Then they said, 'Come, let us build ourselves a city, and a tower with its top in the heavens, and let us make a name for ourselves.'[1] Absalom said . . . 'Oh that I were judge in the land!'[2] Would that this people were under my hand![3] But they were silent; for on the way they had discussed with one another who was the greatest.[4] Diotrephes, who likes to put himself first, does not acknowledge my authority.[5] Thus says the Lord: . . . 'Do you seek great things for yourself? Seek them not.'[6]

One thing . . . will I seek after; that I may dwell in the house of the Lord all the days of my life, to behold the beauty of the Lord, and to inquire in His temple.[7] One thing I do, forgetting what lies behind and straining forward to what lies ahead, I press on toward the goal for the prize of the upward call of God in Christ Jesus.[8]

Train yourself in godliness.[9] Strive for . . . the holiness without which no one will see the Lord.[10] We make it our aim to please Him.[11] Do your best to present yourself to God as one approved.[12] Making it my ambition to preach the gospel.[13] For this I toil, striving with all the energy which He mightily inspires within me.[14]

**Phil. 3:13.* [1]*Gen. 11:4.* [2]*2 Sam. 15:4.* [3]*Judg. 9:29.* [4]*Mk. 9:34.* [5]*3 Jn. 9.* [6]*Jer. 45:4, 5.* [7]*Ps. 27:4.* [8]*Phil. 3:13, 14.* [9]*1 Tim. 4:7.* [10]*Heb. 12:14.* [11]*2 Cor. 5:9.* [12]*2 Tim. 2:15.* [13]*Rom. 15:20.* [14]*Col. 1:29.*

SEPTEMBER 4

*The Master**

No one can serve two masters; for either he will hate the one and love the other, or he will be devoted to the one and despise the other. You cannot serve God and mammon.[1] For you have one Master, the Christ.[2] No one who puts his hand to the plow and looks back is fit for the kingdom of God.[3]

A bruised reed He will not break, and a dimly burning wick He will not quench.[4] Who are you to pass judgment on the servant of another? It is before his own master that he stands or falls. And he will be upheld, for the Master is able to make him stand.[5] The Lord redeems the life of His servants; none of those who take refuge in Him will be condemned.[6]

Remember the word that I said to you, 'A servant is not greater than his master.' If they persecuted Me, they will persecute you; if they kept My word, they will keep yours also.[7] Take My yoke upon you . . . for My yoke is easy, and My burden is light.[8] We are fellow workmen for God.[9] Working together with Him.[10]

**Rom. 14:4.* [1]*Mt. 6:24.* [2]*Mt. 23:10.* [3]*Lk. 9:62.* [4]*Isa. 42:3.* [5]*Rom. 14:4.* [6]*Ps. 34:22.* [7]*Jn. 15:20.* [8]*Mt. 11:29, 30.* [9]*1 Cor. 3:9.* [10]*2 Cor. 6:1.*

*Publius . . . entertained us hospitably**

Abraham lifted up his eyes . . . and behold, three men stood in front of him. When he saw them, he ran from the tent door to meet them, and bowed himself to the earth, and said . . . 'Let a little water be brought, and wash your feet, and rest yourselves under the tree, while I fetch a morsel of bread, that you may refresh yourselves.'[1] Do not neglect to show hospitality to strangers, for thereby some have entertained angels unawares.[2]

Jesus said to Simon . . . 'I entered your house, you gave Me no water for My feet . . . You gave me no kiss . . . You did not anoint My head with oil.[3] And when Lydia was baptized . . . she besought us, saying, 'If you have judged me to be faithful to the Lord, come to my house and stay.' And she prevailed upon us.[4] They constrained Him, saying, Stay with us, for it is toward evening and the day is now far spent. So He went in to stay with them.[5]

The sojourner has not lodged in the street; I have opened my doors to the wayfarer.[6] So then, as we have opportunity, let us do good to all men, and especially to those who are of the household of faith.[7] Practice hospitality.[8]

**Acts 28:7. [1]Gen. 18:2–5. [2]Heb. 13:2. [3]Lk. 7:44–46. [4]Acts 16:15. [5]Lk. 24:29. [6]Job 31:32. [7]Gal. 6:10. [8]Rom. 12:13.*

SEPTEMBER 6

*Increase our faith!**

Faith comes from what is heard, and what is heard comes by the preaching of Christ.[1] Many of those who heard the word believed; and the number of the men came to about five thousand.[2] When they believed Philip as he preached good news about the kingdom of God and the name of Jesus Christ, they were baptized, both men and women.[3]

What does it profit, my brethren, if a man says he has faith but has not works? Can his faith save him? . . . So faith by itself, if it has no works, is dead.[4] We are bound to give thanks to God always for you, brethren, as is fitting, because your faith is growing abundantly, and the love of every one of you for one another is increasing.[5] For in Christ Jesus neither circumcision nor uncircumcision is of any avail, but faith working through love.[6]

For this very reason make every effort to supplement your faith with virtue, and virtue with knowledge, and knowledge with self-control, and self-control with steadfastness, and steadfastness with godliness, and godliness with brotherly affection, and brotherly affection with love. For if these things are yours and abound, they keep you from being ineffective or unfruitful in the knowledge of our Lord Jesus Christ.[7]

**Lk. 17:5.* [1]*Rom. 10:17.* [2]*Acts 4:4.* [3]*Acts 8:12.* [4]*Jas. 2:14, 17.* [5]*2 Thess. 1:3.* [6]*Gal. 5:6.* [7]*2 Pet. 1:5–8.*

*I have loved you, says the Lord**

Are the consolations of God too small for you?[1] I have loved you with an everlasting love; therefore I have continued My faithfulness to you.[2] For the mountains may depart and the hills be removed, but My steadfast love shall not depart from you, . . . says the Lord, who has compassion on you.[3] It was I who taught Ephraim to walk, I took them up in My arms; but they did not know that I healed them. I led them with cords of compassion, with the bands of love.[4]

In this the love of God was made manifest among us, that God sent His only Son into the world, so that we might live through Him.[5] God shows His love for us in that while we were yet sinners Christ died for us.[6] For God so loved the world that He gave His only Son, that whoever believes in Him should not perish but have eternal life.[7]

The steadfast love of the Lord never ceases.[8] For I am sure that neither death, nor life, nor angels, nor principalities, nor things present, nor things to come, nor powers, nor height, nor depth, nor anything else in all creation, will be able to separate us from the love of God in Christ Jesus our Lord.[9]

**Mal. 1:2.* [1]*Job 15:11.* [2]*Jer. 31:3.* [3]*Is. 54:10.* [4]*Hos. 11:3, 4.* [5]*1 Jn. 4:9.* [6]*Rom. 5:8.* [7]*Jn. 3:16.* [8]*Lam. 3:22.* [9]*Rom. 8:38, 39.*

SEPTEMBER 8

*Pray at all times**

Jesus was praying in a certain place, and when He ceased, one of His disciples said to Him, 'Lord, teach us to pray, as John taught his disciples.' And He said to them, 'When you pray, say: "Father, hallowed be Thy name. Thy kingdom come. Give us each day our daily bread; and forgive us our sins, for we ourselves forgive every one who is indebted to us; and lead us not into temptation." '[1] Pray then like this.[2]

Daniel . . . went to his house . . . and he got down upon his knees three times a day and prayed and gave thanks before his God, as he had done previously.[3] Evening and morning and at noon I utter my complaint and moan, and He will hear my voice.[4] O Lord, in the morning Thou dost hear my voice.[5] In the morning my prayer comes before Thee.[6] Let my prayer be . . . as an evening sacrifice.[7] At midnight I rise to praise Thee.[8] I rise before dawn and cry for help.[9]

And Jesus told them a parable, to the effect that they ought always to pray and not lose heart.[10] Pray constantly, give thanks in all circumstances; for this is the will of God in Christ Jesus for you.[11]

**Eph. 6:18.* [1]*Lk. 11:1–4.* [2]*Mt. 6:9.* [3]*Dan. 6:10.* [4]*Ps. 55:17.* [5]*Ps. 5:3.* [6]*Ps. 88:13.* [7]*Ps. 141:2.* [8]*Ps. 119:62.* [9]*Ps. 119:147.* [10]*Lk. 18:1.* [11]*1 Thess. 5:17, 18.*

SEPTEMBER 9

*Every day I will bless Thee**

And Jesus said to all, 'If any man would come after Me, let him deny himself and take up his cross daily and follow Me.'[1] I protest, brethren, by my pride in you which I have in Christ Jesus our Lord, I die every day![2] For Thy sake we are being killed all the day long.[3] Always carrying in the body the death of Jesus, so that the life of Jesus may also be manifested in our bodies.[4]

Now these Jews . . . received the word with all eagerness, examining the scriptures daily to see if these things were so [5] Oh, how I love Thy law! It is my meditation all the day.[6] His delight is in the law of the Lord, and on His law he meditates day and night.[7]

Blessed be the Lord, who daily bears us up; God is our salvation.[8] The steadfast love of the Lord never ceases, His mercies never come to an end; they are new every morning; great is Thy faithfulness.[9] As your days, so shall your strength be.[10]

**Ps. 145:2.* [1]*Lk. 9:23.* [2]*1 Cor. 15:31.* [3]*Rom. 8:36.* [4]*2 Cor. 4:10.* [5]*Acts. 17:11.* [6]*Ps. 119:97.* [7]*Ps. 1:2.* [8]*Ps. 68:19.* [9]*Lam. 3:22, 23.* [10]*Deut. 33:25.*

SEPTEMBER 10

*A faithful Creator**

The Spirit of God has made me, and the breath of the Almighty gives me life.[1] It is He that made us, and not we ourselves.[2] We are the clay, and Thou art our potter; we are all the work of Thy hand.[3] Have we not all one Father? Has not one God created us? Why then are we faithless to one another?[4]

Thy hands fashioned and made me.... Thou didst clothe me with skin and flesh, and knit me together with bones and sinews. Thou hast granted me life and steadfast love; and Thy care has preserved my spirit.[5] For Thou didst form my inward parts, Thou didst knit me together in my mother's womb. I praise Thee, for Thou art fearful and wonderful. Wonderful are Thy works! Thou knowest me right well.[6]

When God created man, He made him in the likeness of God.[7] Bringing many sons to glory.[8] Now thus says the Lord, He who created you, O Jacob, He who formed you, O Israel: 'Fear not, for I have redeemed you; I have called you by name, you are Mine.'[9] Called by My name... created for My glory.[10]

**I Pet. 4:19.* [1]*Job 33:4.* [2]*Ps. 100:3.* [3]*Isa. 64:8.* [4]*Mal. 2:10.* [5]*Job 10:8, 11, 12.* [6]*Ps. 139:13, 14.* [7]*Gen. 5:1.* [8]*Heb. 2:10.* [9]*Isa. 43:1.* [10]*Isa. 43:7.*

*Jesus increased . . . in favor with God and man**

And all who believed were together . . . praising God and having favor with all the people.[1] The patriarchs, jealous of Joseph, sold him into Egypt; but God was with him . . . and gave him favor and wisdom before Pharaoh, king of Egypt.[2] God gave Daniel favor and compassion in the sight of the chief of the eunuchs.[3]

You know what kind of men we proved to be among you for your sake.[4] You are witnesses, and God also, how holy and righteous and blameless was our behavior.[5] Keep your conscience clear, so that, when you are abused, those who revile your good behavior in Christ may be put to shame.[6] Maintain good conduct among the Gentiles, so that . . . they may see your good deeds and glorify God.[7] Let your light so shine before men, that they may see your good works and give glory to your Father who is in heaven.[8]

These are the things that you shall do: Speak the truth to one another, render in your gates judgments that are true and make for peace, do not devise evil in your hearts against one another, and love no false oath, for all these things I hate, says the Lord.[9]

**Lk.* 2:52. [1]*Acts* 2:44, 47. [2]*Acts* 7:9, 10. [3]*Dan.* 1:9. [4]*1 Thess.* 1:5. [5]*1 Thess.* 2:10. [6]*1 Pet.* 3:16. [7]*1 Pet.* 2:12. [8]*Mt.* 5:16. [9]*Zech.* 8:16, 17.

SEPTEMBER 12

*The friend of God**

Abraham believed God, and it was reckoned to him as righteousness; and he was called the friend of God.[1] Abraham, My friend.[2] No longer do I call you servants, for the servant does not know what his master is doing; but I have called you friends, for all that I have heard from My Father I have made known to you.[3] He who has the bride is the bridegroom; the friend of the bridegroom, who stands and hears him, rejoices greatly at the bridegroom's voice; therefore this joy of mine is now full.[4]

Do you not know that friendship with the world is enmity with God? Therefore whoever wishes to be a friend of the world makes himself an enemy of God.[5] Do not love the world or the things in the world. If any one loves the world, love for the Father is not in him.[6] If a man loves Me, he will keep My word, and My Father will love him, and We will come to him and make Our home with him.[7] If you love Me, you will keep My commandments.[8] You are My friends if you do what I command you.[9]

**Jas. 2:23.* [1]*Jas. 2:23.* [2]*Is. 41:8.* [3]*Jn. 15:15.* [4]*Jn. 3:29.* [5]*Jas. 4:4.* [6]*1 Jn. 2:15.* [7]*Jn. 14:23.* [8]*Jn. 14:15.* [9]*Jn. 15:14.*

SEPTEMBER 13

*The soul that sins shall die**

When you were slaves of sin, you were free in regard to righteousness. But then what return did you get from the things of which you are now ashamed? The end of those things is death. . . . . For the wages of sin is death, but the free gift of God is eternal life in Christ Jesus our Lord.[1]

He who believes in the Son has eternal life; he who does not obey the Son shall not see life, but the wrath of God rests upon him.[2] Let no one deceive you with empty words, for it is because of these things that the wrath of God comes upon the sons of disobedience.[3] For Thou art not a God who delights in wickedness; evil may not sojourn with Thee.[4]

Those eighteen upon whom the tower in Siloam fell and killed them, do you think that they were worse offenders than all the others who dwelt in Jerusalem? I tell you, No; but unless you repent you will all likewise perish.[5] See that you do not refuse Him who is speaking. For if they did not escape when they refused Him who warned them on earth, much less shall we escape if we reject Him who warns from heaven . . . Thus let us offer to God acceptable worship, with reverence and awe; for our God is a consuming fire.[6]

**Ezek. 18:4.* [1]*Rom. 6:20, 21, 23.* [2]*Jn. 3:36.* [3]*Eph. 5:6.* [4]*Ps. 5:4.* [5]*Lk. 13:4, 5.* [6]*Heb. 12:25, 28, 29.*

SEPTEMBER 14

*Be content**

The whole congregation of the people of Israel murmured against Moses and Aaron in the wilderness, and said to them, 'Would that we had died by the hand of the Lord in the land of Egypt.'[1] There was no water for the people to drink. Therefore the people found fault with Moses.[2] There is no food and no water, and we loathe this worthless food.[3] O that we had meat to eat![4] They spoke against God, saying, 'Can God spread a table in the wilderness?'[5]

Better is a little with the fear of the Lord than great treasure and trouble with it. Better is a dinner of herbs where love is than a fatted ox and hatred with it.[6] Give me neither poverty nor riches; feed me with the food that is needful for me.[7]

There is great gain in godliness with contentment; for we brought nothing into the world, and we cannot take anything out of the world; but if we have food and clothing, with these we shall be content.[8] Not that I complain of want; for I have learned, in whatever state I am, to be content.[9]

**Phil. 4:11.* [1]*Ex. 16:2, 3.* [2]*Ex. 17:1, 2.* [3]*Num. 21:5.* [4]*Num. 11:4.* [5]*Ps. 78:19.* [6]*Prov. 15:16, 17.* [7]*Prov. 30:8.* [8]*1 Tim. 6:6–8.* [9]*Phil. 4:11.*

*You have overcome the evil one**

Little children, you are of God, and have overcome them; for He who is in you is greater than he who is in the world.[1] What then shall we say to this? If God is for us, who is against us?[2] If it had not been the Lord who was on our side . . . then they would have swallowed us up alive.[3] With the Lord on my side I do not fear. What can man do to me?[4] Strengthened with might through His Spirit in the inner man.[5] Be of good cheer, I have overcome the world.[6]

Whatever is born of God overcomes the world; and this is the victory that overcomes the world, our faith. Who is it that overcomes the world but he who believes that Jesus is the Son of God?[7] Above all taking the shield of faith, with which you can quench all the flaming darts of the evil one.[8] Thus says the Lord to you, 'Fear not, and be not dismayed at this great multitude; for the battle is not yours but God's. . . . You will not need to fight in this battle; take your position, stand still, and see the victory of the Lord on your behalf . . . Fear not, and be not dismayed; tomorrow go out against them, and the Lord will be with you.[9] Thanks be to God, who gives us the victory through our Lord Jesus Christ.[10]

**1 Jn. 2:13. [1]1 Jn. 4:4. [2]Rom. 8:31. [3]Ps. 124:2, 3. [4]Ps. 118:6. [5]Eph. 3:16. [6]Jn. 16:33. [7]1 Jn. 5:4, 5. [8]Eph. 6:16. [9]2 Chron. 20: 15, 17. [10]1 Cor. 15:57.*

SEPTEMBER 16

*There they crucified Him**

Now . . . there was darkness over all the land . . . And about the ninth hour Jesus cried with a loud voice . . . 'My God, My God, why hast Thou forsaken Me?'[1] For our sake God made Him to be sin who knew no sin, so that in Him we might become the righteousness of God.[2] Christ redeemed us from the curse of the law, having become a curse for us.[3] Smitten by God, and afflicted.[4] Yet it was the will of the Lord to bruise Him.[5]

When Jesus had received the vinegar, He said, 'It is finished.'[6] I glorified Thee on earth, having accomplished the work which Thou gavest Me to do.[7] Christ . . . offered for all time a single sacrifice for sins.[8] And behold, the curtain of the temple was torn in two, from top to bottom.[9]

Then Jesus . . . said, 'Father, into Thy hands I commit My spirit!' And having said this He breathed His last.[10] I lay down My life, that I may take it again. No one takes it from Me, but I lay it down of My own accord. I have power to lay it down, and I have power to take it again; this charge I have received from My Father.[11]

**Lk. 23:33. [1]Mt. 27:45, 46. [2]2 Cor. 5:21. [3]Gal. 3:13. [4]Is. 53:4. [5]Is. 53:10. [6]Jn. 19:30. [7]Jn. 17:4. [8]Heb. 10:12. [9]Mt. 27:51. [10]Lk. 23:46. [11]Jn. 10:17, 18.*

*A man of sorrows, and acquainted with grief**

Godly grief produces a repentance that leads to salvation and brings no regret, but worldly grief produces death.[1] The Lord turned and looked at Peter. And Peter remembered the word of the Lord . . . and he went out and wept bitterly.[2] I confess my iniquity, I am sorry for my sin.[3]

We would not have you ignorant, brethren, concerning those who are asleep, that you may not grieve as others do who have no hope.[4] Truly, truly, I say to you, you will weep and lament . . . you will be sorrowful, but your sorrow will turn into joy . . . And no one will take your joy from you.[5]

How long, O Lord? Wilt Thou forget me for ever? How long wilt Thou hide Thy face from me? How long must I . . . have sorrow in my heart all the day?[6] He will wipe away every tear from their eyes, and death shall be no more, neither shall there be mourning nor crying nor pain any more.'[7]

Is it nothing to you, all you who pass by? Look and see if there is any sorrow like my sorrow.[8] Surely He has borne our griefs and carried our sorrows.[9]

**Is. 53:3.* [1]*2 Cor. 7:10.* [2]*Lk. 22:61, 62.* [3]*Ps. 38:18.* [4]*1 Thess. 4:13.* [5]*Jn. 16:20, 22.* [6]*Ps. 13:1, 2.* [7]*Rev. 21:4.* [8]*Lam. 1:12.* [9]*Is. 53:4.*

SEPTEMBER 18

*Your companion and your wife by covenant**

The Lord God said,

'It is not good that the man should be alone; I will make him a helper fit for him.'[1] Therefore a man leaves his father and his mother and cleaves to his wife, and they become one flesh.[2] So they are no longer two but one. What therefore God has joined together, let no man put asunder.[3]

A good wife who can find? She is far more precious than jewels.[4] House and wealth are inherited from fathers, but a prudent wife is from the Lord.[5] Charm is deceitful, and beauty is vain, but a woman who fears the Lord is to be praised.[6] Do not be mismated with unbelievers.[7] He who finds a wife finds a good thing.[8]

Let marriage be held in honor among all.[9] The Lord was witness to the covenant between you and the wife of your youth . . . And what does He desire? Godly offspring. So take heed to yourselves, and let none be faithless to the wife of his youth. For I hate divorce, says the Lord.[10] Jesus said . . . 'Whoever divorces his wife and marries another, commits adultery against her; and if she divorces her husband and marries another, she commits adultery.'[11]

**Mal.* 2:14. [1]*Gen.* 2:18. [2]*Gen.* 2:24. [3]*Mt.* 19:6. [4]*Prov.* 31:10. [5]*Prov.* 19:14. [6]*Prov.* 31:30. [7]2 *Cor.* 6:14. [8]*Prov.* 18:22. [9]*Heb.* 13:4. [10]*Mal.* 2:14–16. [11]*Mk.* 10:11, 12.

*A testimony to all nations**

The kingdom of heaven is like a grain of mustard seed which a man took and sowed in his field; it is the smallest of all seeds, but when it has grown it is the greatest of shrubs and becomes a tree, so that birds of the air come and make nests in its branches . . . The kingdom of heaven is like leaven which a woman took and hid in three measures of meal, till it was all leavened.[1]

Jesus said to them, 'Go into all the world and preach the gospel to the whole creation.'[2] This gospel of the kingdom will be preached throughout the whole world, as a testimony to all nations; and then the end will come.[3] For 'Every one who calls upon the name of the Lord will be saved.' But how are men to call upon Him in whom they have not believed? And how are they to believe in Him of whom they have never heard? And how are they to hear without a preacher?[4]

I do not account my life of any value . . . to myself, if only I may accomplish my course and the ministry which I received from the Lord Jesus, to testify to the gospel of the grace of God.[5] For if I preach the gospel, that gives me no ground for boasting. For necessity is laid upon me. Woe to me if I do not preach the gospel![6]

**Mt. 24:14.* [1]*Mt. 13:31–33.* [2]*Mk. 16:15.* [3]*Mt. 24:14.* [4]*Rom. 10:13, 14.* [5]*Acts 20:24.* [6]*1 Cor. 9:16.*

SEPTEMBER 20

*Well versed in the scriptures**

Examining the scriptures daily.[1] Jesus answered them, 'You are wrong, because you know neither the scriptures nor the power of God.'[2] But as for you . . . from childhood you have been acquainted with the sacred writings which are able to instruct you for salvation through faith in Christ Jesus. All scripture is inspired by God and profitable for teaching, for reproof, for correction, and for training in righteousness, that the man of God may be complete, equipped for every good work.[3] How can a young man keep his way pure? By guarding it according to Thy word.[4]

Showing by the scriptures that the Christ was Jesus.[5] Beginning with Moses and all the prophets, Jesus interpreted to them in all the scriptures the things concerning Himself . . . He opened their minds to understand the scriptures.[6] Philip ran to him, and heard him reading Isaiah the prophet, and asked, 'Do you understand what you are reading?' And he said, 'How can I, unless some one guides me?' . . . Then Philip opened his mouth, and beginning with this scripture he told him the good news of Jesus.[7] Paul went in, as was his custom, and for three weeks he argued with them from the scriptures.[8]

**Acts 18:24.* [1]*Acts 17:11.* [2]*Mt. 22:29.* [3]*2 Tim. 3:14–17.* [4]*Ps. 119:9.* [5]*Acts 18:28.* [6]*Lk. 24:27, 45.* [7]*Acts 8:30, 31, 35.* [8]*Acts 17:2.*

SEPTEMBER 21

*Jesus . . . saw . . . Matthew**

After this Jesus went out, and saw a tax collector, named Levi, sitting at the tax office.[1] Those who are well have no need of a physician, but those who are sick; I have not come to call the righteous, but sinners to repentance.[2] The Son of man has authority on earth to forgive sins.[3]

And Jesus said to him. 'Follow Me.' And he left everything, and rose and followed Him.[4] Whatever gain I had, I counted as loss for the sake of Christ. Indeed I count everything as loss because of the surpassing worth of knowing Christ Jesus my Lord.[5] Truly, I say to you, there is no man who has left house or wife or brothers or parents or children, for the sake of the kingdom of God, who will not receive manifold more in this time, and in the age to come eternal life.[6]

And Levi made Him a great feast in his house; and there was a large company of tax collectors and others sitting at table with them.[7] And I have other sheep, that are not of this fold; I must bring them also, and they will heed My voice. So there shall be one flock, one Shepherd.[8]

**Mt. 9:9.* [1]*Lk. 5:27.* [2]*Lk. 5:31, 32.* [3]*Mk. 2:10.* [4]*Lk. 5:27, 28.* [5]*Phil. 3:7, 8.* [6]*Lk. 18:29, 30.* [7]*Lk. 5:29.* [8]*Jn. 10:16.*

SEPTEMBER 22

*The grace of the Lord Jesus Christ and the love of God and the fellowship of the Holy Spirit be with you all**

For you know the grace of our Lord Jesus Christ, that though He was rich, yet for your sake He became poor, so that by His poverty you might become rich.[1] In Him we have redemption through His blood, the forgiveness of our trespasses, according to the riches of His grace which He lavished upon us.[2]

The earth, O Lord, is full of Thy steadfast love.[3] The Lord is good to all, and His compassion is over all that He has made.[4] In this the love of God was made manifest among us, that God sent His only Son into the world, so that we might live through Him.[5]

Eager to maintain the unity of the Spirit in the bond of peace.[6] Have unity of spirit, sympathy, love of the brethren, a tender heart and a humble mind.[7] So if there is any encouragement in Christ, any incentive of love, any participation in the Spirit, any affection and sympathy, complete my joy by being of the same mind, having the same love, being in full accord and of one mind.[8]

**2 Cor. 13:14.* [1]*2 Cor. 8:9.* [2]*Eph. 1:7, 8.* [3]*Ps. 119:64.* [4]*Ps. 145, 9.* [5]*1 Jn. 4:9.* [6]*Eph. 4:3.* [7]*1 Pet. 3:8.* [8]*Phil. 2:1, 2.*

*Be at peace with one another**

If possible, so far as it depends upon you, live peaceably with all.[1] Behold, how good and pleasant it is when brothers dwell in unity![2] Blessed are the peacemakers, for they shall be called sons of God.[3]

The wisdom from above is first pure, then peaceable, gentle, open to reason, full of mercy and good fruits, without uncertainty or insincerity.[4] Strive for peace with all men, and for the holiness without which no one will see the Lord.[5]

Too long have I had my dwelling among those who hate peace. I am for peace; but when I speak, they are for war![6] 'Lord, do You want us to bid fire come down from heaven and consume them?' But He . . . rebuked them.[7] And He said, 'You do not know what manner of spirit you are of.'[7] The Lord's servant must not be quarrelsome but . . . forbearing, correcting his opponents with gentleness.[8] When a man's ways please the Lord, He makes even his enemies to be at peace with him.[9] Agree with one another, live in peace, and the God of love and peace will be with you.[10]

**Mk. 9:50.* [1]*Rom. 12:18.* [2]*Ps. 133:1.* [3]*Mt. 5:9.* [4]*Jas. 3:17.* [5]*Heb. 12:14.* [6]*Ps. 120:6, 7.* [7]*Lk. 9:54, 55.* [8]*2 Tim. 2:24, 25.* [9]*Prov. 16:7.* [10]*2 Cor. 13:11.*

SEPTEMBER 24

*Seek first His kingdom**

Jesus said to His disciples, 'Truly, I say to you, it will be hard for a rich man to enter the kingdom of heaven . . . It is easier for a camel to go through the eye of a needle than for a rich man to enter the kingdom of God.'[1] Blessed are you poor, for yours is the kingdom of God.[2]

And calling to Him a child, He put him in the midst of them, and said, 'Truly, I say to you, unless you turn and become like children, you will never enter the kingdom of heaven.'[3] Jesus answered him, 'Truly, truly, I say to you, unless one is born anew, he cannot see the kingdom of God.'[4]

Another said, 'I will follow You, Lord; but let me first say farewell to those at my home.' Jesus said to him, 'No one who puts his hand to the plow and looks back is fit for the kingdom of God.'[5] They returned to . . . Antioch, strengthening the souls of the disciples, exhorting them to continue in the faith, and saying that through many tribulations we must enter the kingdom of God.[6]

And when Jesus saw that he answered wisely, He said to him, 'You are not far from the kingdom of God.'[7]

**Mt. 6:33. [1]Mt. 19:23, 24. [2]Lk. 6:20. [3]Mt. 18:2, 3. [4]Jn. 3:3. [5]Lk. 9:61, 62. [6]Acts 14:21, 22. [7]Mk. 12:34.*

*The delight in riches**

Thus says the Lord: . . . 'Let not the rich man glory in his riches.'[1] Do not toil to acquire wealth; be wise enough to desist. When your eyes light upon it, it is gone; for suddenly it takes to itself wings, flying like an eagle toward heaven.[2]

Jesus looking upon him loved him, and said to him, 'You lack one thing; go, sell what you have, and give to the poor, and you will have treasure in heaven; and come, follow Me.' At that saying his countenance fell, and he went away sorrowful: for he had great possessions. And Jesus looked around and said to His disciples, 'How hard it will be for those who have riches to enter the kingdom of God!'[3]

Those who desire to be rich fall into temptation, into a snare, into many senseless and hurtful desires that plunge men into . . . destruction. For the love of money is the root of all evils; it is through this craving that some have wandered away from the faith and pierced their hearts with many pangs.[4] See the man who would not make God his refuge, but trusted in the abundance of his riches, and sought refuge in his wealth![5]

**Mt. 13:22.* [1]*Jer. 9:23.* [2]*Prov. 23:4, 5.* [3]*Mk. 10:21–23.* [4]*1 Tim. 6:9, 10.* [5]*Ps. 52:7.*

SEPTEMBER 26

*Not because of works, lest any man should boast**

A man is not justified by works of the law but through faith in Jesus Christ.[1] God . . . saved us and called us with a holy calling, not in virtue of our works but in virtue of His own purpose and the grace which He gave us in Christ Jesus.[2]

Do not say in your heart . . ., 'It is because of my righteousness that the Lord has brought me in.'[3] Then the king said to his servants, 'The wedding is ready, but those invited were not worthy. Go therefore to the thoroughfares, and invite to the marriage feast as many as you find.' And those servants went out into the streets and gathered all whom they found, both bad and good; so the wedding hall was filled with guests. But when the king came in to look at the guests, he saw there a man who had no wedding garment; and he said to him, 'Friend, how did you get in here without a wedding garment?' And he was speechless.[4]

The Son of man came to seek and to save the lost.[5] Why, one will hardly die for a righteous man—though perhaps for a good man one will dare even to die. But God shows His love for us in that while we were yet sinners Christ died for us.[6]

**Eph. 2:9. [1]Gal. 2:16. [2]2 Tim. 1:8, 9. [3]Deut. 9:4. [4]Mt. 22:8–12. [5]Lk. 19:10. [6]Rom. 5:7, 8.*

*The will of the Lord be done**

Lo, I have come to do Thy will, O God.[1] Jesus said to them, 'My food is to do the will of Him who sent Me, and to accomplish His work.[2] I seek not My own will but the will of Him who sent Me.[3] And He who sent Me is with Me; He has not left Me alone, for I always do what is pleasing to Him.[4] My Father, if it be possible, let this cup pass from Me; nevertheless, not as I will, but as Thou wilt.[5]

By faith Abraham obeyed when he was called to go out to a place which he was to receive as an inheritance; and he went out, not knowing where he was to go.[6] God raised up David to be their king; of whom He testified and said, 'I have found in David the son of Jesse a man after My heart, who will do all My will.[7] We and the people there begged Paul not to go up to Jerusalem. Then Paul answered . . . 'I am ready not only to be imprisoned but even to die at Jerusalem for the name of the Lord Jesus.' And when he would not be persuaded, we ceased and said, 'The will of the Lord be done.'[8] Obedient unto death.[9] Doing the will of God from the heart, rendering service with a good will as to the Lord and not to men.[10]

**Acts 21:14.* [1]*Heb. 10:7.* [2]*Jn. 4:34.* [3]*Jn. 5:30.* [4]*Jn. 8:29.* [5]*Mt. 26:39.* [6]*Heb. 11:8.* [7]*Acts 13:22.* [8]*Acts 21:12–14.* [9]*Phil. 2:8.* [10]*Eph. 6:6, 7.*

SEPTEMBER 28

*God is spirit**

Will God indeed dwell on the earth? Behold, heaven and highest heaven cannot contain Thee; how much less this house which I have built![1] Thus says the Lord: 'Heaven is My throne and the earth is My footstool; what is the house which you would build for Me, and what is the place of My rest?'[2]

Such knowledge is too wonderful for me; it is high, I cannot attain it. Whither shall I go from Thy Spirit? Or whither shall I flee from Thy presence? If I ascend to heaven, Thou art there! If I make my bed in Sheol, Thou art there! If I take the wings of the morning and dwell in the uttermost parts of the sea, even there Thy hand shall lead me, and Thy right hand shall hold me.[3] 'Can a man hide himself in secret places so that I cannot see him? . . . Do I not fill heaven and earth?' says the Lord.[4]

Thus says the high and lofty One who inhabits eternity, whose name is Holy: 'I dwell in the high and holy place, and also with him who is of a contrite and humble spirit . . . to revive the heart of the contrite.'[5]

**Jn. 4:24. [1]1 Kings 8:27. [2]Is. 66:1. [3]Ps. 139:6–10. [4]Jer. 23:24. [5]Is. 57:15.*

*The angels of God . . . ascending and descending**

Are they not all ministering spirits sent forth to serve, for the sake of those who are to obtain salvation?[1]

And the angel said to them, 'Be not afraid; for behold, I bring you good news of a great joy . . . for to you is born this day . . . a Savior.[2] Then the devil left Him, and behold, angels came and ministered to Him.[3] Jesus . . . prayed, 'Father, . . . not My will, but Thine, be done.' And there appeared to Him an angel from heaven, strengthening Him.[4] An angel of the Lord descended from heaven and came and rolled back the stone, and sat upon it.[5]

The angel of the Lord encamps around those who fear Him, and delivers them[6] For He will give His angels charge of you to guard you in all your ways. On their hands they will bear you up, lest you dash your foot against a stone.[7] See that you do not despise one of these little ones; for I tell you that in heaven their angels always behold the face of My Father who is in heaven.[8] And Peter came to himself, and said, 'Now I am sure that the Lord has sent His angel and rescued me from the hand of Herod.'[9]

**Gen. 28:12.* [1]*Heb. 1:14.* [2]*Lk. 2:10, 11.* [3]*Mt. 4:11.* [4]*Lk. 22:41–43.* [5]*Mt. 28:2.* [6]*Ps. 34:7.* [7]*Ps. 91:11, 12.* [8]*Mt. 18:10.* [9]*Acts 12:11.*

SEPTEMBER 30

*Wait for the Lord**

Be still, and know that I am God. I am exalted among the nations, I am exalted in the earth![1] All these with one accord devoted themselves to prayer . . . When the day of Pentecost had come, they were all together in one place. And suddenly a sound came from heaven like the rush of a mighty wind . . . And they were all filled with the Holy Spirit. . . . And there were added that day about three thousand souls.[2]

Will not God vindicate His elect, who cry to Him day and night? Will He delay long over them? I tell you, He will vindicate them speedily. Nevertheless, when the Son of man comes, will He find faith on earth?[3] Fear not, Daniel, for from the first day that you set your mind to understand and humbled yourself before your God, your words have been heard, and I have come because of your words. The prince of the kingdom of Persia withstood me twenty-one days.[4]

I wait for the Lord, my soul waits, and in His word I hope; my soul waits for the Lord more than watchmen for the morning.[5] Be still before the Lord, and wait patiently for Him; fret not yourself.[6]

**Ps. 27:14.* [1]*Ps. 46:10.* [2]*Acts 1:14, 2:1, 2, 4, 41.* [3]*Lk. 18:7, 8.* [4]*Dan. 10:12, 13.* [5]*Ps. 130:5. 6.* [6]*Ps. 37:7.*

OCTOBER 1

*His perfect patience**

What man of you, having a hundred sheep, if he has lost one of them, does not leave the ninety-nine in the wilderness, and go after the one which is lost, until he finds it?[1] The saying is sure and worthy of full acceptance, that Christ Jesus came into the world to save sinners. And I am the foremost of sinners; but I received mercy for this reason, that in me, as the foremost, Jesus Christ might display His perfect patience for an example to those who were to believe in Him for eternal life.[2]

O Jerusalem, Jerusalem, killing the prophets and stoning those who are sent to you! How often would I have gathered your children together as a hen gathers her brood under her wings, and you would not![3] The Lord is not slow about His promise as some count slowness, but is forbearing toward you, not wishing that any should perish, but that all should reach repentance.[4] You have seen the purpose of the Lord, how the Lord is compassionate and merciful.[5] God's patience waited in the days of Noah.[6] Therefore the Lord waits to be gracious to you.[7]

**1 Tim. 1:16. [1]Lk. 15:4. [2]1 Tim. 1:15, 16. [3]Lk. 13:34. [4]2 Pet. 3:9. [5]Jas. 5:11. [6]1 Pet. 3:20. [7]Is. 30:18.*

OCTOBER 2

*They turned aside from following Him**

They forgot what He had done, and the miracles that He had shown them.[1] He forsook God who made him, and scoffed at the Rock of his salvation . . . and you forgot the God who gave you birth.[2] You have abandoned the love you had at first.[3] You have been weary of Me.[4]

The younger son gathered all he had and took his journey into a far country, and there he squandered his property in loose living. And when he had spent everything, a great famine arose in that country, and he began to be in want . . . When he came to himself he said, 'How many of my father's hired servants have bread enough and to spare, but I perish here with hunger! I will arise and go to my father, and I will say to him, "Father, I have sinned against heaven and before you; I am no longer worthy to be called your son." '[5]

Beloved . . . beware lest you be carried away with the error of lawless men and lose your own stability.[6] I am afraid that as the serpent deceived Eve by his cunning, your thoughts will be led astray from a sincere and pure devotion to Christ.[7] Take care, brethren, lest there be in any of you an evil, unbelieving heart, leading you to fall away from the living God.[8]

**Job 34:27.* [1]*Ps. 78:11.* [2]*Deut. 32:15, 18.* [3]*Rev. 2:4.* [4]*Is. 43:22.* [5]*Lk. 15:13, 14, 17 19.* [6]*2 Pet. 3:17.* [7]*2 Cor. 11:3.* [8]*Heb. 3:12.*

OCTOBER 3

*Fighting the battles of the Lord**

Take your share of suffering as a good soldier of Christ Jesus. No soldier on service gets entangled in civilian pursuits, since his aim is to satisfy the one who enlisted him.[1] For it has been granted to you that for the sake of Christ you should not only believe in Him but also suffer for His sake, engaged in the same conflict which you saw and now hear to be mine.[2]

Be watchful, stand firm in your faith, be courageous, be strong.[3] Set up a standard against the walls of Babylon; make the watch strong; set up watchmen; prepare the ambushes.[4] And we prayed to our God and set a guard as a protection against them day and night.[5] So neither I nor . . . the men of the guard who followed me, none of us took off our clothes; each kept his weapon in his hand.[6]

They have conquered him by the blood of the Lamb and by the word of their testimony, for they loved not their lives even unto death.[7] He who conquers, I will grant him to sit with Me on My throne, as I Myself conquered and sat down with My Father on His throne.[8]

**I Sam. 25:28.* [1]*2 Tim. 2:3, 4.* [2]*Phil. 1:29, 30.* [3]*1 Cor. 16:13.* [4]*Jer. 51:12.* [5]*Neh. 4:9.* [6]*Neh. 4:23.* [7]*Rev. 12:11.* [8]*Rev. 3:21.*

OCTOBER 4

*God is not far from each one of us**

For the Lord your God is He that goes with you, to fight for you against your enemies, to give you the victory.[1] He will not fail you or forsake you.[2] Forty years didst Thou sustain them in the wilderness, and they lacked nothing.[3]

When you pass through the waters I will be with you; and through the rivers, they shall not overwhelm you; when you walk through fire you shall not be burned, and the flame shall not consume you. For I am the Lord your God.[4] Even there Thy hand shall lead me.[5] Waters shall break forth in the wilderness, and streams in the desert; the burning sand shall become a pool, and the thirsty ground springs of water.[6] It is the Lord who goes before you; He will be with you, He will not fail you or forsake you; do not fear or be dismayed.[7]

And the Lord said, 'My presence will go with you, and I will give you rest.' And Moses said to Him, 'If Thy presence will not go with me, do not carry us up from here.'[8]

**Acts 17:27.* [1]*Deut. 20:4.* [2]*Deut. 31:6.* [3]*Neh. 9:21.* [4]*Is. 43:2, 3.* [5]*Ps. 139:10.* [6]*Is. 35:6, 7.* [7]*Deut. 31:8.* [8]*Ex. 33:14, 15.*

*Partakers of the divine nature**

Put off your old nature which belongs to your former manner of life and is corrupt through deceitful lusts, and be renewed in the spirit of your minds, and put on the new nature, created after the likeness of God in true righteousness and holiness.[1]

For as many of you as were baptized into Christ have put on Christ.[2] I have been crucified with Christ; it is no longer I who live, but Christ who lives in me.[3] He who is united to the Lord becomes one spirit with Him.[4] Therefore, if any one is in Christ, he is a new creation; the old has passed away, behold, the new has come.[5] And we all, with unveiled face, beholding the glory of the Lord, are being changed into His likeness from one degree of glory to another; for this comes from the Lord who is the Spirit.[6]

Put on then, as God's chosen ones, holy and beloved, compassion, kindness, lowliness, meekness and patience, forbearing one another and, if one has a complaint against another, forgiving each other; as the Lord has forgiven you, so you also must forgive. And above all these put on love, which binds everything together in perfect harmony.[7]

**2 Pet. 1:4. [1]Eph. 4:22–24. [2]Gal. 3:27. [3]Gal. 2:20. [4]1 Cor. 6:17. [5]2 Cor. 5:17. [6]2 Cor. 3:18. [7]Col. 3:12–14.*

OCTOBER 6

*Encourage one another**

After this the Lord appointed seventy others, and sent them on ahead of Him, two by two, into every town and place where He Himself was about to come.[1] Two are better than one . . . for if they fall, one will lift up his fellow; but woe to him who is alone when he falls, and has not another to lift him up.[2]

Taking with Him Peter and the two sons of Zebedee, Jesus began to be sorrowful and troubled. Then He said to them, 'My soul is very sorrowful, even to death; remain here, and watch with Me.'[3] And so we came to Rome. And the brethren there, when they heard of us, came as far as the Forum of Appius and Three Taverns to meet us. On seeing them Paul thanked God and took courage.[4]

That we may be mutually encouraged by each other's faith.[5] That you, being rooted and grounded in love, may have power to comprehend with all the saints what is the breadth and length and height and depth, and to know the love of Christ which surpasses knowledge.[6] Therefore encourage one another and build one another up, just as you are doing.[7]

**1 Thess. 5:11.* [1]*Lk. 10:1.* [2]*Eccl. 4:9, 10.* [3]*Mt. 26:37, 38.* [4]*Acts 28:14, 15.* [5]*Rom. 1:12.* [6]*Eph. 3:17–19.* [7]*1 Thess. 5:11.*

OCTOBER 7

*The power of Satan**

Now the serpent was more subtle than any other wild creature that the Lord God had made. He said to the woman, 'Did God say, "You shall not eat of any tree of the garden"?' And the woman said to the serpent, 'We may eat of the fruit of the trees of the garden; but God said, "You shall not eat of the fruit of the tree which is in the midst of the garden, neither shall you touch it, lest you die."' But the serpent said to the woman, 'You will not die.'[1] The Lord God said to the woman, 'What is this that you have done?' The woman said, 'The serpent beguiled me, and I ate.'[2] The serpent deceived Eve by his cunning.[3] He . . . has nothing to do with the truth, because there is no truth in him . . . for he is a liar and the father of lies.[4]

Your adversary the devil prowls around like a roaring lion, seeking some one to devour.[5] He was a murderer from the beginning.[6] The devil . . . put it into the heart of Judas Iscariot . . . to betray Jesus.[7] Then . . . Satan entered into him.[8]

God may perhaps grant that they will repent and come to know the truth, and they may escape from the snare of the devil, after being captured by him to do his will.[9]

**Acts 26:18.* [1]*Gen. 3:1–4.* [2]*Gen. 3:13.* [3]*2 Cor. 11:3.* [4]*Jn. 8:44.* [5]*1 Pet. 5:8.* [6]*Jn. 8:44.* [7]*Jn. 13:2.* [8]*Jn. 13:27.* [9]*2 Tim. 2:25, 26.*

OCTOBER 8

*Fruitful labor**

By this My Father is glorified, that you bear much fruit, and so prove to be My disciples.[1] You did not choose Me, but I chose you and appointed you that you should go and bear fruit and that your fruit should abide.[2]

I want you to know, brethren, that I often intended to come to you . . . in order that I may reap some harvest among you as well as among the rest of the Gentiles.[3] For though I am free from all men, I have made myself a slave to all, that I might win the more. To the Jews I became as a Jew, in order to win Jews . . . To the weak I became weak, that I might win the weak. I have become all things to all men, that I might by all means save some.[4]

My little children, with whom I am again in travail until Christ be formed in you![5] I became your father in Christ Jesus through the gospel.[6] Timothy, my true child in the faith.[7] Onesimus, whose father I have become in my imprisonment.[8]

What then is Apollos? What is Paul? Servants through whom you believed . . . I planted, Apollos watered, but God gave the growth.[9]

**Phil. 1:22. [1]Jn. 15:8. [2]Jn. 15:16. [3]Rom. 1:13. [4]1 Cor. 9:19, 20, 22. [5]Gal. 4:19. [6]1 Cor. 4:15. [7]1 Tim. 1:2. [8]Philem. 10. [9]1 Cor. 3:5, 6.*

OCTOBER 9

*Love is not jealous**

Wrath is cruel, anger is overwhelming; but who can stand before jealousy?[1]

And the patriarchs, jealous of Joseph, sold him into Egypt.[2] Pilate knew that it was out of envy that they had delivered Jesus up.[3] When the Jews saw the multitudes, they were filled with jealousy, and contradicted what was spoken by Paul, and reviled him.[4]

Jesus said, 'What comes out of a man is what defiles a man. For from within, out of the heart of man, come evil thoughts . . . wickedness . . . envy . . .'[5] But I, brethren, could not address you as spiritual men, but as men of the flesh, as babes in Christ . . . For while there is jealousy and strife among you, are you not of the flesh, and behaving like ordinary men?[6]

So put away all malice and all guile and insincerity and envy and all slander.[7] If we live by the Spirit, let us also walk by the Spirit. Let us have no self-conceit, no provoking of one another, no envy of one another.[8]

**I Cor. 13:4.* [1]*Prov. 27:4.* [2]*Acts 7:9.* [3]*Mt. 27:18.* [4]*Acts 13:45.* [5]*Mk. 7:20–22.* [6]*I Cor. 3:1, 3.* [7]*I Pet. 2:1.* [8]*Gal. 5:25, 26.*

OCTOBER 10

*How . . . can man . . . be clean?**

We have all become like one who is unclean, and all our righteous deeds are like a polluted garment. We all fade like a leaf, and our iniquities, like the wind, take us away.[1] Wash yourselves; make yourselves clean; remove the evil of your doings from before My eyes; cease to do evil, learn to do good.[2] How then can man be righteous before God? How can he who is born of woman be clean?[3]

On that day there shall be a fountain opened for the house of David and the inhabitants of Jerusalem to cleanse them from sin and uncleanness.[4] I will sprinkle clean water upon you, and you shall be clean from all your uncleannesses, and from all your idols I will cleanse you.[5]

Behold, now is the day of salvation.[6] For the grace of God has appeared for the salvation of all men . . . Jesus Christ, who gave Himself for us to redeem us from all iniquity and to purify for Himself a people of His own.[7] They have washed their robes and made them white in the blood of the Lamb.[8] The blood of Jesus His Son cleanses us from all sin.[9] To Him who loves us and has freed us from our sins by His blood . . . be glory and dominion for ever and ever. Amen.[10]

**Job 25:4.* [1]*Is. 64:6.* [2]*Is. 1:16, 17.* [3]*Job 25:4.* [4]*Zech. 13:1.* [5]*Ezek. 36:25.* [6]*2 Cor. 6:2.* [7]*Tit. 2:11, 13, 14.* [8]*Rev. 7:14.* [9]*1 Jn. 1:7.* [10]*Rev. 1:5, 6.*

OCTOBER 11

*Serve Him with a whole heart and with a willing mind**

You yourselves know how I lived among you all the time from the first day that I set foot in Asia, serving the Lord with all humility and with tears and with trials which befell me through the plots of the Jews.[1] If I then, your Lord and Teacher, have washed your feet, you also ought to wash one another's feet. For I have given you an example, that you also should do as I have done to you.[2] Through love be servants of one another.[3] Humility goes before honor.[4]

Upon a watchtower I stand, O Lord, continually by day, and at my post I am stationed whole nights.[5] For three years I did not cease night or day to admonish every one with tears.[6] Preach the word, be urgent in season and out of season, convince, rebuke, and exhort, be unfailing in patience and in teaching.[7] Always be prepared to make a defense to any one who calls you to account for the hope that is in you, yet do it with gentleness and reverence.[8] Paul expounded the matter to them from morning till evening, testifying to the kingdom of God and trying to convince them about Jesus.[9] So we are ambassadors for Christ, God making His appeal through us.[10]

**1 Chron. 28:9.* [1]*Acts 20:18, 19.* [2]*Jn. 13:14, 15.* [3]*Gal. 5:13.* [4]*Prov. 15:33.* [5]*Is. 21:8.* [6]*Acts 20:31.* [7]*2 Tim. 4:2.* [8]*1 Pet. 3:15.* [9]*Acts 28:23.* [10]*2 Cor. 5:20.*

OCTOBER 12

*Take heed to the path of your feet**

Blessed is the man who walks not in the counsel of the wicked, nor stands in the way of sinners.[1] My son, if sinners entice you, do not consent. If they say, 'Come with us' . . . do not walk in the way with them, hold back your foot from their paths; for their feet run to evil, and they make haste to shed blood.[2] I will run in the way of Thy commandments.[3] I hold back my feet from every evil way, in order to keep Thy word.[4]

My eyes are ever toward the Lord, for He will pluck my feet out of the net.[5] For Thou hast delivered my soul from death, yea, my feet from falling, that I may walk before God in the light of life.[6]

How beautiful upon the mountains are the feet of him who brings good tidings, who publishes peace, who brings good tidings of good, who publishes salvation, who says to Zion, 'Your God reigns.'[7] Stand therefore, having girded your loins with truth . . . and having shod your feet with the equipment of the gospel of peace.[8]

**Prov. 4:26.* [1]*Ps. 1:1.* [2]*Prov. 1:10, 11, 15, 16.* [3]*Ps. 119:32.* [4]*Ps. 119:101.* [5]*Ps. 25:15.* [6]*Ps. 56:13.* [7]*Is. 52:7.* [8]*Eph. 6:14, 15.*

OCTOBER 13

*He led them in safety, so that they were not afraid**

Jesus the pioneer and perfecter of our faith.[1] Then after this He said to the disciples, 'Let us go into Judea again.' The disciples said to Him, 'Rabbi, the Jews were but now seeking to stone You, and are You going there again?' . . . Thomas, called the Twin, said to his fellow disciples, 'Let us also go, that we may die with Him.'[2] And they were on the road, going up to Jerusalem, and Jesus was walking ahead of them; and they were amazed, and those who followed were afraid.[3]

Thou didst bring us into the net; Thou didst lay affliction on our loins; Thou didst let men ride over our heads; we went through fire and through water; yet Thou hast brought us forth to a spacious place.[4] The following night the Lord stood by Paul and said, 'Take courage, for as you have testified about Me at Jersusalem, so you must bear witness also at Rome.'[5]

I have taught you the way of wisdom; I have led you in the paths of uprightness.[6] Thou dost guide me with Thy counsel, and afterward Thou wilt receive me to glory.[7]

**Ps. 78:53.* [1]*Heb. 12:2.* [2]*Jn. 11:7, 8, 16.* [3]*Mk. 10:32.* [4]*Ps. 66:11, 12.* [5]*Acts 23:11.* [6]*Prov. 4:11.* [7]*Ps. 73:24.*

OCTOBER 14

*I am the bread of life**

Why do you spend your money for that which is not bread, and your labor for that which does not satisfy?[1] He who loves money will not be satisfied with money; nor he who loves wealth, with gain; this also is vanity.[2] The eye is not satisfied with seeing, nor the ear filled with hearing.[3] Jesus said to her, 'You are right in saying, "I have no husband"; for you have had five husbands, and he whom you now have is not your husband; this you said truly.'[4]

Every one who drinks of this water will thirst again, but whoever drinks of the water that I shall give him will never thirst.[5] Do not labor for the food which perishes, but for the food which endures to eternal life, which the Son of man will give to you.[6] I am the bread of life; he who comes to Me shall not hunger, and he who believes in Me shall never thirst.[7] O that My people would listen to Me, that Israel would walk in My ways! . . . I would feed you with the finest of the wheat, and with honey from the rock I would satisfy you.[8]

**Jn. 6:35.* [1]*Is. 55:2.* [2]*Eccl. 5:10.* [3]*Eccl. 1:8.* [4]*Jn. 4:16–18.* [5]*Jn. 4:13, 14.* [6]*Jn. 6:27.* [7]*Jn. 6:35.* [8]*Ps. 81:13, 16.*

*Helpers**

Now a Jew named Apollos, a native of Alexandria, came to Ephesus . . . He began to speak boldly in the synagogue; but when Priscilla and Aquila heard him, they took him and expounded to him the way of God more accurately. And when he wished to cross to Achaia, the brethren encouraged him, and wrote to the disciples to receive him.[1] Onesiphorus . . . often refreshed me; he was not ashamed of my chains, but when he arrived in Rome he searched for me eagerly and found me . . . and you well know all the service he rendered at Ephesus.[2] When you come, bring the cloak that I left with Carpus at Troas, also the books, and above all the parchments.[3]

I delivered the poor who cried, and the fatherless who had none to help him. The blessing of him who was about to perish came upon me, and I caused the widow's heart to sing for joy . . . I was eyes to the blind, and feet to the lame.[4] I smiled on them when they had no confidence; and the light of my countenance they did not cast down.[5]

And we exhort you, brethren . . . encourage the fainthearted, help the weak, be patient with them all.[6] Bear one another's burdens, and so fulfil the law of Christ.[7]

* *1 Cor. 12:28.* [1] *Acts 18:24, 26, 27.* [2] *2 Tim. 1:16–18.* [3] *2 Tim. 4:13.* [4] *Job 29:12, 13, 15.* [5] *Job 29:24.* [6] *1 Thess. 5:14.* [7] *Gal. 6:2.*

OCTOBER 16

*What . . . must I do, to have eternal life?**

You search the scriptures, because you think that in them you have eternal life; and it is they that bear witness to Me; yet you refuse to come to Me that you may have life.[1] And this is the testimony, that God gave us eternal life, and this life is in His Son. He who has the Son has life; he who has not the Son has not life.[2] The free gift of God is eternal life in Christ Jesus our Lord.[3]

Truly, truly, I say to you, he who hears My word and believes Him who sent Me, has eternal life; he does not come into judgment, but has passed from death to life.[4] I am the living bread . . . If any one eats of this bread, he will live for ever; and the bread which I shall give for the life of the world is My flesh.[5] He who eats Me will live because of Me.[6]

Then he showed me the river of the water of life, bright as crystal, flowing from the throne of God and of the Lamb through the middle of the street of the city.[7] Let him who is thirsty come, let him who desires take the water of life without price.[8]

**Mt. 19:16. [1]Jn. 5:39, 40. [2]1 Jn. 5:11, 12. [3]Rom. 6:23. [4]Jn. 5:24. [5]Jn. 6:35, 51. [6]Jn. 6:57. [7]Rev. 22:1, 2. [8]Rev. 22:17.*

OCTOBER 17

*Fret not yourself because of the wicked**

Why do the wicked live, reach old age, and grow mighty in power?[1] Why does the way of the wicked prosper? Why do all who are treacherous thrive?[2] For I was envious of the arrogant, when I saw the prosperity of the wicked.[3]

Fret not yourself because of the wicked, be not envious of wrongdoers! For they will soon fade like the grass and wither like the green herb.[4] Be still before the Lord, and wait patiently for Him; fret not yourself over him who prospers in his way, over the man who carries out evil devices![5] Fret not yourself because of evildoers, and be not envious of the wicked; for the evil man has no future; the lamp of the wicked will be put out.[6]

Though a sinner does evil a hundred times and prolongs his life, yet I know that it will be well with those who fear God, because they fear before Him; but it will not be well with the wicked, neither will he prolong his days like a shadow, because he does not fear before God.[7]

**Ps. 37:1.* [1]*Job 21:7.* [2]*Jer. 12:1.* [3]*Ps. 73:3.* [4]*Ps. 37:1, 2.* [5]*Ps. 37:7.* [6]*Prov. 24:19, 20.* [7]*Eccl. 8:12, 13.*

OCTOBER 18

*Luke the beloved physician**

'You are My witnesses,' says the Lord, 'and My servant whom I have chosen.'[1] Now there are varieties of service, but the same Lord.[2] And God has appointed in the church first apostles, second prophets . . . then healers, helpers . . .[3]

Epaphras, my fellow prisoner in Christ Jesus, sends greetings to you, and so do Mark, Aristarchus, Demas and Luke, my fellow workers.[4] They have labored side by side with me in the gospel.[5] Do your best to come to me soon. For Demas . . . has deserted me and gone to Thessalonica; Crescens has gone to Galatia, Titus to Dalmatia. Luke alone is with me.[6] Luke the beloved physician.[7]

It seemed good to me (Luke) also, having followed all things closely for some time past, to write an orderly account for you, most excellent Theophilus, that you may know the truth concerning the things of which you have been informed.[8] For we did not follow cleverly devised myths when we made known to you the power and coming of our Lord Jesus Christ, but we were eye-witnesses of His majesty.[9] That your faith might not rest in the wisdom of men but in the power of God.[10]

Col. 4:14. [1]Is. 43:10. [2]1 Cor. 12:5. [3]1 Cor. 12:28. [4]Philem. 23. [5]Phil. 4:3. [6]2 Tim. 4:9–11. [7]Col. 4:14. [8]Lk. 1:3, 4. [9]2 Pet. 1:16. [10]1 Cor. 2:5.

OCTOBER 19

*The promise of the Spirit**

That we might receive the promise of the Spirit through faith.[1] The Holy Spirit whom God has given to those who obey Him.[2] In Him you . . . who have heard the word of truth, the gospel of your salvation, and have believed in Him, were sealed with the promised Holy Spirit.[3]

The wind blows where it wills, and you hear the sound of it, but you do not know whence it comes or whither it goes; so it is with every one who is born of the Spirit. Nicodemus said to Him, 'How can this be?'[4] The Spirit of truth . . . will be in you. I will not leave you desolate; I will come to you.[5] He saved us . . . by the washing of regeneration and renewal in the Holy Spirit, which He poured out upon us richly through Jesus Christ our Savior.[6]

The water that I shall give him will become in him a spring of water welling up to eternal life.[7] For the promise is to you and to your children and to all that are far off, every one whom the Lord our God calls to Him.[8]

**Gal. 3:14. [1]Gal. 3:14. [2]Acts 5:32. [3]Eph. 1:13. [4]Jn. 3:8, 9. [5]Jn. 14:17, 18. [6]Tit. 3:5, 6. [7]Jn. 4:14. [8]Acts 2:39.*

OCTOBER 20

*You ask and do not receive, because you ask wrongly**

We do not present our supplications before Thee on the ground of our righteousness, but on the ground of Thy great mercy.[1] We have confidence to enter the sanctuary by the blood of Jesus.[2]

We receive from Him whatever we ask, because we keep His commandments and do what pleases Him.[3] And whenever you stand praying, forgive, if you have anything against any one; so that your Father also who is in heaven may forgive you your trespasses.[4]

Pray at all times in the Spirit, with all prayer and supplication.[5] The Spirit helps us in our weakness; for we do not know how to pray as we ought, but the Spirit Himself intercedes for us with sighs too deep for words.[6]

Whatever you ask in My name, I will do it, that the Father may be glorified in the Son; if you ask anything in My name, I will do it.[7] And this is the confidence which we have in Him, that if we ask anything according to His will He hears us. And if we know that He hears us in whatever we ask, we know that we have obtained the requests made of Him.[8]

**Jas. 4:3. [1]Dan. 9:18. [2]Heb. 10:19. [3]1 Jn. 3:22. [4]Mk. 11:25. [5]Eph. 6:18. [6]Rom. 8:26. [7]Jn. 14:13, 14. [8]1 Jn. 5:14, 15.*

OCTOBER 21

*I will protect him**

He who dwells in the shelter of the Most High, who abides in the shadow of the Almighty, will say to the Lord, 'My refuge and my fortress; my God, in whom I trust.'[1] Those who trust in the Lord are like Mount Zion, which cannot be moved, but abides for ever. As the mountains are round about Jerusalem, so the Lord is round about His people, from this time forth and for evermore.[2]

You will not fear the terror of the night, nor the arrow that flies by day, nor the pestilence that stalks in darkness, nor the destruction that wastes at noonday.[3] No weapon that is fashioned against you shall prosper, and you shall confute every tongue that rises against you in judgment.[4] The Lord is faithful; He will strengthen you and guard you from evil.[5]

Because he cleaves to Me in love, I will deliver him; I will protect him, because he knows My name.[6] Let all who take refuge in Thee rejoice, let them ever sing for joy; and do Thou defend them, that those who love Thy name may exult in Thee. For Thou dost bless the righteous, O Lord; Thou dost cover him with favor as with a shield.[7]

**Ps. 91:14. [1]Ps. 91:1, 2. [2]Ps. 125:1, 2. [3]Ps. 91:5, 6. [4]Is. 54:17. [5]2 Thess. 3:3. [6]Ps. 91:14. [7]Ps. 5:11, 12.*

OCTOBER 22

*For the gifts and the call of God are irrevocable**

And passing along by the Sea of Galilee, Jesus saw Simon and Andrew the brother of Simon casting a net in the sea, for they were fishermen. And Jesus said to them, 'Follow Me and I will make you become fishers of men.' And immediately they left their nets and followed Him.[1] Then Amos answered Amaziah, 'I am no prophet, nor a prophet's son; but I am a herdsman, and a dresser of sycamore trees, and the Lord took me from following the flock, and the Lord said to me, "Go, prophesy to My people Israel." '[2]

Moses, His chosen one.[3] But Moses said to God, 'Who am I that I should go to Pharaoh, and bring the sons of Israel out of Egypt? . . . But behold, they will not believe me or listen to my voice . . . Oh, my Lord, I am not eloquent . . . Oh, my Lord, send, I pray, some other person.'[4] He sent Moses His servant, and Aaron whom He had chosen.[5]

He . . . set me apart before I was born, and . . . called me through His grace.[6] Jesus said, 'You did not choose Me, but I chose you and appointed you that you should go and bear fruit and that your fruit should abide.'[7]

**Rom.* 11:29. [1]*Mk.* 1:16–18. [2]*Amos* 7:14, 15. [3]*Ps.* 106:23. [4]*Ex.* 3:11; 4:1, 10, 13. [5]*Ps.* 105:26. [6]*Gal.* 1:15. [7]*Jn.* 15:16.

OCTOBER 23

*Let all men know your forbearance**

Repay no one evil for evil, but take thought for what is noble in the sight of all. If possible, so far as it depends upon you, live peaceably with all. Beloved, never avenge yourselves, but leave it to the wrath of God; for it is written, Vengeance is Mine, I will repay, says the Lord.[1]

A village of the Samaritans . . . would not receive Him, because His face was set toward Jerusalem. And when His disciples James and John saw it, they said, 'Lord, do You want us to bid fire come down from heaven and consume them?' But He turned and rebuked them, and said, 'You do not know what manner of spirit you are of.'[2] The fruit of the Spirit is . . . gentleness, self-control.[3]

The wisdom from above is first pure, then peaceable, gentle, open to reason.[4] Remind them . . . to speak evil of no one, to avoid quarreling, to be gentle, and to show perfect courtesy toward all men.[5] The patient in spirit is better than the proud in spirit. Be not quick to anger, for anger lodges in the bosom of fools.[6]

**Phil.* 4:5. [1]*Rom.* 12:17–19. [2]*Lk.* 9:52–54, 55 (*mgn.*). [3]*Gal.* 5:22, 23. [4]*Jas.* 3:17. [5]*Tit.* 3:1, 2. [6]*Eccl.* 7:8, 9.

OCTOBER 24

*God was in Christ**

This was why the Jews sought . . . to kill Him, because He . . . called God His Father, making Himself equal with God.[1] The high priest asked Him, 'Are You the Christ, the Son of the Blessed?' Jesus said, 'I am.'[2] Truly, truly, I say to you, before Abraham was, I am.[3]

Great indeed, we confess, is the mystery of our religion: God was manifested in the flesh.[4] No one has ever seen God; the only Son, who is in the bosom of the Father, He has made Him known.[5] He is the image of the invisible God.[6] He reflects the glory of God and bears the very stamp of His nature.[7] For in Him the whole fulness of deity dwells bodily.[8]

Philip said to Him, 'Lord, show us the Father, and we shall be satisfied.' Jesus said to him, 'Have I been with you so long, and yet you do not know Me, Philip? He who has seen Me has seen the Father; how can you say, "Show us the Father"? Do you not believe that I am in the Father and the Father in Me?'[9] I and the Father are one.[10] The glory of God in the face of Christ.[11]

**2 Cor. 5:19.* [1]*Jn. 5:18.* [2]*Mk. 14:61, 62.* [3]*Jn. 8:58.* [4]*1 Tim. 3:16.* [5]*Jn. 1:18.* [6]*Col. 1:15.* [7]*Heb. 1:3.* [8]*Col. 2:9.* [9]*Jn. 14:8–10.* [10]*Jn. 10:30.* [11]*2 Cor. 4:6.*

OCTOBER 25

*We shall all be changed**

God raised the Lord and will also raise us up by His power.[1] Because I live, you will live also.[2] The hour is coming when all who are in the tombs will hear His voice and come forth, those who have done good, to the resurrection of life, and those who have done evil, to the resurrection of judgment.[3]

But someone will ask, 'How are the dead raised? With what kind of body do they come?'[4] We know that if the earthly tent we live in is destroyed, we have a building from God, a house not made with hands, eternal in the heavens.[5] Flesh and blood cannot inherit the kingdom of God . . . This perishable nature must put on the imperishable, and this mortal nature must put on immortality.[6]

Christ . . . will change our lowly body to be like His glorious body.[7] It is sown a physical body, it is raised a spiritual body.[8] It does not yet appear what we shall be, but we know that . . . we shall be like Him.[9] I shall behold Thy face in righteousness; when I awake, I shall be satisfied with beholding Thy form.[10] Behold, I make all things new.[11]

**1 Cor. 15:51.* [1]*1 Cor. 6:14.* [2]*Jn. 14:19.* [3]*Jn. 5:28, 29.* [4]*1 Cor. 15:35.* [5]*2 Cor. 5:1.* [6]*1 Cor. 15:50, 53.* [7]*Phil. 3:20, 21.* [8]*1 Cor. 15:44.* [9]*1 Jn. 3:2.* [10]*Ps. 17:15.* [11]*Rev. 21:5.*

OCTOBER 26

*They all look after their own interests, not those of Jesus Christ**

And James and John, the sons of Zebedee, came forward to Him, and said to Him, 'Teacher, we want You to do for us whatever we ask of You . . . Grant us to sit, one at Your right hand and one at Your left, in Your glory.' But Jesus said to them . . . 'Whoever would be great among you must be your servant, and whoever would be first among you must be slave of all. For the Son of man also came not to be served but to serve, and to give His life as a ransom for many.'[1]

He died for all, that those who live might live no longer for themselves but for Him who for their sake died and was raised.[2] Our beloved Barnabas and Paul, men who have risked their lives for the sake of our Lord Jesus Christ.[3] We were ready to share with you not only the gospel of God but also our own selves, because you had become very dear to us.[4]

Men will be lovers of self . . . lovers of pleasure rather than lovers of God.[5] Let each of you look not only to his own interests, but also to the interests of others.[6]

**Phil.* 2:21. [1]*Mk.* 10:35, 37, 38, 43–45. [2]2 *Cor.* 5:15. [3]*Acts* 15:25, 26. [4]1 *Thess.* 2:8. [5]2 *Tim.* 3:2, 4. [6]*Phil.* 2:4.

OCTOBER 27

*Thy people whom Thou hast chosen**

Therefore Thou art great, O Lord God; for there is none like Thee, and there is no God besides Thee, according to all that we have heard with our ears. What other nation on earth is like Thy people Israel, whom God went to redeem to be His people? . . . And Thou didst establish for Thyself Thy people Israel to be Thy people for ever.[1] And they shall be called The holy people, The redeemed of the Lord.[2] We are His people, and the sheep of His pasture.[3]

Not all are children of Abraham because they are his descendants . . . It is not the children of the flesh who are the children of God, but the children of the promise are reckoned as descendants.[4] Now we, brethren, like Isaac, are children of promise.[5]

But you are a chosen race, a royal priesthood, a holy nation, God's own people, that you may declare the wonderful deeds of Him who called you out of darkness into His marvelous light.[6] The people whom I formed for Myself that they might declare My praise.[7]

** 1 Kings 3:8.* [1] *2 Sam. 7:22–24.* [2] *Is. 62:12.* [3] *Ps. 100:3.* [4] *Rom. 9:7, 8.* [5] *Gal. 4:28.* [6] *1 Pet. 2:9.* [7] *Is. 43:21.*

OCTOBER 28

*Joint heirs of the grace of life**

Husbands, live considerately with your wives, bestowing honor on the woman as the weaker sex.[1] Be subject to one another out of reverence for Christ.[2] Love does not insist on its own way.[3]

The head of every man is Christ, the head of a woman is her husband, and the head of Christ is God.[4] Husbands, love your wives, as Christ loved the church . . . and let the wife see that she respects her husband.[5] A good wife is the crown of her husband.[6] She is far more precious than jewels. The heart of her husband trusts in her . . . She does him good, and not harm, all the days of her life.[7]

Enjoy life with the wife whom you love.[8] And rejoice in the wife of your youth, a lovely hind, a graceful doe. Let her affection fill you at all times with delight, be infatuated always with her love.[9] How sweet is your love, my sister, my bride![10]

If two of you agree on earth about anything they ask, it will be done for them by My Father in heaven.[11] Two are better than one . . . For if they fall, one will lift up his fellow.[12]

**1 Pet. 3:7.* [1] *1 Pet. 3:7.* [2] *Eph. 5:21.* [3] *1 Cor. 13:5.* [4] *1 Cor. 11:3.* [5] *Eph. 5:25, 33.* [6] *Prov. 12:4.* [7] *Prov. 31:10–12.* [8] *Eccl. 9:9.* [9] *Prov. 5:18, 19.* [10] *Song of Sol. 4:10.* [11] *Mt. 18:19.* [12] *Eccl. 4:9, 10.*

*The Lord is your keeper**

He found him in a desert land, and in the howling waste of the wilderness; He encircled him, He cared for him, He kept him as the apple of His eye.[1] Keep me as the apple of the eye; hide me in the shadow of Thy wings.[2] My sheep hear My voice, and I know them, and they follow Me; and I give them eternal life, and they shall never perish, and no one shall snatch them out of My hand.[3]

The Lord will keep you from all evil; He will keep your life. The Lord will keep your going out and your coming in from this time forth and for evermore.[4] He will not let your foot be moved, He who keeps you will not slumber. Behold, He who keeps Israel will neither slumber nor sleep.[5] He will guard the feet of His faithful ones.[6] And will keep your foot from being caught.[7]

Now to Him who is able to keep you from falling and to present you without blemish before the presence of His glory with rejoicing, to the only God, our Savior through Jesus Christ our Lord, be glory, majesty, dominion, and authority, before all time and now and for ever. Amen.[8]

**Ps. 121:5.* [1]*Deut. 32:10.* [2]*Ps. 17:8.* [3]*Jn. 10:27, 28.* [4]*Ps. 121:7, 8.* [5]*Ps. 121:3, 4.* [6]*1 Sam. 2:9.* [7]*Prov. 3:26.* [8]*Jude 24, 25.*

OCTOBER 30

*If we endure, we shall also reign with Him**

For you have need of endurance, so that you may do the will of God and receive what is promised.[1] And because wickedness is multiplied, most men's love will grow cold. But he who endures to the end will be saved.[2] And these . . . are the ones sown upon rocky ground, who . . . have no root in themselves, but endure for a while; then . . . fall away.[3] But we are not of those who shrink back and are destroyed, but of those who have faith and keep their souls.[4]

Which of you, desiring to build a tower, does not first sit down and count the cost, whether he has enough to complete it? Otherwise, when he has laid a foundation, and is not able to finish, all who see it begin to mock him, saying, 'This man began to build, and was not able to finish.'[5]

So Solomon built the house, and finished it.[6] I glorified Thee on earth, having accomplished the work which Thou gavest Me to do.[7] I have fought the good fight, I have finished the race, I have kept the faith. Henceforth there is laid up for me the crown of righteousness.[8]

**2 Tim. 2:12.* [1]*Heb. 10:36.* [2]*Mt. 24:12, 13.* [3]*Mk. 4:16, 17.* [4]*Heb. 10:39.* [5]*Lk. 14:28–30.* [6]*1 Kings 6:14.* [7]*Jn. 17:4.* [8]*2 Tim. 4:7, 8.*

OCTOBER 31

*God's varied grace**

To me, though I am the very least of all the saints, this grace was given, to preach to the Gentiles the unsearchable riches of Christ.[1] And His grace toward me was not in vain. On the contrary, I worked harder than any of them, though it was not I, but the grace of God which is with me.[2]

He said to me, 'My grace is sufficient for you, for My power is made perfect in weakness.' I will all the more gladly boast of my weaknesses, that the power of Christ may rest upon me.[3] For God opposes the proud, but gives grace to the humble.[4]

Our sufficiency is from God.[5] And God is able to provide you with every blessing in abundance, so that you may always have enough of everything and may provide in abundance for every good work.[6]

Let us then with confidence draw near to the throne of grace, that we may receive mercy and find grace to help in time of need.[7]

* *1 Pet. 4:10.* [1] *Eph. 3:8.* [2] *1 Cor. 15:10.* [3] *2 Cor. 12:9.* [4] *1 Pet. 5:5.* [5] *2 Cor. 3:5.* [6] *2 Cor. 9:8.* [7] *Heb. 4:16.*

NOVEMBER 1

*So we shall always be with the Lord**

We would not have you ignorant . . . concerning those who are asleep, that you may not grieve as others do who have no hope.[1] Let not your hearts be troubled; believe in God, believe also in Me. In My Father's house are many rooms; if it were not so, would I have told you that I go to prepare a place for you?[2] My desire is to depart and be with Christ, for that is far better.[3]

I know that my Redeemer lives, and at last He will stand upon the earth; and after my skin has been thus destroyed, then from my flesh I shall see God.[4] As for me, I shall behold Thy face in righteousness; when I awake, I shall be satisfied with beholding Thy form.[5]

Blessed are the dead who die in the Lord henceforth. 'Blessed indeed,' says the Spirit, 'that they may rest from their labors, for their deeds follow them.'[6] Therefore are they before the throne of God, and serve Him day and night within His temple; and He who sits upon the throne will shelter them with His presence.[7]

**I Thess. 4:17.* [1]*I Thess. 4:13.* [2]*Jn. 14:1, 2.* [3]*Phil. 1:23.* [4]*Job 19:25, 26 (mgn.).* [5]*Ps. 17:15.* [6]*Rev. 14:13.* [7]*Rev. 7:15.*

NOVEMBER 2

*The Lord is a God of knowledge**

O Lord, Thou hast searched me and known me! Thou knowest when I sit down and when I rise up; Thou discernest my thoughts from afar. Thou searchest out my path and my lying down, and art acquainted with all my ways. Even before a word is on my tongue, lo, O Lord, Thou knowest it altogether . . . Such knowledge is too wonderful for me; it is high, I cannot attain it.[1] Before Him no creature is hidden, but all are open and laid bare to the eyes of Him with whom we have to do.[2]

O the depth of the riches and wisdom and knowledge of God! How unsearchable are His judgements and how inscrutable His ways! 'For who has known the mind of the Lord, or who has been His counselor?'[3]

The word of the Lord came to me saying, 'Before I formed you in the womb I knew you.'[4] Jesus answered him, 'Before Philip called you, when you were under the fig tree, I saw you.'[5] He knows the secrets of the heart.[6] Lord, You know everything.[7]

**1 Sam. 2:3.* [1]*Ps. 139:1–4, 6.* [2]*Heb. 4:13.* [3]*Rom. 11: 33, 34.* [4]*Jer. 1:4, 5.* [5]*Jn. 1:48.* [6]*Ps. 44:21.* [7]*Jn. 21:17.*

NOVEMBER 3

*The Lord opens the eyes of the blind**

For although they knew God they did not honor Him as God or give thanks to Him, but they became futile in their thinking and their senseless minds were darkened.[1] They are darkened in their understanding, alienated from the life of God because of the ignorance that is in them, due to their hardness of heart.[2]

If your eye is not sound, your whole body will be full of darkness. If then the light in you is darkness, how great is the darkness![3] Woe to those who call evil good and good evil, who put darkness for light and light for darkness, who put bitter for sweet and sweet for bitter![4] Let them alone; they are blind guides. And if a blind man leads a blind man, both will fall into a pit.[5]

Jesus asked him, 'What do you want Me to do for you?' He said, 'Lord, let me receive my sight.'[6] When a man turns to the Lord the veil is removed.[7] God . . . has shone in our hearts to give the light of the knowledge of the glory of God in the face of Christ.[8] One thing I know, that though I was blind, now I see.[9]

**Ps. 146:8.* [1]*Rom. 1:21.* [2]*Eph. 4:18.* [3]*Mt. 6:23.* [4]*Is. 5:20.* [5]*Mt. 15:14.* [6]*Lk. 18:40, 41.* [7]*2 Cor. 3:16.* [8]*2 Cor. 4:6.* [9]*Jn. 9:25.*

*To teach others also**

For though by this time you ought to be teachers, you need someone to teach you again the first principles of God's word. You need milk, not solid food; for every one who lives on milk is unskilled in the word of righteousness, for he is a child.[1] Do your best to present yourself to God as one approved, a workman who has no need to be ashamed, rightly handling the word of truth.[2]

We refuse to practice cunning or to tamper with God's word, but by the open statement of the truth we would commend ourselves to every man's conscience in the sight of God.[3] Come, O sons, listen to me, I will teach you the fear of the Lord.[4] For I long to see you, that I may impart to you some spiritual gift to strengthen you.[5] So, being affectionately desirous of you, we were ready to share with you not only the gospel of God but also our own selves, because you had become very dear to us.[6] And I know that when I come to you I shall come in the fulness of the blessing of Christ.[7]

**2 Tim. 2:2. [1]Heb. 5:12, 13. [2]2 Tim. 2:15. [3]2 Cor. 4:2. [4]Ps. 34:11. [5]Rom. 1:11. [6]1 Thess. 2:8. [7]Rom. 15:29.*

NOVEMBER 5

*We shall all stand before the judgment seat of God**

It is appointed for men to die once, and after that comes judgment.[1] For God will bring every deed into judgment, with every secret thing, whether good or evil.[2] On that day when, according to my gospel, God judges the secrets of men by Christ Jesus.[3] Nothing is covered up that will not be revealed, or hidden that will not be known.[4] Do not be deceived; God is not mocked, for whatever a man sows, that he will also reap.[5]

Then I saw a great white throne and Him who sat upon it; from His presence earth and sky fled away, and no place was found for them. And I saw the dead, great and small, standing before the throne, and books were opened. Also another book was opened, which is the book of life. And the dead were judged by what was written in the books, by what they had done.[6]

God sent the Son into the world, not to condemn the world, but that the world might be saved through Him. He who believes in Him is not condemned; he who does not believe is condemned already, because he has not believed in the name of the only Son of God.[7]

**Rom. 14:10. [1]Heb. 9:27. [2]Eccl. 12:14. [3]Rom. 2:16. [4]Lk. 12:2. [5]Gal. 6:7. [6]Rev. 20:11, 12. [7]Jn. 3:17, 18.*

NOVEMBER 6

*When you pray, say: 'Father . . . forgive us our sins'**

Behold, I have taken upon myself to speak to the Lord, I who am but dust and ashes.[1] I acknowledged my sin to Thee, and I did not hide my iniquity; I said, 'I will confess my transgressions to the Lord'; then Thou didst forgive the guilt of my sin.[2]

If they sin against Thee—for there is no man who does not sin—and Thou art angry with them . . . yet if they lay it to heart . . . and . . . if they repent with all their mind and with all their heart . . . then hear Thou in heaven Thy dwelling-place their prayer . . . and forgive Thy people who have sinned against Thee.[3]

My iniquities have overtaken me, till I cannot see; they are more than the hairs of my head; my heart fails me.[4] I confess my iniquity, I am sorry for my sin.[5] If we say we have no sin, we deceive ourselves, and the truth is not in us. If we confess our sins, He is faithful and just, and will forgive our sins and cleanse us from all unrighteousness.[6] Then man prays to God, and He accepts him, he comes into His presence with joy.[7]

**Lk. 11:2, 4.* [1]*Gen. 18:27.* [2]*Ps. 32:5.* [3]*1 Kings 8:46–50.* [4]*Ps. 40:12.* [5]*Ps. 38:18.* [6]*1 Jn. 1:8, 9.* [7]*Job 33:26.*

NOVEMBER 7

*Checking the indulgence of the flesh**

If you have found honey, eat only enough for you, lest you be sated with it and vomit it.[1] He who loves pleasure will be a poor man; he who loves wine and oil will not be rich.[2] Hear, my son, and be wise, and direct your mind in the way. Be not among winebibbers, or among gluttonous eaters of meat; for the drunkard and the glutton will come to poverty, and drowsiness will clothe a man with rags.[3] He who loves wisdom makes his father glad, but one who keeps company with harlots squanders his substance.[4]

But I say, walk by the Spirit, and do not gratify the desires of the flesh. For the desires of the flesh are against the Spirit, and the desires of the Spirit are against the flesh; for these are opposed to each other, to prevent you from doing what you would.[5] Train yourself in godliness; for while bodily training is of some value, godliness is of value in every way, as it holds promise for the present life and also for the life to come.[6]

Your tackle hangs loose; it cannot hold the mast firm in its place, or keep the sail spread out.[7]

**Col. 2:23.* [1]*Prov. 25:16.* [2]*Prov. 21:17.* [3]*Prov. 23:19–21.* [4]*Prov. 29:3.* [5]*Gal. 5:16, 17.* [6]*1 Tim. 4:7, 8.* [7]*Is. 33:23.*

NOVEMBER 8

*Let them make peace with Me**

You were dead through the trespasses and sins in which you once walked, following the course of this world, following the prince of the power of the air, the spirit that is now at work in the sons of disobedience. Among these we all once lived in the passions of our flesh, following the desires of body and mind, and so we were by nature children of wrath, like the rest of mankind.[1] Let no one deceive you with empty words, for it is because of these things that the wrath of God comes upon the sons of disobedience.[2]

In this is love, not that we loved God but that He loved us and sent His Son to be the expiation for our sins.[3] Making peace by the blood of His cross. And you, who once were estranged and hostile in mind, doing evil deeds, He has now reconciled in His body of flesh by His death.[4] While we were enemies we were reconciled to God by the death of His Son.[5] For He is our peace.[6]

All this is from God, who through Christ reconciled us to Himself and gave us the ministry of reconciliation; that is, God was in Christ reconciling the world to Himself . . . and entrusting to us the message of reconciliation. So we are ambassadors for Christ, God making His appeal through us. We beseech you on behalf of Christ, be reconciled to God.[7]

**Is. 27:5.* [1]*Eph. 2:1–3.* [2]*Eph. 5:6.* [3]*1 Jn. 4:10.* [4]*Col. 1:20–22.* [5]*Rom. 5:10.* [6]*Eph. 2:14.* [7]*2 Cor. 5:18–20.*

NOVEMBER 9

*How long, O Lord? Wilt Thou hide Thyself for ever?**

Why are you cast down, O my soul?[1] Why is my pain unceasing, my wound incurable, refusing to be healed?[2] Why did I not die at birth, come forth from the womb and expire?[3] Why sleepest Thou, O Lord?[4] My God, my God, why hast Thou forsaken me?[5] Has God forgotten to be gracious? Has He in anger shut up His compassion?[6]

His anger is but for a moment, and His favor is for a lifetime. Weeping may tarry for the night, but joy comes with the morning.[7] I believe that I shall see the goodness of the Lord in the land of the living![8] Hope in God; for I shall again praise Him, my help and my God.[9]

So we do not lose heart. Though our outer nature is wasting away, our inner nature is being renewed every day. For this slight momentary affliction is preparing for us an eternal weight of glory beyond all comparison, because we look not to the things that are seen but to the things that are unseen; for the things that are seen are transient, but the things that are unseen are eternal.[10]

**Ps. 89:46.* [1]*Ps. 42:5.* [2]*Jer. 15:18.* [3]*Job 3:11.* [4]*Ps. 44:23.* [5]*Ps. 22:1.* [6]*Ps. 77:9.* [7]*Ps. 30:5.* [8]*Ps. 27:13.* [9]*Ps. 42:11.* [10]*2 Cor. 4:16–18.*

*Hold fast what is good**

The fruit of the Spirit is . . . goodness.[1] I am the vine, you are the branches. He who abides in Me, and I in him, he it is that bears much fruit, for apart from Me you can do nothing.[2]

Joseph . . . was a member of the council, a good and righteous man, who had not consented to their purpose and deed, and he was looking for the kingdom of God.[3] Barnabas was a good man, full of the Holy Spirit and of faith.[4] And the king said, 'Ahimaaz is a good man, and comes with good tidings.'[5] Jesus went about doing good and healing all that were oppressed by the devil, for God was with Him.[6]

Beloved, do not imitate evil but imitate good. He who does good is of God; he who does evil has not seen God.[7] Out of the abundance of the heart the mouth speaks. The good man out of his good treasure brings forth good, and the evil man out of his evil treasure brings forth evil.[8] I know that nothing good dwells within me.[9] God is at work in you, both to will and to work for His good pleasure.[10]

* *1 Thess. 5:21.* [1]*Gal. 5:22.* [2]*Jn. 15:5.* [3]*Lk. 23:50, 51.* [4]*Acts 11:24.* [5]*2 Sam. 18:27.* [6]*Acts 10:38.* [7]*3 Jn. 11.* [8]*Mt. 12:34, 35.* [9]*Rom. 7:18.* [10]*Phil. 2:13.*

NOVEMBER 11

*Arise from the dead**

Do not yield your members to sin as instruments of wickedness, but yield yourselves to God as men who have been brought from death to life, and your members to God as instruments of righteousness.[1] While we were living in the flesh, our sinful passions . . . were at work in our members to bear fruit for death.[2] For the wages of sin is death.[3] Sin came into the world through one man and death through sin, and so death spread to all men because all men sinned.[4]

You were at that time separated from Christ . . . having no hope and without God in the world.[5] Alienated from the life of God.[6] Dead through . . . trespasses and sins.[7] But God . . . out of the great love with which He loved us, even when we were dead through our trespasses, made us alive together with Christ.[8] Have I any pleasure in the death of the wicked, says the Lord God, and not rather that he should turn from his way and live?[9]

He who has the Son has life; he who has not the Son has not life.[10] Therefore choose life.[11] Awake, O sleeper, and arise from the dead, and Christ shall give you light.[12]

**Eph.* 5:14. [1]*Rom.* 6:13. [2]*Rom.* 7:5. [3]*Rom.* 6:23. [4]*Rom.* 5:12. [5]*Eph.* 2:12. [6]*Eph.* 4:18. [7]*Eph.* 2:1. [8]*Eph.* 2:4, 5. [9]*Ezek.* 18:23. [10]*1 Jn.* 5:12. [11]*Deut.* 30:19. [12]*Eph.* 5:14.

*The scriptures . . . bear witness to Me**

But you, O Bethlehem Ephrathah, who are little to be among the clans of Judah, from you shall come forth for me one who is to be ruler in Israel, whose origin is from of old, from ancient days.[1] Behold, a young woman shall conceive and bear a son, and shall call His name Immanuel.[2] To us a child is born, to us a son is given.[3]

The Spirit of the Lord God is upon Me, because the Lord has anointed Me to bring good tidings to the afflicted; He has sent Me to bind up the brokenhearted, to proclaim liberty to the captives, and the opening of the prison to those who are bound; to proclaim the year of the Lord's favor.[4]

But He was wounded for our transgressions, He was bruised for our iniquities; upon Him was the chastisement that made us whole, and with His stripes we are healed.[5] Therefore I will divide Him a portion with the great, and He shall divide the spoil with the strong.[6]

And the government will be upon His shoulder, and His name will be called Wonderful Counselor, Mighty God, Everlasting Father, Prince of Peace. Of the increase of His government and of peace there will be no end.[7]

**Jn. 5:39.* [1]*Mic. 5:2.* [2]*Is. 7:14.* [3]*Is. 9:6.* [4]*Is. 61:1, 2.* [5]*Is. 53:5.* [6]*Is. 53:12.* [7]*Is. 9:6, 7.*

NOVEMBER 13

*Thou art my help and my deliverer**

For Thou hast delivered my soul from death, my eyes from tears, my feet from stumbling; I walk before the Lord in the land of the living.[1] This poor man cried, and the Lord heard him, and saved him out of all his troubles. The angel of the Lord encamps around those who fear Him, and delivers them.[2] When the righteous cry for help, the Lord hears, and delivers them out of all their troubles.[3]

'O Daniel . . . has your God . . . been able to deliver you from the lions?' Then Daniel said . . . 'My God sent His angel and shut the lions' mouths, and they have not hurt me.'[4] And Peter . . . said, 'Now I am sure that the Lord has sent His angel and rescued me from the hand of Herod and from all that the Jewish people were expecting.'[5] But the Lord stood by me and gave me strength to proclaim the word fully . . . So I was rescued from the lion's mouth.[6]

The Lord knows how to rescue the godly from trial.[7] He delivered us from so deadly a peril, and He will deliver us; on Him we have set our hope that He will deliver us again.[8]

**Ps. 40:17.* [1]*Ps. 116:8, 9.* [2]*Ps. 34:6, 7.* [3]*Ps. 34:17.* [4]*Dan. 6:20–22.* [5]*Acts 12:11.* [6]*2 Tim. 4:17.* [7]*2 Pet. 2:9.* [8]*2 Cor. 1:10.*

NOVEMBER 14

*Renewal in the Holy Spirit**

Thus says the Lord God: 'Come from the four winds, O breath, and breathe upon these slain, that they may live.'[1] That which is born of the Spirit is spirit.[2] It is the Spirit that gives life, the flesh is of no avail.[3]

The law of the Spirit of life in Christ Jesus has set me free from the law of sin and death.[4] Now the Lord is the Spirit, and where the Spirit of the Lord is, there is freedom.[5]

The fruit of the Spirit is love, joy, peace, patience, kindness, goodness, faithfulness, gentleness, self-control.[6] God's love has been poured into our hearts through the Holy Spirit which has been given to us.[7] And we all, with unveiled face, beholding the glory of the Lord, are being changed into His likeness from one degree of glory to another; for this comes from the Lord who is the Spirit.[8]

Not by might, nor by power, but by My Spirit, says the Lord.[9] Strengthened with might through His Spirit in the inner man.[10] You shall receive power when the Holy Spirit has come upon you; and you shall be My witnesses . . . to the end of the earth.[11]

**Tit.* 3:5. [1]*Ezek.* 37:9. [2]*Jn.* 3:6. [3]*Jn.* 6:63. [4]*Rom.* 8:2. [5]*2 Cor.* 3:17. [6]*Gal.* 5:22, 23. [7]*Rom.* 5:5. [8]*2 Cor.* 3:18. [9]*Zech.* 4:6. [10]*Eph.* 3:16. [11]*Acts* 1:8.

NOVEMBER 15

*A disciple of Jesus, but secretly**

Whoever is ashamed of Me and of My words, of him will the Son of man be ashamed when He comes in His glory and the glory of the Father and of the holy angels.[1] For fear of the Jews no one spoke openly of Him.[2] Many even of the authorities believed in Him, but for fear of the Pharisees they did not confess it, lest they should be put out of the synagogue: for they loved the praise of men more than the praise of God.[3]

Because, if you confess with your lips that Jesus is Lord and believe in your heart that God raised Him from the dead, you will be saved. For man believes with his heart and so is justified, and he confesses with his lips and so is saved.[4] Do not be ashamed then of testifying to our Lord.[5]

Always be prepared to make a defense to any one who calls you to account for the hope that is in you, yet do it with gentleness and reverence.[6] If one suffers as a Christian, let him not be ashamed, but under that name let him glorify God.[7] God is not ashamed to be called their God.[8]

**Jn. 19:38. [1]Lk. 9:26. [2]Jn. 7:13. [3]Jn. 12:42, 43. [4]Rom. 10:9, 10. [5]2 Tim. 1:8. [6]1 Pet. 3:15. [7]1 Pet. 4:16. [8]Heb. 11:16.*

*Love is patient and kind**

And the king (David) said, 'Is there not still some one of the house of Saul, that I may show the kindness of God to him?' Ziba said to the king, 'There is still a son of Jonathan; he is crippled in his feet' . . . And David said to him, 'Do not fear; for I will show you kindness for the sake of your father Jonathan.'[1]

Love your enemies, and do good, and lend, expecting nothing in return; and your reward will be great, and you will be sons of the Most High; for He is kind to the ungrateful and the selfish.[2] Be kind to one another, tenderhearted, forgiving one another, as God in Christ forgave you.[3]

If a brother or sister is ill-clad and in lack of daily food, and one of you says to them, 'Go in peace, be warmed and filled,' without giving them the things needed for the body, what does it profit?[4] If any one has the world's goods and sees his brother in need, yet closes his heart against him, how does God's love abide in him? Little children, let us not love in word or speech but in deed and in truth.[5] And the King will answer them, 'Truly, I say to you, as you did it to one of the least of these My brethren, you did it to Me.'[6]

** 1 Cor. 13:4.* [1] *2 Sam. 9:3, 7.* [2] *Lk. 6:35.* [3] *Eph. 4:32.* [4] *Jas. 2:15, 16.* [5] *1 Jn. 3:17, 18.* [6] *Mt. 25:40.*

NOVEMBER 17

*Who has known the mind of the Lord?**

O the depth of the riches and wisdom and knowledge of God! How unsearchable are His judgments and how inscrutable His ways![1] For My thoughts are not your thoughts, neither are your ways My ways, says the Lord. For as the heavens are higher than the earth, so are My ways higher than your ways and My thoughts than your thoughts.[2]

Has not God made foolish the wisdom of the world? For since, in the wisdom of God, the world did not know God through wisdom, it pleased God through the folly of what we preach to save those who believe. For Jews demand signs and Greeks seek wisdom, but we preach Christ crucified, a stumbling-block to Jews and folly to Gentiles, but to those who are called, both Jews and Greeks, Christ the power of God and the wisdom of God. For the foolishness of God is wiser than men, and the weakness of God is stronger than men.[3]

At that time Jesus declared, 'I thank Thee, Father, Lord of heaven and earth, that Thou hast hidden these things from the wise and understanding and revealed them to babes . . . No one knows the Father except the Son and any one to whom the Son chooses to reveal Him.'[4]

**Rom. 11:34.* [1]*Rom. 11:33.* [2]*Is. 55:8, 9.* [3]*1 Cor. 1:20–25.* [4]*Mt. 11:25, 27.*

*A double-minded man, unstable in all his ways**

No one who puts his hand to the plow and looks back is fit for the kingdom of God.[1] No one can serve two masters . . . You cannot serve God and mammon.[2] Now when Simon (the magician) saw that the Spirit was given through the laying on of the apostles' hands, he offered them money, saying, 'Give me also this power, that any one on whom I lay my hands may receive the Holy Spirit.' But Peter said to him . . . 'Your heart is not right before God.'[3]

Do you not know that friendship with the world is enmity with God? Therefore whoever wishes to be a friend of the world makes himself an enemy of God.[4] Now Peter was sitting outside in the courtyard. And a maid came up to him, and said, 'You also were with Jesus the Galilean.' But he denied it before them all, saying, 'I do not know what you mean.'[5]

Purify your hearts, you men of double mind.[6] Create in me a clean heart, O God, and put a new and right spirit within me.[7] Seek first His kingdom and His righteousness, and all these things shall be yours as well.[8]

**Jas. 1:8.* [1]*Lk. 9:62.* [2]*Mt. 6:24.* [3]*Acts 8:18–21.* [4]*Jas. 4:4.* [5]*Mt. 26:69, 70.* [6]*Jas. 4:8.* [7]*Ps. 51:10.* [8]*Mt. 6:33.*

NOVEMBER 19

*What do you mean, you sleeper?**

Jesus came to the disciples and found them sleeping; and He said to Peter, 'So, could you not watch with Me one hour?'[1] Watch therefore—for you do not know when the Master of the house will come, in the evening, or at midnight, or at cockcrow, or in the morning—lest He come suddenly and find you asleep.[2] Scoffers will come in the last days . . . saying, 'Where is the promise of His coming?'[3] As the bridegroom was delayed, they all slumbered and slept.[4] Lo, I am coming like a thief! Blessed is he who is awake.[5]

Take no part in the unfruitful works of darkness, but instead expose them . . . Awake, O sleeper, and arise from the dead, and Christ shall give you light.[6] But you are not in darkness, brethren, for that day to surprise you like a thief. For you are all sons of light and sons of the day . . . So then let us not sleep, as others do, but let us keep awake and be sober.[7] Besides this you know what hour it is, how it is full time now for you to wake from sleep. For salvation is nearer to us now than when we first believed; the night is far gone, the day is at hand.[8]

**Jonah 1:6.* [1]*Mt. 26:40.* [2]*Mk. 13:35, 36.* [3]*2 Pet. 3:3, 4.* [4]*Mt. 25:5.* [5]*Rev. 16:15.* [6]*Eph. 5:11, 14.* [7]*1 Thess. 5:4–6.* [8]*Rom. 13:11, 12.*

*I will put My Spirit within you, and you shall live**

The Lord . . . set me down in the midst of the valley; it was full of bones . . . And lo, they were very dry. And He said to me, 'Son of man, can these bones live?'[1] Jesus answered Nicodemus, 'Truly, truly, I say to you, unless one is born of water and the Spirit, he cannot enter the kingdom of God. That which is born of the flesh is flesh, and that which is born of the Spirit is spirit. Do not marvel that I said to you, "You must be born again." '[2]

Again He said to me, 'Prophesy to these bones, and say to them, "O dry bones, hear the word of the Lord." '[3] Receive with meekness the implanted word, which is able to save your souls.[4] You have been born anew . . . through the living and abiding word of God.[5]

Thus says the Lord God to these bones: 'Behold, I will cause breath to enter you, and you shall live.'[6] It is the Spirit that gives life, the flesh is of no avail.[7] I will put My Spirit within you; . . . and you shall be My people, and I will be your God.[8]

**Ezek. 37:14.* [1]*Ezek. 37:1–3.* [2]*Jn. 3:5–7.* [3]*Ezek. 37:4.* [4]*Jas. 1:21.* [5]*1 Pet. 1:23.* [6]*Ezek. 37:5.* [7]*Jn. 6:63.* [8]*Ezek. 36:27, 28.*

NOVEMBER 21

*Lord, increase our faith!**

By faith Noah, being warned by God concerning events as yet unseen, took heed and constructed an ark for the saving of his household.[1] By faith Joseph, at the end of his life, made mention of the exodus of the Israelites and gave directions concerning his burial.[2] By faith Moses left Egypt, not being afraid of the anger of the king; for he endured as seeing Him who is invisible.[3]

A centurion came . . . to Jesus . . . saying, 'Lord, my servant is lying paralyzed at home, in terrible distress.' And He said to him, 'I will come and heal him.' But the centurion answered Him, 'Lord, only say the word, and my servant will be healed . . .' Jesus marvelled, and said to those who followed Him, 'Truly, I say to you, not even in Israel have I found such faith' . . . And to the centurion Jesus said, 'Go; be it done for you as you have believed.' And the servant was healed at that very moment.[4]

When the Son of man comes, will He find faith on earth?[5] Jesus said to them . . . 'Have you no faith?'[6] O man of little faith, why did you doubt?[7] O woman, great is your faith! Be it done for you as you desire.[8]

**Lk. 17:5. [1]Heb. 11:7. [2]Heb. 11:22. [3]Heb. 11:27. [4]Mt. 8:5–8, 10, 13. [5]Lk. 18:8. [6]Mk. 4:40. [7]Mt. 14:31. [8]Mt. 15:28.*

*The holy one, the true one**

The child to be born will be called holy, the Son of God.[1] He commited no sin; no guile was found on His lips.[2] The Word became flesh and dwelt among us, full of grace and truth.[3]

I delight to do Thy will, O my God; Thy law is within my heart.[4] I always do what is pleasing to Him.[5] You love righteousness and hate wickedness. Therefore God, your God, has anointed you with the oil of gladness above your fellows.[6] One who in every respect has been tempted as we are, yet without sinning.[7]

You know that He appeared to take away sins, and in Him there is no sin.[8] A lamb without blemish or spot.[9] For our sake He made Him to be sin who knew no sin, so that in Him we might become the righteousness of God.[10]

Which of you convicts Me of sin?[11] It was fitting that we should have such a high priest, holy, blameless, unstained, separated from sinners, exalted above the heavens.[12] Why does He eat with tax collectors and sinners?[13] I have not come to call the righteous, but sinners to repentance.[14]

**Rev. 3:7.* [1]*Lk. 1:35.* [2]*1 Pet. 2:22.* [3]*Jn. 1:14.* [4]*Ps. 40:8.* [5]*Jn. 8:29.* [6]*Ps. 45:7.* [7]*Heb. 4:15.* [8]*1 Jn. 3:5.* [9]*1 Pet. 1:19.* [10]*2 Cor. 5:21.* [11]*Jn. 8:46.* [12]*Heb. 7:26.* [13]*Mk. 2:16.* [14]*Lk. 5:32.*

NOVEMBER 23

*Crucified with Christ.**

We are convinced that one has died for all; therefore all have died.[1] Those who belong to Christ Jesus have crucified the flesh with its passions and desires.[2] We know that our old self was crucified with Him so that the sinful body might be destroyed, and we might no longer be enslaved to sin.[3]

For he who has died is freed from sin.[4] And, having been set free from sin, (you) have become slaves of righteousness.[5] For whoever has suffered in the flesh has ceased from sin, so as to live for the rest of the time in the flesh no longer by human passions but by the will of God.[6]

He died for all, that those who live might live no longer for themselves but for Him who for their sake died and was raised.[7] I have been crucified with Christ; it is no longer I who live, but Christ who lives in me; and the life I now live in the flesh I live by faith in the Son of God, who loved me and gave Himself for me.[8] So you also must consider yourselves dead to sin and alive to God in Christ Jesus.[9]

**Gal. 2:20.* [1]*2 Cor. 5:14.* [2]*Gal. 5:24.* [3]*Rom. 6:6.* [4]*Rom. 6:7.* [5]*Rom. 6:18.* [6]*1 Pet. 4:1, 2.* [7]*2 Cor. 5:15.* [8]*Gal. 2:20.* [9]*Rom. 6:11.*

*Whoever wishes to be a friend of the world makes himself an enemy of God**

Now King Solomon loved many foreign women . . . from the nations concerning which the Lord had said . . . 'You shall not enter into marriage with them, neither shall they with you, for surely they will turn away your heart after their gods.' Solomon clung to these in love . . . When Solomon was old his wives turned away his heart after other gods, and his heart was not wholly true to the Lord his God.[1]

Do not be mismated with unbelievers. For what partnership have righteousness and iniquity? Or what fellowship has light with darkness? . . . Or what has a believer in common with an unbeliever?[2] An unjust man is an abomination to the righteous, but he whose way is straight is an abomination to the wicked.[3]

There are friends who pretend to be friends.[4] If sinners entice you, do not consent. If they say, 'Come with us. . . . throw in your lot among us, we will all have one purse' . . . do not walk in the way with them.[5] The companion of fools will suffer harm.[6] A companion of gluttons shames his father.[7]

**Jas.* 4:4. [1]*1 Kings* 11:1, 2, 4. [2]*2 Cor.* 6:14, 15. [3]*Prov.* 29:27. [4]*Prov.* 18:24. [5]*Prov.* 1:10, 11, 14, 15. [6]*Prov.* 13:20. [7]*Prov.* 28:7.

NOVEMBER 25

*The Lord, the righteous Judge**

The Father judges no one, but has given all judgment to the Son.[1] And has given Him authority to execute judgment.[2] He is the one ordained by God to be judge of the living and the dead.[3] He has fixed a day on which He will judge the world in righteousness by a man whom He has appointed, and of this He has given assurance to all men by raising Him from the dead.[4]

For we shall all stand before the judgment seat of God.[5] And I saw the dead, great and small, standing before the throne, and books were opened. Also another book was opened, which is the book of life. And the dead were judged by what was written in the books, by what they had done.[6]

Then the King will say to those at His right hand, 'Come, O blessed of My Father, inherit the kingdom prepared for you.'[7] Heirs of the kingdom which He has promised to those who love Him.[8] Do you not know that the unrighteous will not inherit the kingdom of God?[9] Woe to them! . . . for whom the nether gloom of darkness has been reserved for ever.[10]

**2 Tim. 4:8.* [1]*Jn. 5:22.* [2]*Jn. 5:27.* [3]*Acts 10:42.* [4]*Acts 17:31.* [5]*Rom. 14:10.* [6]*Rev. 20:12.* [7]*Mt. 25:34.* [8]*Jas. 2:5.* [9]*1 Cor. 6:9.* [10]*Jude 11, 13.*

*A place of prayer**

Evening and morning and at noon . . . He will hear my voice.[1] I think of Thee upon my bed, and meditate on Thee in the watches of the night.[2] I rise before dawn and cry for help.[3] In the morning, a great while before day, Jesus rose and went out to a lonely place, and there He prayed.[4] And all night He continued in prayer to God.[5]

Isaac went out to meditate in the field.[6] Daniel . . . went to his house . . . and prayed.[7] Peter went up on the housetop to pray.[8] In these days Jesus went out into the hills to pray.[9] Two men went up into the temple to pray.[10] Peter and John were going up to the temple at the hour of prayer.[11] My house shall be called a house of prayer for all peoples.[12]

Peter went to the house of Mary . . . where many were gathered together and were praying.[13] If two of you agree on earth about anything they ask, it will be done for them by My Father in heaven. For where two or three are gathered in My name, there am I in the midst of them.[14]

**Acts 16:13.* [1]*Ps. 55:17.* [2]*Ps. 63:6.* [3]*Ps. 119:147.* [4]*Mk. 1:35.* [5]*Lk. 6:12.* [6]*Gen. 24:63.* [7]*Dan. 6:10.* [8]*Acts 10:9.* [9]*Lk. 6:12.* [10]*Lk. 18:10.* [11]*Acts 3:1.* [12]*Is. 56:7.* [13]*Acts 12:12.* [14]*Mt. 18:19, 20.*

NOVEMBER 27

*A faithful man who can find?**

What is desired in a man is loyalty, and a poor man is better than a liar.[1] Let not loyalty and faithfulness forsake you; bind them about your neck, write them on the tablet of your heart.[2] Love one another with brotherly affection; outdo one another in showing honor.[3]

Why then are we faithless to one another?[4] You shall not go up and down as a slanderer among your people, and you shall not stand forth against the life of your neighbor: I am the Lord.[5] He who goes about as a talebearer reveals secrets, but he who is trustworthy in spirit keeps a thing hidden.[6] Better is open rebuke than hidden love. Faithful are the wounds of a friend.[7]

He who is faithful in a very little is faithful also in much; and he who is dishonest in a very little is dishonest also in much . . . If you have not been faithful in that which is another's, who will give you that which is your own?[8] His master said to him, 'Well done, good and faithful servant; you have been faithful over a little, I will set you over much; enter into the joy of your master.'[9]

**Prov. 20:6.* [1]*Prov. 19:22.* [2]*Prov. 3:3.* [3]*Rom. 12:10.* [4]*Mal. 2:10.* [5]*Lev. 19:16.* [6]*Prov. 11:13.* [7]*Prov. 27:5, 6.* [8]*Lk. 16:10, 12.* [9]*Mt. 25:21.*

*A man attested to you by God**

And when Jesus was baptized . . . behold, the heavens were opened and He saw the Spirit of God descending like a dove, and alighting on Him; and lo, a voice from heaven, saying, 'This is My beloved Son, with whom I am well pleased.'[1]

Jesus Christ, the Son of God.[2] And the angel said to Mary, 'The Holy Spirit will come upon you, and the power of the Most High will overshadow you; therefore the child to be born will be called holy, the Son of God.'[3] Simon Peter replied, 'You are the Christ, the Son of the living God.'[4] And those in the boat worshipped Him, saying, 'Truly You are the Son of God.'[5] Martha said to Him, 'Yes, Lord; I believe that You are the Christ, the Son of God.'[6]

And Jesus, full of the Holy Spirit, returned from the Jordan, and was led by the Spirit for forty days in the wilderness, tempted by the devil.[7] And Jesus returned in the power of the Spirit into Galilee.[8] Jesus stood up to read; and there was given to Him the book of the prophet Isaiah. He opened the book and found the place where it was written, 'The Spirit of the Lord is upon Me.'[9]

**Acts 2:22.* [1]*Mt. 3: 16, 17.* [2]*Mk. 1:1.* [3]*Lk. 1:35.* [4]*Mt. 16:16.* [5]*Mt. 14:33.* [6]*Jn. 11:27.* [7]*Lk. 4:1, 2.* [8]*Lk. 4:14.* [9]*Lk. 4: 16–18.*

NOVEMBER 29

*Perfect through suffering**

Beloved, do not be surprised at the fiery ordeal which comes upon you to prove you, as though something strange were happening to you. But rejoice in so far as you share Christ's sufferings, that you may also rejoice and be glad when His glory is revealed.[1] For it has been granted to you that for the sake of Christ you should . . . suffer.[2] They left the presence of the council, rejoicing that they were counted worthy to suffer dishonor for the name.[3] If one suffers as a Christian, let him not be ashamed, but under that name let him glorify God.[4]

It was fitting that He . . . in bringing many sons to glory, should make the pioneer of their salvation perfect through suffering.[5] Although He was a Son, He learned obedience through what He suffered.[6]

I consider that the sufferings of this present time are not worth comparing with the glory that is to be revealed to us.[7] And after you have suffered a little while, the God of all grace, who has called you to His eternal glory in Christ, will Himself restore, establish, and strengthen you.[8]

**Heb.* 2:10. [1] *1 Pet.* 4:12, 13. [2] *Phil.* 1:29. [3] *Acts* 5:41. [4] *1 Pet.* 4:16. [5] *Heb.* 2:10. [6] *Heb.* 5:8. [7] *Rom.* 8:18. [8] *1 Pet.* 5:10.

*As Jesus walked . . . He saw . . . Andrew**

Andrew . . . first found his brother Simon, and . . . brought him to Jesus.[1] What man of you, having a hundred sheep . . . does not leave the ninety-nine in the wilderness, and go after the one which is lost until he finds it? And when he has found it, he lays it on his shoulders rejoicing.[2]

One of His disciples, Andrew, Simon Peter's brother, said to Him, 'There is a lad here who has five barley loaves and two fish; but what are they among so many?' Jesus said, 'Make the people sit down.'[3] With men this is impossible, but with God all things are possible.[4] It may be that the Lord will work for us; for nothing can hinder the Lord from saving by many or by few.[5] And they all ate and were satisfied.[6]

Some Greeks . . . came to Philip . . . and said to him, 'Sir, we wish to see Jesus.' Philip went and told Andrew; Andrew went with Philip and they told Jesus.[7] Servants through whom you believed.[8] Fellow workmen for God.[9] Working together with Him, then, we entreat you not to accept the grace of God in vain.[10]

**Mt. 4:18. [1]Jn. 1:40–42. [2]Lk. 15:4, 5. [3]Jn. 6:8–10. [4]Mt. 19:26. [5]1 Sam. 14:6. [6]Mt. 14:20. [7]Jn. 12:20–22. [8]1 Cor. 3:5. [9]1 Cor. 3:9. [10]2 Cor. 6:1.*

DECEMBER 1

*Sin . . . deceived me and . . . killed me**

The woman saw that the tree was good for food, and that it was a delight to the eyes, and that the tree was to be desired to make one wise.[1] Each person is tempted when he is lured and enticed by his own desire. Then desire when it has conceived gives birth to sin; and sin when it is full-grown brings forth death.[2]

The serpent said to the woman, 'Did God say, "You shall not eat of any tree of the garden?" ' . . . So . . . she took of its fruit and ate.[3] If it had not been for the law, I should not have known sin. I should not have known what it is to covet if the law had not said, 'You shall not covet.' But sin, finding opportunity in the commandment, wrought in me all kinds of covetousness.[4]

The woman said, 'The serpent beguiled me, and I ate.'[5] Even Satan disguises himself as an angel of light.[6] There is a way which seems right to a man, but its end is the way to death.[7]

Take care, brethren, lest there be in any of you an evil, unbelieving heart, leading you to fall away from the living God. But exhort one another every day . . . that none of you may be hardened by the deceitfulness of sin.[8]

**Rom. 7:11. [1]Gen. 3:6. [2]Jas. 1:14, 15. [3]Gen. 3:1, 6. [4]Rom. 7:7, 8. [5]Gen. 3:13. [6]2 Cor. 11:14. [7]Prov. 16:25. [8]Heb. 3:12, 13.*

DECEMBER 2

*Walk . . . according to the Spirit**

You stiff-necked people . . . you always resist the Holy Spirit.[1] By your hard and impenitent heart you are storing up wrath for yourself on the day of wrath when God's righteous judgment will be revealed.[2] Therefore, as the Holy Spirit says, 'Today, when you hear His voice, do not harden your hearts as in the rebellion.'[3] All who are led by the Spirit of God are sons of God.[4]

And do not grieve the Holy Spirit of God, in whom you were sealed for the day of redemption.[5] But they rebelled and grieved His Holy Spirit; therefore He turned to be their enemy, and Himself fought against them.[6] The man who has . . . outraged the Spirit of grace.[7] If we live by the Spirit, let us also walk by the Spirit. Let us have no self-conceit, no provoking of one another, no envy of one another.[8]

Do not quench the Spirit.[9] Never flag in zeal, be aglow with the Spirit, serve the Lord.[10] Love is strong as death . . . Many waters cannot quench love, neither can floods drown it.[11] And . . . God's love has been poured into our hearts through the Holy Spirit which has been given to us.[12]

**Rom. 8:4.* [1]*Acts 7:51.* [2]*Rom. 2:5.* [3]*Heb. 3:7, 8.* [4]*Rom. 8:14.* [5]*Eph. 4:30.* [6]*Is. 63:10.* [7]*Heb. 10:29.* [8]*Gal. 5:25, 26.* [9]*1 Thess. 5:19.* [10]*Rom. 12:11.* [11]*Song of Sol. 8:6, 7.* [12]*Rom. 5:5.*

DECEMBER 3

*I will come again**

The Son of man is coming at an hour you do not expect.[1] But of that day or that hour no one knows, not even the angels in heaven, nor the Son, but only the Father.[2] The day of the Lord will come like a thief in the night.[3]

This Jesus, who was taken up from you into heaven, will come in the same way as you saw Him go into heaven.[4] They will see the Son of man coming on the clouds of heaven with power and great glory.[5] For as the lightning comes from the east and shines as far as the west, so will be the coming of the Son of man.[6]

Christ . . . will appear a second time, not to deal with sin but to save those who are eagerly waiting for Him.[7] I will come again and will take you to Myself, that where I am you may be also.[8] When Christ who is our life appears, then you also will appear with Him in glory.[9] Abide in Him, so that when He appears we may have confidence and not shrink from Him in shame at His coming.[10]

'Surely I am coming soon.' Amen. Come, Lord Jesus![11]

**Jn. 14:3.* [1]*Mt. 24:44.* [2]*Mk. 13:32.* [3]*1 Thess. 5:2.* [4]*Acts 1:11.* [5]*Mt. 24:30.* [6]*Mt. 24:27.* [7]*Heb. 9:28.* [8]*Jn. 14:3.* [9]*Col. 3:4.* [10]*1 Jn. 2:28.* [11]*Rev. 22:20.*

*Do nothing from selfishness**

None of us lives to himself, and none of us dies to himself. If we live, we live to the Lord, and if we die, we die to the Lord; so then, whether we live or whether we die, we are the Lord's.[1] But if any one has the world's goods and sees his brother in need, yet closes his heart against him, how does God's love abide in him? Little children, let us not love in word or speech but in deed and in truth.[2]

Decide never to put a stumbling-block or hindrance in the way of a brother . . . If your brother is being injured by what you eat, you are no longer walking in love.[3] Thus, sinning against your brethren and wounding their conscience when it is weak, you sin against Christ.[4] It is right not to eat meat or drink wine or do anything that makes your brother stumble.[5]

We who are strong ought to bear with the failings of the weak, and not to please ourselves; let each of us please his neighbor for his good, to edify him. For Christ did not please Himself.[6] Love does not insist on its own way.[7]

**Phil. 2:3. [1]Rom. 14:7, 8. [2]1 Jn. 3:17, 18. [3]Rom. 14:13, 15. [4]1 Cor. 8:12. [5]Rom. 14:21. [6]Rom. 15:1–3. [7]1 Cor. 13:5.*

DECEMBER 5

*Good stewards of God's varied grace**

And the Lord said, 'Who then is the faithful and wise steward, whom his master will set over his household, to give them their portion of food at the proper time? Blessed is that servant whom his master when he comes will find so doing.'[1] This is how one should regard us, as servants of Christ and stewards of the mysteries of God. Moreover it is required of stewards that they be found trustworthy.[2]

The glorious gospel of the blessed God with which I have been entrusted.[3] The preaching with which I have been entrusted by command of God our Savior.[4] Entrusting to us the message of reconciliation.[5] O Timothy, guard what has been entrusted to you.[6]

Necessity is laid upon me. Woe to me if I do not preach the gospel! . . . I am entrusted with a commission.[7] As we have been approved by God to be entrusted with the gospel, so we speak, not to please men, but to please God.[8] We refuse to practice cunning or to tamper with God's word, but by the open statement of the truth we would commend ourselves to every man's conscience in the sight of God.[9]

**1 Pet. 4:10. [1]Lk. 12:42, 43. [2]1 Cor. 4:1, 2. [3]1 Tim. 1:11. [4]Tit. 1:3. [5]2 Cor. 5:19. [6]1 Tim. 6:20. [7]1 Cor. 9:16, 17. [8]1 Thess. 2:4. [9]2 Cor. 4:2.*

*All scripture is inspired by God**

First of all you must understand this, that no prophecy of scripture is a matter of one's own interpretation, because no prophecy ever came by the impulse of man, but men moved by the Holy Spirit spoke from God.[1]

The Spirit of the Lord speaks by me, His word is upon my tongue.[2] The word that God puts in my mouth, that must I speak.[3] And the Lord put a word in Balaam's mouth.[4] I will raise up . . . a prophet . . . and I will put My words in his mouth, and he shall speak to them all that I command him.[5] For I am the Lord your God . . . And I have put My words in your mouth.[6] Then the Lord put forth His hand and touched my mouth; and the Lord said to me, 'Behold, I have put My words in your mouth.'[7]

I have yet many things to say to you, but you cannot bear them now. When the Spirit of truth comes, He will guide you into all the truth; for He will not speak on His own authority, but whatever He hears He will speak, and He will declare to you the things that are to come.[8] When you received the word of God which you heard from us, you accepted it not as the word of men but as what it really is, the word of God.[9]

**2 Tim. 3:16.* [1]*2 Pet. 1:20, 21.* [2]*2 Sam. 23:2.* [3]*Num. 22:38.* [4]*Num. 23:5.* [5]*Deut. 18:18.* [6]*Is. 51:15, 16.* [7]*Jer. 1:9.* [8]*Jn. 16:12, 13.* [9]*1 Thess. 2:13.*

DECEMBER 7

*Pray for one another**

Pray at all times in the Spirit, with all prayer and supplication. To that end keep alert with all perseverance, making supplication for all the saints.[1] You have heard that it was said, 'You shall love your neighbor and hate your enemy.' But I say to you, 'Love your enemies and pray for those who persecute you.'[2] The prayer of a righteous man has great power in its effects.[3]

To this end we always pray for you, that our God may make you worthy of His call, and may fulfil every good resolve and work of faith by His power, so that the name of our Lord Jesus may be glorified in you, and you in Him.[4] And it is my prayer that your love may abound more and more, with knowledge and all discernment.[5] We pray God that you may not do wrong . . . What we pray for is your improvement.[6]

So Peter was kept in prison; but earnest prayer for him was made to God by the church.[7] Epaphras, who is one of yourselves, a servant of Christ Jesus, greets you, always remembering you earnestly in his prayers, that you may stand mature and fully assured in all the will of God.[8]

**Jas. 5:16. [1]Eph. 6:18. [2]Mt. 5:43, 44. [3]Jas. 5:16. [4]2 Thess. 1:11, 12. [5]Phil. 1:9. [6]2 Cor. 13:7, 9. [7]Acts 12:5. [8]Col. 4:12.*

*Put . . . away anger, wrath, malice . . .**

Now Esau hated Jacob because of the blessing with which his father had blessed him, and Esau said to himself, 'The days of mourning for my father are approaching; then I will kill my brother Jacob.'[1] When Joseph's brothers saw that their father loved him more than all his brothers, they hated him, and could not speak peaceably to him.[2] They hated Me without a cause.[3]

Any one who hates his brother is a murderer, and you know that no murderer has eternal life abiding in him.[4] You have heard that it was said . . . 'You shall not kill' . . . But I say to you that every one who is angry with his brother shall be liable to judgment.[5]

If any one says, 'I love God,' and hates his brother, he is a liar; for he who does not love his brother whom he has seen, cannot love God whom he has not seen.[6] You have heard that it was said, 'You shall love your neighbor and hate your enemy.' But I say to you, Love your enemies and pray for those who persecute you.[7]

**Col. 3:8.* [1]*Gen. 27:41.* [2]*Gen. 37:4.* [3]*Jn. 15:25.* [4]*1 Jn. 3:15.* [5]*Mt. 5:21, 22.* [6]*1 Jn. 4:20.* [7]*Mt. 5:43, 44.*

DECEMBER 9

*Man is born to trouble as the sparks fly upward**

We know that the whole creation has been groaning in travail together until now.[1] How long will the land mourn, and the grass of every field wither? For the wickedness of those who dwell in it the beasts and the birds are swept away.[2] The whole land is made desolate, but no man lays it to heart.[3]

You will hear of wars and rumors of wars . . . For nation will rise against nation, and kingdom against kingdom, and there will be famines and earthquakes in various places.[4] And there will be . . . distress of nations . . . men fainting with fear and with foreboding of what is coming on the world.[5] In those times there was no peace to him who went out or to him who came in, for great disturbances afflicted all the inhabitants of the lands. They were broken in pieces, nation against nation, and city against city, for God troubled them with every sort of distress.[6]

The righteous will never be moved . . . He is not afraid of evil tidings; his heart is firm, trusting in the Lord. His heart is steady, he will not be afraid.[7] In Me you may have peace. In the world you have tribulation; but be of good cheer, I have overcome the world.[8] Your life is hid with Christ in God.[9]

**Job 5:7.* [1]*Rom. 8:22.* [2]*Jer. 12:4.* [3]*Jer. 12:11.* [4]*Mt. 24:6, 7.* [5]*Lk. 21:25, 26.* [6]*2 Chron. 15:5, 6.* [7]*Ps. 112:6–8.* [8]*Jn. 16:33.* [9]*Col. 3:3.*

*Apart from Me you can do nothing**

For I know that nothing good dwells within me, that is, in my flesh. I can will what is right, but I cannot do it.[1] The spirit indeed is willing, but the flesh is weak.[2] For the desires of the flesh are against the Spirit . . . to prevent you from doing what you would.[3]

Be strong in the Lord and in the strength of His might.[4] Be strong in the grace that is in Christ Jesus.[5] With God we shall do valiantly.[6] Yea, by Thee I can crush a troop, and by my God I can leap over a wall.[7] God, the Lord, is my strength; He makes my feet like hinds' feet.[8] I can do all things in Him who strengthens me.[9]

When I am weak, then I am strong.[10] Strengthened with might through His Spirit in the inner man.[11] Blessed are the men whose strength is in Thee.[12] May you be strengthened with all power, according to His glorious might, for all endurance and patience with joy, giving thanks to the Father, who has qualified us to share in the inheritance of the saints in light.[13]

**Jn. 15:5.* [1]*Rom. 7:18.* [2]*Mt. 26:41.* [3]*Gal. 5:17.* [4]*Eph. 6:10.* [5]*2 Tim. 2:1.* [6]*Ps. 60:12.* [7]*2 Sam. 22:30.* [8]*Hab. 3:19.* [9]*Phil. 4:13.* [10]*2 Cor. 12:10.* [11]*Eph. 3:16.* [12]*Ps. 84:5.* [13]*Col. 1:11, 12.*

DECEMBER 11

*I always do what is pleasing to Him**

There are six things which the Lord hates, seven which are an abomination to Him: haughty eyes, a lying tongue, and hands that shed innocent blood, a heart that devises wicked plans, feet that make haste to run to evil, a false witness who breathes out lies, and a man who sows discord among brothers.[1] Those who are in the flesh cannot please God.[2]

But the Lord takes pleasure in those who fear Him, in those who hope in His steadfast love.[3] Who choose the things that please Me.[4] With what shall I come before the Lord, and bow myself before God on high? Shall I come before Him with burnt offerings, with calves a year old? Will the Lord be pleased with thousands of rams, with ten thousands of rivers of oil?[5] Behold, to obey is better than sacrifice, and to hearken than the fat of rams.[6] And without faith it is impossible to please Him.[7]

Finally, brethren, we beseech and exhort you in the Lord Jesus that as you learned from us how you ought to live and to please God, just as you are doing, you do so more and more.[8]

**Jn. 8:29.* [1]*Prov. 6:16–19.* [2]*Rom. 8:8.* [3]*Ps. 147:11.* [4]*Isa. 56:4.* [5]*Mic. 6:6, 7.* [6]*1 Sam. 15:22.* [7]*Heb. 11:6.* [8]*1 Thess. 4:1.*

*Then I saw a new heaven and a new earth**

According to His promise we wait for new heavens and a new earth in which righteousness dwells.[1] And the ransomed of the Lord shall return, and come to Zion with singing, with everlasting joy upon their heads; they shall obtain joy and gladness, and sorrow and sighing shall flee away.[2] And a highway shall be there, and it shall be called the Holy Way; the unclean shall not pass over it, and fools shall not err therein.[3]

The wolf and the lamb shall feed together, the lion shall eat straw like the ox; and dust shall be the serpent's food. They shall not hurt or destroy in all My holy mountain, says the Lord.[4] Woe to you, destroyer, who yourself have not been destroyed; . . . when you have ceased to destroy, you will be destroyed.[5]

God will wipe away every tear from their eyes, and death shall be no more, neither shall there be mourning nor crying nor pain any more, for the former things have passed away.[6] For behold, I create new heavens and a new earth; and the former things shall not be remembered or come into mind.[7]

**Rev. 21:1.* [1]*2 Pet. 3:13.* [2]*Is. 35:10.* [3]*Is. 35:8.* [4]*Is. 65:25.* [5]*Is. 33:1.* [6]*Rev. 21:4.* [7]*Is. 65:17.*

DECEMBER 13

*Rejoice in the Lord always; again I will say, Rejoice**

I will sing to the Lord as long as I live; I will sing praise to my God while I have being. May my meditation be pleasing to Him, for I rejoice in the Lord.[1] Satisfy us in the morning with Thy steadfast love, that we may rejoice and be glad all our days.[2]

Thou hast turned for me my mourning into dancing; Thou hast loosed my sackcloth and girded me with gladness, that my soul may praise Thee and not be silent.[3] Thou preparest a table before me in the presence of my enemies; Thou anointest my head with oil, my cup overflows.[4] Thou dost show me the path of life; in Thy presence there is fullness of joy, in Thy right hand are pleasures for evermore.[5]

Without having seen Him you love Him; though you do not now see Him you believe in Him and rejoice with unutterable and exalted joy.[6] Look to Him, and be radiant.[7] A glad heart makes a cheerful countenance.[8]

**Phil. 4:4.* [1]*Ps. 104:33, 34.* [2]*Ps. 90:14.* [3]*Ps. 30:11, 12.* [4]*Ps. 23:5.* [5]*Ps. 16:11.* [6]*1 Pet. 1:8.* [7]*Ps. 34:5.* [8]*Prov. 15:13.*

DECEMBER 14

*We were eyewitnesses of His majesty**

And after six days Jesus took with Him Peter and James and John his brother, and led them up a high mountain apart. And He was transfigured before them, and His face shone like the sun, and His garments became white as light . . . A bright cloud overshadowed them, and a voice from the cloud said, 'This is My beloved Son, with whom I am well pleased; listen to Him.' When the disciples heard this, they fell on their faces, and were filled with awe. But Jesus came and touched them, saying, 'Rise, and have no fear.'[1]

Then I turned to see the voice that was speaking to me, and on turning I saw seven golden lampstands, and in the midst of the lampstands one like a Son of man, clothed with a long robe and with a golden girdle round His breast; His head and His hair were white as white wool, white as snow; His eyes were like a flame of fire, His feet were like burnished bronze, refined as in a furnace, and His voice was like the sound of many waters; in His right hand He held seven stars, from His mouth issued a sharp two-edged sword, and His face was like the sun shining in full strength. When I saw Him, I fell at His feet as though dead. But He laid His right hand upon me, saying, 'Fear not.'[2]

**2 Pet. 1:16.* [1]*Mt. 17:1, 2, 5–7.* [2]*Rev. 1:12–17.*

DECEMBER 15

*In many and various ways God spoke of old to our fathers by the prophets**

The Lord saw that the wickedness of man was great in the earth . . . and the Lord was sorry that He had made man.[1] And God said to Noah, 'I have determined to make an end of all flesh . . . Make yourself an ark of gopher wood.'[2] Then the Lord said to Noah, 'Go into the ark, you and all your household, for I have seen that you are righteous before Me.'[3] And the Lord shut him in.[4] There is therefore now no condemnation for those who are in Christ Jesus.[5]

Then Moses . . . said . . . 'Kill the passover lamb . . . and touch the lintel and the two doorposts with the blood . . . For the Lord will pass through to slay the Egyptians; and when He sees the blood . . . the Lord will pass over the door, and will not allow the destroyer to enter.'[6] Behold, the Lamb of God, who takes away the sin of the world.[7] For Christ, our paschal Lamb, has been sacrificed.[8]

Moses made a bronze serpent, and set it on a pole; and if a serpent bit any man, he would look at the bronze serpent and live.[9] And as Moses lifted up the serpent in the wilderness, so must the Son of man be lifted up, that whoever believes in Him may have eternal life.[10]

**Heb.* 1:1. [1]*Gen.* 6:5, 6. [2]*Gen.* 6:13, 14. [3]*Gen.* 7:1. [4]*Gen.* 7:16. [5]*Rom.* 8:1. [6]*Ex.* 12:21–23. [7]*Jn.* 1:29. [8]*1 Cor.* 5:7. [9]*Num.* 21:9. [10]*Jn.* 3:14, 15.

*You shall love the Lord your God . . . with all your mind**

Be renewed in the spirit of your minds.[1] Now we have received not the spirit of the world, but the Spirit which is from God, that we might understand the gifts bestowed on us by God.[2] See to it that no one makes a prey of you by philosophy and empty deceit, according to human tradition, according to the elemental spirits of the universe, and not according to Christ.[3] Jesus answered them, 'To you it has been given to know the secrets of the kingdom of heaven, but to them it has not been given.'[4]

And if I have prophetic powers, and understand all mysteries and all knowledge . . . but have not love, I am nothing.[5] Knowledge puffs up, but love builds up. If any one imagines that he knows something, he does not yet know as he ought to know.[6]

Finally, brethren, whatever is true, whatever is honorable, whatever is just, whatever is pure, whatever is lovely, whatever is gracious, if there is any excellence, if there is anything worthy of praise, think about these things.[7] Brethren, do not be children in your thinking; be babes in evil, but in thinking be mature.[8]

**Lk. 10:27. [1]Eph. 4:23. [2]1 Cor. 2:12. [3]Col. 2:8. [4]Mt. 13:11. [5]1 Cor. 13:2. [6]1 Cor. 8:1, 2. [7]Phil. 4:8. [8]1 Cor. 14:20.*

DECEMBER 17

*I will not leave you desolate**

I lie awake, I am like a lonely bird on the housetop.[1] I look to the right and watch, but there is none who takes notice of me; no refuge remains to me, no man cares for me.[2] Turn Thou to me, and be gracious to me; for I am lonely and afflicted.[3]

Elijah . . . pleads with God . . . 'Lord, they have killed Thy prophets, they have demolished Thy altars, and I alone am left, and they seek my life.' But what is God's reply to him? 'I have kept for Myself seven thousand men who have not bowed the knee to Baal.'[4] Joseph's master took him and put him into the prison . . . But the Lord was with Joseph.[5] This very night there stood by me an angel of the God to whom I belong and whom I worship, and He said, 'Do not be afraid, Paul.'[6]

After this many of His disciples drew back and no longer went about with Him. Jesus said to the twelve, 'Will you also go away?'[7] Then all the disciples forsook Him and fled.[8] My God, My God, why hast Thou forsaken Me?[9] I have trodden the wine press alone, and from the peoples no one was with Me.[10] He was . . . rejected by men.[11] Smitten by God, and afflicted.[12]

**Jn. 14:18.* [1]*Ps. 102:7.* [2]*Ps. 142:4.* [3]*Ps. 25:16.* [4]*Rom. 11:2–4.* [5]*Gen. 39:20, 21.* [6]*Acts 27:23, 24.* [7]*Jn. 6:66, 67.* [8]*Mt. 26:56.* [9]*Mt. 27:46.* [10]*Is. 63:3.* [11]*Is. 53:3.* [12]*Is. 53:4.*

*The grace of God has appeared for the salvation of all men**

Jesus looked up and said to him, 'Zacchaeus, make haste and come down; for I must stay at your house today.' So he made haste and came down, and received Him joyfully. And when they saw it they all murmured, 'He has gone in to be the guest of a man who is a sinner' . . . And Jesus said to him, 'Today salvation has come to this house.'[1]

Behold . . . a friend of . . . sinners![2] I formerly blasphemed and persecuted and insulted Him; but I received mercy because I had acted ignorantly in unbelief, and the grace of our Lord overflowed for me with the faith and love that are in Christ.[3] And such were some of you. But you were washed, you were sanctified, you were justified in the name of the Lord Jesus Christ.[4] While we were yet sinners Christ died for us.[5]

God, who is rich in mercy, out of the great love with which He loved us, even when we were dead through our trespasses, made us alive together with Christ (by grace you have been saved).[6] I have seen his ways, but I will heal him.[7] I . . . I am He who blots out your transgressions for My own sake, and I will not remember your sins.[8]

**Tit.* 2:11. [1]*Lk.* 19:5–7, 9. [2]*Lk.* 7:34. [3]*1 Tim.* 1:13, 14. [4]*1 Cor.* 6:11. [5]*Rom.* 5:8. [6]*Eph.* 2:4, 5. [7]*Is.* 57:18. [8]*Is.* 43:25.

DECEMBER 19

*Lead us not into temptation**

Be sober, be watchful. Your adversary the devil prowls around like a roaring lion, seeking someone to devour. Resist him, firm in your faith.[1] Even Satan disguises himself as an angel of light.[2] Give no opportunity to the devil.[3]

Do not love the world or the things in the world . . . For all that is in the world, the lust of the flesh and the lust of the eyes and the pride of life, is not of the Father but is of the world.[4] Do Thou, O Lord, protect us, guard us ever from this generation. On every side the wicked prowl, as vileness is exalted among the sons of men.[5] Do not enter the path of the wicked, and do not walk in the way of evil men. Avoid it; do not go on it; turn away from it and pass on.[6]

Watch and pray that you may not enter into temptation; the spirit indeed is willing, but the flesh is weak.[7] Each person is tempted when he is lured and enticed by his own desire.[8] Make no provision for the flesh, to gratify its desires.[9]

Therefore let any one who thinks that he stands take heed lest he fall.[10]

**Lk. 11:4.* [1]*1 Pet. 5:8, 9.* [2]*2 Cor. 11:14.* [3]*Eph. 4:27.* [4]*1 Jn. 2:15, 16.* [5]*Ps. 12:7, 8.* [6]*Prov. 4:14, 15.* [7]*Mt. 26:41.* [8]*Jas. 1:14.* [9]*Rom. 13:14.* [10]*1 Cor. 10:12.*

*The God in whose hand is your breath**

There is one God, the Father, from whom are all things and for whom we exist, and one Lord, Jesus Christ, through whom are all things and through whom we exist.[1] All things are from God.[2] In Him all things were created, in heaven and on earth, visible and invisible . . . all things were created through Him and for Him. He is before all things, and in Him all things hold together.[3] Upholding the universe by His word of power.[4] For from Him and through Him and to Him are all things. To Him be glory forever. Amen.[5]

He . . . gives to all men life and breath and everything.[6] For 'in Him we live and move and have our being.'[7] These all look to Thee, to give them their food in due season . . . When Thou takest away their breath, they die and return to their dust. When Thou sendest forth Thy Spirit, they are created; and Thou renewest the face of the ground.[8] In His hand is the life of every living thing, and the breath of all mankind.[9] If He should take back His spirit to Himself, and gather to Himself His breath, all flesh would perish together, and man would return to dust.[10]

**Dan. 5:23.* [1]*1 Cor. 8:6.* [2]*1 Cor. 11:12.* [3]*Col. 1:16, 17.* [4]*Heb. 1:3.* [5]*Rom. 11:36.* [6]*Acts 17:25.* [7]*Acts 17:28.* [8]*Ps. 104:27, 29, 30.* [9]*Job 12:10.* [10]*Job 34:14, 15.*

DECEMBER 21

*O man of little faith, why did you doubt?**

Thomas . . . said to his fellow disciples, 'Let us also go, that we may die with Him.'[1] Lord, I am ready to go with You to prison and to death.[2] Then Jesus said to them, 'You will all fall away because of Me . . . for it is written, "I will strike the shepherd, and the sheep of the flock will be scattered." '[3] But you shall receive power when the Holy Spirit has come upon you; and you shall be My witnesses . . . to the end of the earth.[4] Faithful unto death.[5]

Thomas said to Him, 'Lord, we do not know where You are going; how can we know the way?' Jesus said to him, 'I am the way . . . no one comes to the Father, but by Me.'[6] The new and living way which He opened for us through . . . His flesh.[7]

Thomas . . . was not with them when Jesus came . . . He said to them, 'Unless I see . . . I will not believe' . . . Eight days later . . . Jesus came . . . and said . . . to Thomas . . . 'Have you believed because you have seen Me? Blessed are those who have not seen and yet believe.'[8] For we walk by faith, not by sight.[9] Without having seen Him you love Him; though you do not now see Him You believe in Him and rejoice with unutterable and exalted joy.[10]

**Mt. 14:31.* [1]*Jn. 11:16.* [2]*Lk. 22:33.* [3]*Mt. 26:31.* [4]*Acts 1:8.* [5]*Rev. 2:10.* [6]*Jn. 14:5, 6.* [7]*Heb. 10:20.* [8]*Jn. 20:24–29.* [9]*2 Cor. 5:7.* [10]*1 Pet. 1:8.*

*The way of salvation**

All have turned aside, together they have gone wrong; no one does good, not even one . . . For there is no distinction; since all have sinned and fall short of the glory of God.[1] The soul that sins shall die.[2] For the wages of sin is death.[3] He who conceals his transgressions will not prosper, but he who confesses and forsakes them will obtain mercy.[4]

All we like sheep have gone astray; we have turned every one to his own way; and the Lord has laid on Him the iniquity of us all.[5] For Christ . . . died for sins once for all, the righteous for the unrighteous, that He might bring us to God.[6] He Himself bore our sins in His body on the tree.[7] The free gift of God is eternal life in Christ Jesus our Lord.[8]

The jailer fell down before Paul and Silas . . . and said, 'Men, what must I do to be saved?' And they said, 'Believe in the Lord Jesus, and you will be saved.'[9] Because, if you confess with your lips that Jesus is Lord and believe in your heart that God raised Him from the dead, you will be saved.[10] Behold, I stand at the door and knock; if any one hears My voice and opens the door, I will come in to him.[11] Christ in you, the hope of glory.[12]

**Acts 16:17.* [1]*Rom. 3:12, 22, 23.* [2]*Ezek. 18:4.* [3]*Rom. 6:23.* [4]*Prov. 28:13.* [5]*Is. 53:6.* [6]*1 Pet. 3:18.* [7]*1 Pet. 2:24.* [8]*Rom. 6:23.* [9]*Acts 16:29–31.* [10]*Rom. 10:9.* [11]*Rev. 3:20.* [12]*Col. 1:27.*

DECEMBER 23

*You also must help us by prayer**

Continue steadfastly in prayer, being watchful in it with thanksgiving; and pray for us also.[1] Brethren, pray for us, that the word of the Lord may speed on and triumph, as it did among you.[2] Strive together with me in your prayers to God on my behalf, that I may be delivered from the unbelievers in Judea.[3] Remember your leaders, those who spoke to you the word of God.[4]

Then came Amalek and fought with Israel at Rephidim . . . So Joshua . . . fought with Amalek; and Moses, Aaron, and Hur went up to the top of the hill. Whenever Moses held up his hand, Israel prevailed; and whenever he lowered his hand, Amalek prevailed. But Moses' hands grew weary; so . . . Aaron and Hur held up his hands, one on one side, and the other on the other side; so his hands were steady until the going down of the sun.[5]

If two of you agree on earth about anything they ask, it will be done for them by My Father in heaven. For where two or three are gathered in My name, there am I in the midst of them.[6] The end of all things is at hand; therefore keep sane and sober for your prayers.[7]

**2 Cor. 1:11. [1]Col. 4:2, 3. [2]2 Thess. 3:1. [3]Rom. 15:30, 31. [4]Heb. 13:7. [5]Ex. 17:8–12. [6]Mt. 18:19, 20. [7]1 Pet. 4:7.*

*God loves a cheerful giver**

They still kept bringing Moses freewill offerings every morning, so that all the able men . . . said to Moses, 'The people bring much more than enough for doing the work which the Lord has commanded us to do' . . . So the people were restrained from bringing.[1] Then the people rejoiced because these had given willingly, for with a whole heart they had offered freely to the Lord.[2]

And the disciples determined, every one according to his ability, to send relief to the brethren who lived in Judea.[3] For they gave according to their means, as I can testify, and beyond their means, of their own free will.[4] All day long the wicked covets, but the righteous gives and does not hold back.[5] Remembering the words of the Lord Jesus, how He said, 'It is more blessed to give than to receive.'[6] Each one must do as he has made up his mind, not reluctantly or under compulsion, for God loves a cheerful giver.[7]

But who am I, and what is my people, that we should be able thus to offer willingly? For all things come from Thee, and of Thy own have we given Thee.[8]

*[*] *2 Cor. 9:7.* [1] *Ex. 36:3–6.* [2] *1 Chron. 29:9.* [3] *Acts 11:29.* [4] *2 Cor. 8:3.* [5] *Prov. 21:26.* [6] *Acts 20:35.* [7] *2 Cor. 9:7.* [8] *1 Chron. 29:14.*

DECEMBER 25

*He has visited . . . His people**

I have set the crown upon one who is mighty, I have exalted one chosen from the people.[1] He will be great, and will be called the Son of the Most High . . . and of His kingdom there will be no end.[2] For to us a child is born, to us a Son is given; and the government will be upon His shoulder, and His name will be called 'Wonderful Counselor, Mighty God, Everlasting Father, Prince of Peace.'[3] Sing and rejoice, O daughter of Zion; for lo, I come and I will dwell in the midst of you, says the Lord.[4]

When the time had fully come, God sent forth His Son, born of woman, born under the law, to redeem those who were under the law, so that we might receive adoption as sons.[5] Christ Jesus . . . though He was in the form of God, did not count equality with God a thing to be grasped, but emptied Himself, taking the form of a servant, being born in the likeness of men.[6] It will be said on that day, 'Lo, this is our God; we have waited for Him, that He might save us. This is the Lord; we have waited for Him; let us be glad and rejoice in His salvation.'[7] For mine eyes have seen Thy salvation.[8]

* *Lk. 1:68.* [1]*Ps. 89:19.* [2]*Lk. 1:32, 33.* [3]*Is. 9:6.* [4]*Zech. 2:10.* [5]*Gal. 4:4, 5.* [6]*Phil. 2:5–7.* [7]*Is. 25:9.* [8]*Lk. 2.30.*

DECEMBER 26

*A man of God**

They chose Stephen, a man full of faith and of the Holy Spirit.[1] And Stephen, full of grace and power, did great wonders and signs among the people.[2] A man after My heart, who will do all My will.[3] This is a holy man of God.[4]

And gazing at him, all who sat in the council saw that his face was like the face of an angel.[5] Look to Him and be radiant; so your faces shall never be ashamed.[6] And we all, with unveiled face, beholding the glory of the Lord, are being changed into His likeness from one degree of glory to another.[7]

And Stephen said, 'Behold, I see the heavens opened, and the Son of man standing at the right hand of God.'[8] And as they were stoning Stephen, he prayed, 'Lord Jesus, receive my spirit . . . and when he had said this, he fell asleep.[9] These all died in faith.[10] Looking to Jesus the pioneer and perfecter of our faith, who for the joy that was set before Him endured the cross, despising the shame, and is seated at the right hand of the throne of God.[11]

**Judg. 13:6.* [1]*Acts 6:5.* [2]*Acts 6:8.* [3]*Acts 13:22.* [4]*2 Kings 4:9.* [5]*Acts 6:15.* [6]*Ps. 34:5.* [7]*2 Cor. 3:18.* [8]*Acts 7:56.* [9]*Acts 7:59, 60.* [10]*Heb. 11:13.* [11]*Heb. 12:2.*

DECEMBER 27

*The disciple whom Jesus loved**

When Jesus saw His mother, and the disciple whom He loved standing near, He said to His mother, 'Woman, behold your son!' Then He said to the disciple, 'Behold your mother!' And from that hour the disciple took her to his own home.[1]

Now when they saw the boldness of Peter and John, and perceived that they were uneducated, common men, they wondered; and they recognized that they had been with Jesus.[2] Peter and John answered them, 'Whether it is right in the sight of God to listen to you rather than to God, you must judge; for we cannot but speak of what we have seen and heard.'[3]

The revelation of Jesus Christ, which God gave Him to show to His servants what must soon take place; and He made it known by sending His angel to His servant John, who bore witness to the word of God and to the testimony of Jesus Christ, even to all that he saw.[4] I John, your brother, who share with you in Jesus the tribulation and the kingdom and the patient endurance, was on the island called Patmos on account of the word of God and the testimony of Jesus. I was in the Spirit on the Lord's day, and I heard behind me a loud voice like a trumpet saying, 'Write . . .'[5] This is the disciple who . . . has written these things; and we know that his testimony is true.[6]

**Jn. 19:26.* [1]*Jn. 19:26, 27.* [2]*Acts 4:13.* [3]*Acts 4:19, 20.* [4]*Rev. 1:1, 2.* [5]*Rev. 1:9–11.* [6]*Jn. 21:24.*

*The name which is above every name**

Behold, a virgin shall conceive and bear a son, and His name shall be called Emmanuel (which means, God with us).[1] But will God indeed dwell on the earth?[2] The Word became flesh and dwelt among us, full of grace and truth.[3]

She will bear a son, and you shall call His name Jesus, for He will save His people from their sins.[4] And we have seen and testify that the Father has sent His Son as the Savior of the world.[5] We know that this is indeed the Savior of the world.[6]

His name will be called 'Wonderful Counselor, Mighty God, Everlasting Father, Prince of Peace.'[7] And this is the name by which He will be called: 'The Lord is our righteousness.'[8] He will be great, and will be called the Son of the Most High.[9]

God has highly exalted Him and bestowed on Him the name which is above every name.[10] O Lord, our Lord, how majestic is Thy name in all the earth![11] O magnify the Lord with me, and let us exalt His name together![12] Ascribe to the Lord the glory due His name.[13] Blessed be His glorious name for ever; may His glory fill the whole earth![14]

**Phil. 2:9.* [1]*Mt. 1:23.* [2]*1 Kings 8:27.* [3]*Jn. 1:14.* [4]*Mt. 1:21.* [5]*1 Jn. 4:14.* [6]*Jn. 4:42.* [7]*Is. 9:6.* [8]*Jer. 23:6.* [9]*Lk. 1:32.* [10]*Phil. 2:9.* [11]*Ps. 8:1.* [12]*Ps. 34:3.* [13]*1 Chron. 16:29.* [14]*Ps. 72:19.*

DECEMBER 29

*Made like His brethren in every respect**

Christ Jesus, who, though He was in the form of God, did not count equality with God a thing to be grasped, but emptied Himself, taking the form of a servant, being born in the likeness of men.[1] We see Jesus, who for a little while was made lower than the angels . . . so that by the grace of God He might taste death for every one.[2] Since . . . the children share in flesh and blood, He Himself likewise partook of the same nature, that through death He might destroy him who has the power of death, that is, the devil.[3]

And being found in human form He humbled Himself and became obedient unto death, even death on a cross.[4] Christ redeemed us from the curse of the law, having become a curse for us—for it is written, 'Cursed be every one who hangs on a tree.'[5] For our sake He made Him to be sin who knew no sin, so that in Him we might become the righteousness of God.[6] He poured out His soul to death, and was numbered with the transgressors.[7]

**Heb. 2:17.* [1]*Phil. 2:5–7.* [2]*Heb. 2:9.* [3]*Heb. 2:14.* [4]*Phil. 2:8.* [5]*Gal. 3:13.* [6]*2 Cor. 5:21.* [7]*Is. 53:12.*

*Exalted at the right hand of God**

Therefore God has highly exalted Him and bestowed on Him the name which is above every name, that at the name of Jesus every knee should bow, in heaven and on earth and under the earth, and every tongue confess that Jesus Christ is Lord, to the glory of God the Father.[1]

When Christ had offered for all time a single sacrifice for sins, He sat down at the right hand of God, then to wait until His enemies should be made a stool for His feet.[2] Jesus Christ, who has gone into heaven and is at the right hand of God, with angels, authorities, and powers subject to Him.[3] Thou didst make Him for a little while lower than the angels, Thou hast crowned Him with glory and honor, putting everything in subjection under His feet.[4]

As it is, we do not yet see everything in subjection to Him. But we see Jesus . . . crowned with glory and honor.[5] Then comes the end, when He delivers the kingdom to God the Father after destroying every rule and every authority and power. For He must reign until He has put all His enemies under His feet.[6]

**Acts 2:33.* [1]*Phil. 2:9–11.* [2]*Heb. 10:12, 13.* [3]*1 Pet. 3:21, 22.* [4]*Heb. 2:7, 8.* [5]*Heb. 2:8, 9.* [6]*1 Cor. 15:24, 25.*

DECEMBER 31

*Hitherto the Lord has helped us**

You shall remember all the way which the Lord your God has led you.[1] You know in your hearts and souls, all of you, that not one thing has failed of all the good things which the Lord your God promised concerning you; all have come to pass for you, not one of them has failed.[2] For the Lord your God has blessed you in all the work of your hands; . . . you have lacked nothing.[3]

Moses my servant is dead; now therefore arise, go over this Jordan . . . No man shall be able to stand before you all the days of your life; as I was with Moses, so I will be with you; I will not fail you or forsake you. Be strong and of good courage . . . for the Lord your God is with you wherever you go.[4] One thing I do, forgetting what lies behind and straining forward to what lies ahead, I press on toward the goal for the prize of the upward call of God in Christ Jesus.[5] There remains yet very much land to be possessed. This is the land that yet remains . . .[6] That I may gain Christ and . . . that I may know Him and the power of His resurrection, and may share His sufferings, becoming like Him in His death, that if possible I may attain the resurrection from the dead.[7]

**1 Sam. 7:12.* [1]*Deut. 8:2.* [2]*Josh. 23:14.* [3]*Deut. 2:7.* [4]*Josh. 1:2, 5, 6, 9.* [5]*Phil. 3:13, 14.* [6]*Josh. 13:1, 2.* [7]*Phil. 3:8, 10, 11.*

INDEX

INDEX